WELCOME TO

it's GREEK to me!

A MELANGE OF TRADITIONAL AND FAMILY RECIPES FROM *G*REECE AND OTHER COUNTRIES EMBRACING THE *E*ASTERN *O*RTHODOX *R*ELIGION

They came to America...

...Immigrants from diverse countries, bringing with them their hopes and dreams, their cherished traditions, and—most precious of all—their religion, the Eastern Orthodox Faith, which brings our various cultures together.

The recipes in this book have made the transition from open hearth to modern kitchen, in spoken tradition from generation to generation, reflecting the use of the ingredients available to each particular region.

Immigrants still come to America. We celebrate them and their recipes.

Come, enjoy our inheritance! καλή όρεξη **(Good Appetite!)**
Greek

Ethiopian

Lebanese

Serbian

Russian

Armenian

IT'S GREEK TO ME!

573 North Highland
Memphis, Tennessee 38122

©Copyright 1981
ISBN #09625267-0-3
ISBN #978-0-9625-2670-1

First Printing, November 1981
Second Printing, Revised, November 1988
Third Printing, Revised, March 2001
Fourth Printing, Revised, March 2013

IT'S GREEK TO ME! is based on our previous publication
"Grecian Gourmet" 1963.

Cover photography: Michael T. Grehl;
Kastro Church, the Island of Sifnos, Greece, copyrighted.

Published by
Toof Cookbook Division

TOOF

670 South Cooper Street
Memphis, Tennessee 38104

COOKBOOK COMMITTEES

FIRST PRINTING
Mrs. Mary V. Lenis, *Chairman*
Ms. Scottie Koleas
Mrs. Tina T. Liollio
Mrs. Helen K. Ostrosky
Mrs. Carolyn I. Speros
Mrs. Bessie V. Taras
Mrs. Anastasia V. Vergos

SECOND PRINTING
Mrs. Mary V. Lenis, *Chairman*
Mrs. Jane C. Futris
Mrs. Katherine D. Futris
Ms. Anne Pekovich
Mrs. Sophie M. Sousoulas
Mrs. Bessie V. Taras
Mrs. Sarah C. Touliatos
Mrs. Anastasia V. Vergos

Proofreaders and Typists
Ms. Sue Donnelly
Mrs. Jane C. Futris
Mrs. Elaine F. Hardesty
Ms. Lynda Liollio
Ms. Anne Pekovich
Mrs. Nancy K. Taras

THIRD PRINTING
Mrs. Doris V. Anagnos
Mrs. Helen S. Gresham
Mrs. Mary Ann Koch
Mrs. Mary V. Lenis
Mrs. Bessie V. Taras
Mrs. Anastasia V. Vergos

FOURTH PRINTING
Mrs. Helen C. Erskine
Mrs. Linda Farrell
Mrs. Georgia S. Karris
Mrs. Linda Nichols
Mrs. Angela Tobias
Mrs. Elaine Otto

This book was compiled by the above members of the Philoptochos Society of the Annunciation Greek Orthodox Church, Memphis, Tennessee.

The Philoptochos Society is the national philanthropic society of the Ladies of the Greek Orthodox Church in North and South America.

With great love, respect and gratitude, we dedicate
this book to our parents, the immigrants who
bridged two continents and two cultures with
their devotion to faith and family. We thank
them for persevering against almost insurmountable
odds to preserve our rich heritage, that we and
future generations may enjoy this priceless gift.

We love you,

Your grateful children

ACKNOWLEDGEMENTS

We wish to recognize and thank the earlier cookbook committees. The one which printed the first GRECIAN GOURMET 1960 at the church under the direction of Mrs. Loretta C. Taras, chairman, and the one which gave the parish its first real "cookbook," under the direction of Mrs. Zoe T. Futris, chairman. These works formed the basis for IT'S GREEK TO ME.

THE CONTRIBUTORS OF RECIPES have our sincere thanks and gratitude for sharing their treasured legacies not only with us but with future generations of cooks.

MICHAEL T. GREHL for unselfishly sharing his love of Greece with us through his extraordinary photography of our favorite subject.

MICHAEL C. SPEROS for his support and advice in decision making. Who also unselfishly researched the wines of Greece, relished every minute of it, and was kind enough to write about it.

GENE McCOWN for his technical assistance and direction, and patience.

FATHER NICHOLAS L. VIERON for his love and spiritual guidance.

ARISTOTLE W. DAMASCUS, Youth Director and newest member of our parish, whose generous offer to assist us was gratefully accepted.

KENETH T. ROME, Rome Advertising/Design, for his consultation and technical assistance.

LAST, BUT NOT LEAST, we wish to thank our husbands and families for their patience and understanding, and enduring the many nights of non-gourmet dinners and the disruption of their normal routine.

SECOND PRINTING 1988 Special thanks to our Philoptochos Presidents, Sophie Theodore (1985-87) and Georgia S. Karris (1987-89), for their invaluable assistance.

THIRD PRINTING 2001 Special thanks to Helen Stamson Gresham for volunteering to assist with this third edition. Helen also headed the committee responsible for the beautiful television coverage which featured our own parishioners demonstrating various recipes and cooking methods found in this cookbook. Brava, Eleni!

CHUCK COON, TOOF COMMERCIAL PRINTING. Thank you for your guidance and continued support of our cookbook.

FOURTH PRINTING 2012 Special thanks to our Elpis Philoptochos Society and especially to Elaine Otto for her committed leadership and devotion toward the continuation of our beloved *it's Greek to me!* Cookbook. With respect, "Axia, Elaine."

TABLE OF CONTENTS

SPECIAL OCCASIONS 9

    Liturgical and Traditional Offerings to the Church
    Traditions and Customs
    Classic Menus

BASIC TECHNIQUES 25

APPETIZERS 33

SOUPS 39

SALADS 45

CHEESE DISHES 49

SEAFOOD 57

POULTRY 65

MEATS/MEAT COMBINATIONS 73

SAUCES 99

VEGETABLES 105

BREADS 113

DESSERTS/PRESERVES 123

WINES AND CHEESES/BEVERAGES 165

ET CETERA 169

INDEX 197

Brand names have been used only when the donor of the recipe bases the success of the recipe on that particular brand.

"Therefore, brethren, stand fast, and hold the traditions which ye have been taught, whether by word, or our epistle."

– The Second Epistle of Paul to the Thessalonians, Chapter 2:15

SPECIAL OCCASIONS

LITURGICAL AND TRADITIONAL OFFERINGS
TO THE CHURCH

PROSPHORA/ANTIDORON, the Bread of Oblation, is the bread which is offered for consecration in the Divine Liturgy of the Greek Orthodox Church. This is the bread which is distributed after the Divine Liturgy and represents "breaking bread" after a fast. Christians have been fasting to receive Holy Communion. It is the remainder of the bread from which the sfragetha "seal" has been removed for the preparation of Holy Communion.

ARTOS FOR ARTOKLASIA is the service in which the five loaves of bread are blessed by the Priest in commemoration of the Miracle of the Feeding of the Multitude by Jesus. The distribution of the blessed bread to the congregation is symbolic of God's blessings to the faithful.

KOLIVA are offered by the bereaved in memory of the deceased at a memorial service held the third, ninth or fortieth day and then again the sixth month or year following the death. During the memorial service, prayers are offered for the salvation of the soul of the departed.

PROSPHORA
Antidoron

GREEK

Temperature: 350°
Pan Size: 9" round
Yield: 3 loaves

**3 packages of yeast,
   granulated or cake
4 to 6 cups lukewarm water
1-1/2 Tbsp. salt
5 pounds plain flour, sifted
Sfragetha (Religious Seal)**

Step 1. Dissolve yeast in 4 cups lukewarm water. Reserve 1 cup flour (use to flour board, dust baking pans, etc.) and sift the rest with salt. Make a well in the center of the flour, pour in warm yeast mixture, mixing until liquid is absorbed. Add as much of the two extra cups warm water as needed to moisten all flour and have a smooth and elastic dough.

Step 2. Divide into three portions, form into round loaves and place in lightly floured 9" pans. Dip seal in flour, tap seal to remove excess, and press gently, but firmly, into dough so that the impression will hold while loaf rises. Cover and allow to rise in warm place until almost double in bulk.

Step 3. Bake in 350° oven for 30 to 40 minutes. Do not allow loaves to become too brown. Remove from oven and brush top with water. Remove from pans and cool.

Grecian Gourmet

PROSCURI
Individual Church Altar Breads

Temperature: 350°
Yield: Approximately 18

1 cake fresh yeast
1/2 cup warm water
4 cups flour

Step 1. Mix the yeast and warm water. Add flour and enough warm water to make a stiff dough. Let rise in a warm place in a covered bowl. Knead after first rising; then let rise again.

Step 2. After second rising, roll out on a board to about 1" thickness. Cut into 2-1/2" rounds with a heavy water glass. Place on cookie sheet. Press seal on center of each. Pierce 4 times with a toothpick, so it will rise evenly. Let rise again for 1/2 hour. Bake for 15 to 20 minutes at 350,° until just baked, but not brown.

At the traditional Easter Blessing of Baskets after midnight service, each family places a Proscura and a lighted candle in their basket of food. Then after the priest blesses the food, it is taken home, where the family shares the Proscura and breaks the 40 day fast.

Mrs. Anna Ostrosky
Coaldale, Pennsylvania

ARTOS I
For Artoklasia

GREEK

Temperature: 350° for 20 minutes
300° for 40 minutes
Pan Size: 9" round
Yield: 5 loaves

5 cakes yeast
1/2 cup lukewarm water
3 cups milk, scalded
1 pound butter
5 eggs
1/2 cup orange juice
1 cup water
1 Tbsp. whole cloves
1 stick cinnamon
5 pounds plain flour, sifted
2-1/2 cups sugar
1-1/2 tsp. salt
1 egg yolk for glaze, beaten
Sesame seeds
Honey
Powdered sugar

Step 1. Boil cinnamon and cloves in 1 cup water for 15 minutes. Strain spiced water and combine all liquids.

Step 2. Dissolve yeast in 1/2 cup lukewarm water. Add butter to scalded milk and cool to lukewarm.

Step 3. Beat eggs with orange juice.

Step 4. Sift flour, sugar and salt into large bowl. Make a well in center and add liquids, stirring until well mixed. Knead on floured surface until very smooth.

Step 5. Place in greased bowl, cover, and let rise until double in size.

Step 6. Divide dough, form into 5 round loaves and place in greased pans. Cover and let rise in warm place until double in size, for about an hour.

Step 7. Brush top of bread with beaten egg yolk. Sprinkle with sesame seeds. Bake in 350° oven for 20 minutes, then reduce heat to 300° and bake for 40 minutes longer.

Step 8. After removing loaves from oven, allow to cool 5 minutes, then remove from pans and brush with honey. When loaves have cooled, dust with powdered sugar.

Mrs. Bill Taras (Bessie)

ARTOS II
For Artoklasia

Temperature: 350°
Pan Size: 10" or 12" round
Yield: 5 large loaves

1 quart milk
1 pound butter
2 Tbsp. Crisco
2 sticks margarine
1 pound yeast
1/2 cup warm water
5 cups sugar
2 Tbsp. salt
1 tsp. mastiha, crushed
2 dozen eggs, beaten
10 pounds all purpose flour
1 egg, beaten
Honey
Powdered sugar

Step 1. Scald milk. Add butter, Crisco, and margarine; set aside to cool to lukewarm.

Step 2. Dissolve yeast in 1/2 cup warm water.

Step 3. Pour lukewarm milk mixture into large mixing bowl; add sugar, salt, mastiha, beaten eggs, yeast, and begin adding flour until dough is smooth and not sticky. Place dough in greased bowl large enough to accommodate when doubled in bulk; cover and let rise in warm place until doubled.

Step 4. Punch down dough. Divide into 5 equal parts. Shape dough into round loaves and place in greased pans. Cover and let rise again to double.

Step 5. Before baking, brush tops with beaten egg. Bake 45 to 60 minutes or until a toothpick comes out clean. Brush tops lightly with honey and dust with powdered sugar.

Mrs. D. G. Anaston (Zoie)

KOLIVA
Memorial Wheat Offering
(See Page 10 for History)

The recipe on page 14 is a large quantity for special memorials, which are celebrated during the Sunday Liturgy, to be shared with the congregation.

Koliva is also offered in smaller amounts on All Souls Saturdays. A smaller amount of Koliva may be prepared using one or three pounds of wheat and reducing the other ingredients accordingly. Follow steps 1 through 3 on page 14. Place the mixture into a bowl and dust with powdered sugar. We add sugar and spices to the boiled wheat symbolizing the church's prayers for a sweet resurrection of the deceased.

The offering of Koliva is based on the words of Jesus, "Truly, truly, I say to you, unless a grain of wheat falls into the earth and dies, it remains alone, but if it dies it bears much fruit." (John 12:24, 31-35)

KOLIVA

Memorial Wheat Offering

Yield: 100 servings

5 pounds hard wheat, whole grain
1 pound sesame seeds
1 pound almonds, blanched
2 cups walnuts, chopped
1 cup pecans, chopped
1 cup currants (optional)
1 pound raisins, white, seedless
1 pound raisins, dark, seedless
3 Tbsp. cinnamon, ground
1 Tbsp. cloves, ground
1/2 cup parsley, chopped (straight leaf type)
Seeds of 1 pomegranate (optional)
2 6 oz. boxes Zwieback, finely crushed and sifted
3 to 4 boxes confectioners' sugar
1 pound white Jordan almonds
3 ounces silver dragees (candies)

ICING:
4 cups sugar
2 cups water
6 egg whites
1/2 tsp. cream of tartar
1 tsp. vanilla

Presuming memorial service will be held on a Sunday morning, begin preparation of Koliva on Friday evening.

Step 1. Pick over wheat to remove foreign objects. Put wheat in a large pot, fill with water and let water run slowly into pot to overflow, stirring grain so that any loose chaff and dust will be washed away. Fill pot with clean water and allow to stand overnight. The next morning drain and put soaked wheat in pot large enough to accommodate 2 parts water and 1 part wheat. Cook over medium heat until tender and skin splits, stirring often with wooden spoon to prevent sticking.

Step 2. Drain wheat, rinse and spread on table covered with several thicknesses of clean cloth to completely absorb moisture. Occasionally turn wheat to facilitate drying. This process takes from 2 to 4 hours.

Step 3. While wheat is drying, prepare other ingredients. Blanch almonds, split and toast in moderate oven until golden brown. Place sesame seeds in shallow baking pan and toast in moderate oven until golden brown, stirring often. Transfer wheat to large, clean cloth. Add toasted sesame seeds and almonds, chopped nuts, cinnamon, cloves, raisins, currants, parsley and pomegranate seeds. With hands and broad spatula, mix gently but thoroughly.

Step 4. Line tray (21" x 15" or larger) with foil. White or silver paper doilies may be placed around tray extending beyond edge of tray. Mound wheat mixture on tray beginning in form of a cross. Finish by covering tray completely. (If all wheat mixture cannot be placed on tray, the remainder may be placed in a bowl and taken to church along with the decorated tray.)

Continued…

Step 5. Place sheet of waxed paper over wheat. Press firmly into a smooth mound. Sift zwieback over entire surface. Zwieback layer should be 1/8" deep. Sift confectioners' sugar over entire surface. Press firmly with waxed paper. Sift more sugar and press firmly with waxed paper until sugar is 1/4" deep. Make sure surface is firmly and smoothly packed.

Step 6. Decoration: Desired shape of cross is drawn on paper and cut out (stencil). Position cross on mound and outline in the sugar with toothpick. Remove paper pattern. With tip of teaspoon, carefully remove confectioners' sugar within outline down to zwieback layer. Use same procedure for initials of deceased.

Step 7. Icing: Boil sugar and water (without stirring) to 242° F. or until a small amount dropped from tip of spoon spins a thread. Beat egg whites until stiff but not dry and pour hot syrup in a thin stream, while beating constantly. Add cream of tartar and vanilla and beat until cool and stiff enough to hold shape when forced through pastry tube.

Step 8. Place icing in pastry bag with decorating tube, fill in hollowed out cross and initials of the decreased to about 1/2 inch above surface. Decorate cross and initials as desired with dragees, using tweezers to place them. Using remaining icing to make 2 or 3 rows around base of mound, decorate with Jordan almonds and dragees as desired.

Note: Wheat mixture is very perishable and must be kept cool, preferably refrigerated, especially if it is to be kept overnight.
Also note: Tradition dictates that one must always use odd number of pounds of wheat; i.e., 3, 5, 7, 9, or 11 pounds.

Mrs. Bill Taras (Bessie)

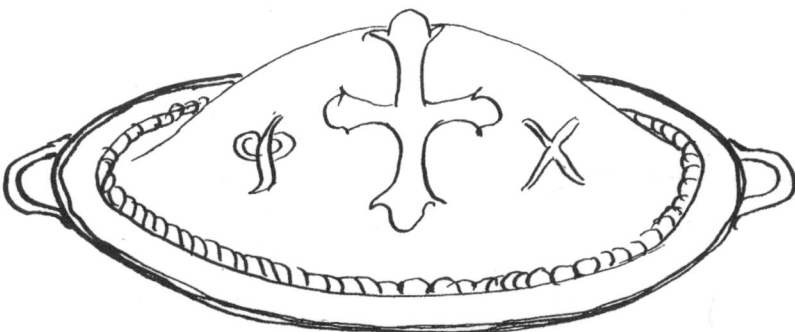

SERBIAN CHRISTMAS CUSTOMS

Most Christians celebrate Christmas on the 25th of December in various customs and traditions of their individual ethnic heritages.

Others celebrate the event on the 7th of January, which is December 25th by the Julian calendar. Serbians are among the latter, and this story will show how we have observed it since childhood days.

Preparations for the great day begin anytime after New Year's Day. Anything which can be cooked or baked in advance, without fear of spoilage, is done as early as possible. These preparations involve much work but at this time there is no need to rush about shopping for gifts. It is a great relief not to be obliged to do so, for it has become more time consuming than any other aspect of the approaching Holy Event.

At our home, Mother prepares a Lenten meal for our Christmas Eve dinner. She has everything in readiness at sundown for her family, but it doesn't seem that way; she is alone in her kitchen-dining room and the table is absolutely bare. Only the scent of tamjan (incense) makes one aware that this night something special is about to happen.

Soon enough, there is a tap on the door. After Mother inquires "Who is there?," Father answers, "We come to greet you on this eve of Christ's Birth, with hope that He will bless us with good health and happiness." She welcomes him and the children in by showering grains of wheat on them saying, "May He also bless us with the necessities of life," to which we respond with, "God grant."

Father then reaches into the large bag he is carrying, which is filled with hay, and gives Mother the first handful. She places some of it on the bare table. The rest is strewn all over the floor. As she strews hers, she imitates a mother hen, and the children following her with their hands full of hay pretend to be her chicks, and they just love spreading their share anywhere they please. For them it was a lot of fun to start Christmas Eve this way, but there was something else there which left a deeper impression on us. The meaning of it all grew stronger as we grew older. That "something" was that by strewing the hay in our home, we humbled ourselves and again remembered that our Lord was born in humble surroundings. To this day, regardless of the sort of home we live in, there will be hay on our table and floor from Christmas Eve until the third day of Christmas.

As soon as the hay is strewn, the table is covered and the first item placed there is a dish upon which wheat has been growing since December 18th. Around it, the Serbian tri-color ribbon is held in place with a small gold cross. In the center of the dish, a small glass holds a vigil light which floats on oil. The wheat is the symbol of the daily bread, for which we pray and give thanks each day, and the Lord alone provides.

A candle is also placed on the table with a special loaf of bread, Kolach, which won't be eaten until the next day. The candle represents Jesus, the Light of the World. These three items and the hay are the extent of our decorations for Christmas, but they have a special beauty of their own and are quite sufficient and appropriate for the occasion.

Mother then gives each one of us the honor of helping to set the table and placing the various foods on it. That way everything is ready in short order. The meal consists of fish, cooked vegetables, potato salad, green salad, fruit, nuts, and honey. No meats or dairy products are included at this meal.

As we all come to the table, Father asks the blessing, "In the name of the Father, Son, and Holy Spirit," and we all repeat the Lord's Prayer together and then immediately sing the two Christmas Hymns which are sung in every Orthodox Church in the world: "Thy Birth, O Christ Our God" and "Today the Virgin Gave Birth." Before we partake of the meal, Father again blesses all of us and each corner of his home by tossing walnuts in all four directions. After dinner the children join others to go into as many Serbian homes as possible to sing the Hymn of Christmas. Parents stay home to greet and reward them with fruit, nuts, cookies, and coins while, in the meantime, they keep an eye on the Badnjak (Yule log) and the piglet (the pechenitsa) on a spit, if they have one (otherwise it will be roasted at the Serbian bakery). Pechenitsa will be the main dish at almost every Serbian table on the next day.

Christmas morning, Mother's first task is the making and baking of the Chesnitsa, the pastry very similar to Baklava, to which white raisins are added to the nuts. Somewhere between one of the layers, the good luck coin has been placed. After the meal this will be the first dessert offered and will be served according to the age of each one present, starting with the eldest down to the youngest. Some Serbs make a flat bread instead of this previous version.

Mother also has a large pot full of ingredients that will make delicious homemade chicken or duck noodle soup. A large roaster contains sarme (stuffed cabbage), cooked the day before–they always taste better the next day. Deliciously browned potatoes will also be served with the pechenitsa, plus salad and hot peppers.

While Mother is busy at home, the family is attending Divine Liturgy with Father, which on Christmas is lengthier than on other days. By the time they come home, they will have huge appetites; Mother will be waiting at the door, where she usually waits when unable to attend services; the children each kiss her hand. This day they greet her with the words "Hristos se Rodi," "Christ is Born," and she responds, "Vo Istinu se Rodi," "Truly He is Born." The family again sets the table where the wheat, candle and Kolach remain as they were placed the night before. When all are assembled at the table, Father summons his sons to his side and picks up the Kolach, and each one places a hand under it and rotates it while we all sing the Christmas Hymns. When they are finished, Father turns the Kolach upside down, makes a cut crosswise and separates the sections partially, into which he drips a little wine, saying three times, "In the name of the Father, Son and Holy Spirit, Christ is with us," and we answer, "He is and ever shall be." The bread is then broken in small pieces and passed to everyone present. Father then picks up his wine glass and says, "Mir Bozi, Hristos se Rodi," "God's Peace, Christ is Born," and we respond, picking up the bread and wine saying, "Truly He is Born." Father and sons kiss each other. This ends the ritual of Christ's Birth in our home, and the feast begins.

Though we honor many loved ones in our lifetime on their birthdays, none should surpass this one, to the Loved One who loves us most.

Mrs. Rodney Arnokovich
Tucson, Arizona

A CARPATHO-RUSSIAN CHRISTMAS EVE

MENU

PIVPACHO (Bread)
HONEY, SALT, GARLIC
MUSHROOM SOUP
BAKED FISH
PIROHI, Stuffed with Potatoes,
Sauerkraut, or Prunes
KUTYA (Sweetened Wheat), GREEN PEAS
OVEN-BROWNED POTATOES
COLE SLAW
SOFT DRINKS   RUSSIAN TEA
STEWED FRUIT   MIXED NUTS
KOLACHKY (Nut Roll Bread)
A TOAST TO GOOD HEALTH WITH VODKA
OR WHISKEY

In Europe, the traditional "Holy Supper" (Christmas Eve Supper) was prepared with foods that were grown on their own land. Twelve foods were prepared, to represent the 12 disciples. Here in America, the cultures of many countries such as Austria, Poland, Czechoslovakia, Hungary, Romania, Carpatho-Russia (in the Carpathian Mountains) and The Ukraine, were melted together, as America became known as "The Melting Pot" during the turn of the century. From these immigrants we have received the tradition, which is carried on even to this day.

Christmas was a religious holiday, with only a few little gifts being exchanged, but love, food, and companionship were very much in abundance. There was always room at the table for the old bachelor without a family, or the uncle who had left a family in Europe, or the new immigrant without friends.

Preparations for this day began by fasting during Advent; this meant eating meatless meals and also abstaining from dancing and music. The homes were spotlessly cleaned, and the linens washed and pressed. It was also a custom to pay your debts before this night.

Early in the morning of Christmas Eve Day, the special lenten bread is baked by Mama; a large round bread just a few inches high, with garlic buds decorating the top. This will be the first food served and is to be eaten with salt and honey. This represents the bitter and the sweet. Dried mushrooms are prepared by washing and breaking into small pieces, then boiled until tender, and delicately seasoned. Wheat is cooked all day and then seasoned with honey. The pirochi (stuffed dumplings) are made with potatoes, sauerkraut, or prunes and lightly sautéed with onion and oil. These are also known as vareniki in the Ukraine. The potatoes are first boiled, and then oven browned. By now, evening is near. The table is set with a white cloth, the foods are set on the table, and a white candle is set in a dish of grain, usually rice. In some homes, hay is placed under the table, to remind us of the manger where Jesus was born. Everyone washes his hands in cold water for good luck. Sometimes a silver coin is placed in the washing bowl for good luck. All lights are then extinguished, and the candle is lit. Truly it is the Light of the World, Jesus, come to visit with us as we sing The Lord's Prayer and the Christmas Troparion. Papa gives a blessing and also remembers all those who have departed from this life, and those who could not be with us for other reasons. The lights are turned on and the bread is broken by Mama, and The Holy Supper begins. Everyone must at least taste everything that is served, even the garlic.

After supper, traditional European Christmas carols are sung, and then the candle flame is blown out. If the smoke goes straight up, all will be present again next year. If the smoke goes toward the door, someone will be missing.

The Christmas holiday season lasts for 13 days, with much singing and feasting. During this time, people greet each other with Christ is Born! to which we reply, Praise Him!

CHRISTOS RAZHEAETSIA! SLAVETE YEHO!

PHANOUROPITA
St. Phanourios Cake

GREEK

St. Phanourios is the Patron Saint of lost articles. This cake is prepared in prayerful silence in memory of St. Phanourios' mother and offered in fulfillment of a promise to the Saint for revealing a "lost" article.

Temperature: 350° for 30 minutes
Pan Size: 10" round (Must use round pan)

3/4 cup corn oil
1-1/2 cups sugar
3 cups all purpose flour
2-1/2 tsp. baking powder
1-1/2 tsp. cinnamon
1-1/2 tsp. vanilla
1 can 7-up or Sprite*

Step 1. Place oil in large mixing bowl. With mixer at low speed, _slowly_ add ingredients one at a time.

Step 2. Bake at 350° until golden brown and the center is cooked. At 30 minutes begin testing with toothpick until toothpick comes out clean.

Step 3. Slice cake to yield as many pieces as possible to distribute to the congregation.

*Note: 1-1/2 cup orange juice may be substituted for Sprite. Also raisins or nuts may be substituted for vanilla. Make sure that the total number of ingredients is 7.

Mrs. Tom Mitchell (Phani)

GREEK MENUS

EASTER SUNDAY FEAST

Mayeritsa
(Traditional Easter Soup)

Salata
(Greek Salad)

Arni tis Souflas
(Roast Lamb on the Spit)

OR

Arni Psito Me Patates
(Roast Leg of Lamb with Oven Baked Potatoes)

Spanakopeta
(Spinach Pie)

Pastitso
(Macaroni-Meat Casserole)

Yaourti
(Yogurt)

Psomi
(Greek Bread)

Lambropsomo
(Easter Bread with Dyed Red Eggs)

Koulourakia
(Easter Cookies)

Galatobouriko
(Custard Pastry)

For the Orthodox Christian the most glorious feast of the Church is Easter, "the Feast of Feasts." Easter is our key to salvation. If Christ had not risen from the dead, His death would have gone down in history as just another death; but, because He rose from the dead, He gave us eternal life. As the beautiful hymn states: "Christ is risen from the dead, trampling down death by death, and upon those in the tomb bestowing life."

LENTEN MEAL

Faki
(Lentil Soup)

OR

Psarosoupa
(Fish Soup)

Marithes Me Skorthalia
(Fried Smelts with Garlic Sauce)

Spanakorizo
(Sautéed Spinach and Rice)

Psomi
(Greek Bread)

Paximathia
(Tea Cookies)

Stafili Gliko
(Grape Preserves)

SUNDAY LUNCH AT HOME

Horiatiki Salata
(Provincial Salad)

Kota Riganato Me Patates
(Chicken Riganato with Potatoes)

OR

Kota Kapama
(Chicken in Tomato Sauce with Spaghetti)

Kolokithakia Me Domates
(Squash with Tomatoes)

Psomi
(Greek Bread)

Yaourtopeta
(Yogurt-Nut Cake)

AEGEAN COCKTAIL BUFFET

Orektika
(Assorted Greek Cheeses and Olives)

Taramousalata
(Caviar Dip with Toasts)

Psari Mayonnaisa
(Chilled Snapper with Mayonnaise Sauce)

Kalamaria Yemista
(Stuffed Squid)

Spanakopetakia
(Spinach Triangles)

Kreatopetakia
(Meat Triangles)

Amegthalota Flogeres
(Almond Flutes)

LUNCHEON WITH FRIENDS

Salata
(Greek Salad)

Kotopetakia Me Avgholemono
(Chicken Rolls with Egg-Lemon Sauce)

Rizi Me Manitaria
(Rice with Mushrooms)

Crema Karamela
(Caramel Custard)

Kafe
(Coffee)

IONIAN DINNER

Avgholemono Soupa
(Egg-Lemon Soup)

Panzaria Salata
(Marinated Beet Salad)

Breezoles tis Skaras
(Charcoal Broiled Lamb Chops)

Rizi Pilaf
(Rice Pilaf)

Fasolakia Yiahni
(Sautéed Green Beans with Tomatoes)

Psomi
(Greek Bread)

Baklava
(Honey Nut Pastry)

Kafe
(Coffee)

TRADITION OF THE VASILOPETA GREEK

The tradition of giving is perpetuated by the families. Each year when the New Year Bread is being prepared, coins which have been boiled (or wrapped in aluminum foil) are kneaded into the dough just before placing it in the pans to rise. When the bread is served at midnight or the following day, it is cut in a prescribed manner; naming each slice as it is cut, the first slice is for the house, then one slice is cut for each member of the family beginning with the oldest and most respected. When all of the family names have been called, the courtesy is then extended to all guests. Legend has it that the person finding the coin in his slice of bread will have good luck in the new year.

St. Basil was a true philanthropist who helped the needy people of his village by distributing loaves of bread into which he had baked money; thus originated the tradition of the New Year's Vasilopeta. St. Basil was a bishop of the Church who is also remembered as an eloquent speaker and for a Divine Liturgy that he wrote which is celebrated on his feast day, January 1, since this is the day he fell asleep in the Year of our Lord 379 A.D.

ST. BASIL'S FEAST DAY DINNER
(New Year's Day)

Saganaki
(Fried Cheese Flambé)

Dolmathakia Yialandji
(Grape Leaves filled with Rice)

Hirino Psito Me Patates
(Roast Pork Grecian Style with Potatoes)

Mavromatika Fasolia Salata
(Black-eyed Pea Salad)

Spanakopeta
(Spinach Pie)

Psomi
(Greek Bread)

Vasilopeta
(Traditional Greek Sweet Bread)

Diples
(Rolled Honey Pastry)

BASIC TECHNIQUES

BASIC TECHNIQUES

Many traditional Greek dishes use thin layers of flaky pastry. This flaky pastry is referred to as "filo," a special dough in tissue thin sheets. Filo is very difficult to make at home, and most Greek cooks now rely on the commercially prepared and packaged dough which can be purchased at large grocery stores in their gourmet or frozen food sections. Though the packages may differ, most contain 16-20 sheets, approximately 17" x 14" in size.

WORKING WITH FILO

Filo is purchased frozen and _must_ be thawed before being used. Faithfully follow the thawing directions on the package and your filo will be cool and pliable when you are ready to use it. Keep the filo wrapped in the plastic package until time to be used. Unroll the package and unfold the stack of sheets. Cover completely with plastic wrap, and then cover with a damp towel to prevent it from drying out. Remember while using the filo, you should work very quickly!

1. Pan Preparation

Use a pastry brush or nylon paint brush—yes, a new, soft, clean paint brush—to grease bottom and sides of the pan with melted butter. Line the pan as illustrated below:

When creamy, moist fillings are used; line pan as shown in fig. 1.

When dry filling is used, line the pan using single filo that overlaps as in fig. 2

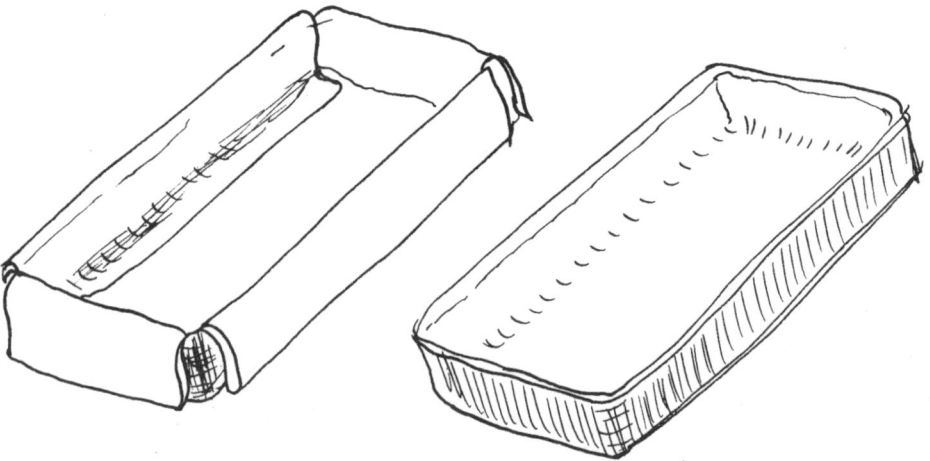

"Paint" or thoroughly drizzle each sheet of filo with melted butter until approximately 6-8 sheets have been placed in the pan. Add filling; continue adding individual sheets of filo, buttering each, until 8-12 sheets form the top layer. Score through the top layers to mark serving pieces before baking, otherwise top filo will crumble and servings will look ragged. Carefully follow individual recipe instructions as to number of filo and scoring.

The following methods of cutting are used for all desserts made in pans, those which are "cake" type, as well as filo pastries. Petes (pies made with filo) are usually cut in squares.

Several traditional methods of cutting are used, depending on individual preference.

Method 1: This method yields square or triangular pieces. There is no waste nor odd-shaped edges left.

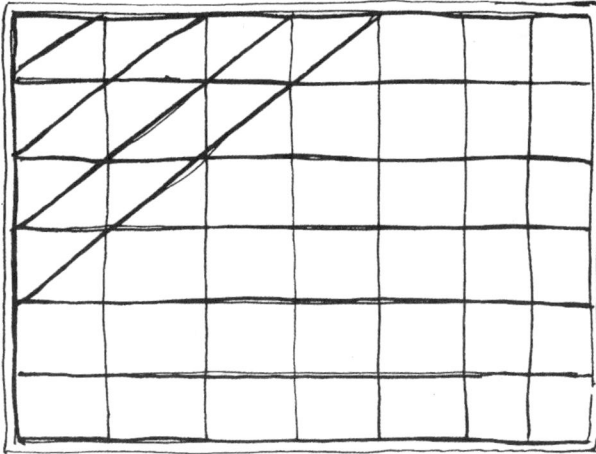

Method 2: Yields the greatest number of pieces, all the same size, provided the measurements are precise. Make lengthwise cuts first, then make diagonal cuts. A 9" x 13" pan yields 36 pieces and some edge pieces.

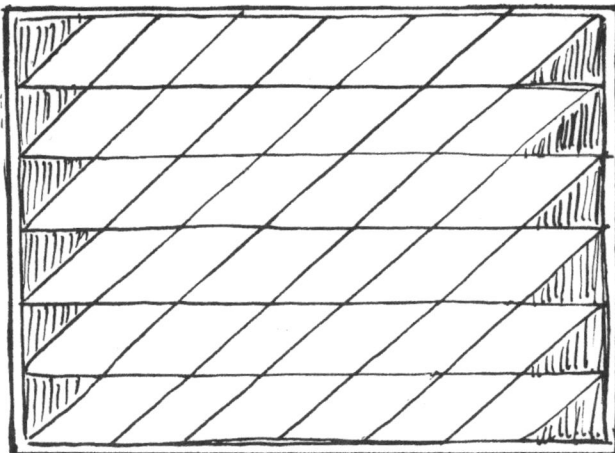

2. Directions for method of folding trigona/triangles:

Step 1. Lay out full package of filo, measure 5" strips (approximately). Cut through all layers. Take one section of strips to begin work; cover the rest with plastic wrap and lay a damp cloth over plastic to keep filo from drying out. Have melted butter and soft pastry brushes ready. Work on a non-absorbent, easy to clean surface.

Step 2. Butter one filo strip. Place filling about 1" from bottom of lower right hand corner.

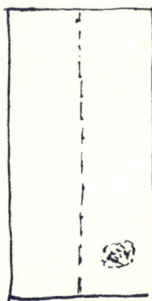

Step 3. Fold other side over to cover filling; butter surface.

Step 4. Begin folding as shown in diagram until all filo is folded over and a "trigono" (triangle) is completed. Butter entire surface and place on baking sheet.

If trigona are to be frozen, prepare sheets of aluminum foil (preferably heavy duty) approximately 18" long, arrange 12 trigona close together on one half of the sheet, fold other half over the trigona (press to remove air pockets) and seal the open edges with a double fold. Place flat on freezer shelf as each dozen is wrapped. When ready to use, unfold package on a cookie sheet and bake according to recipe. The freezer life of trigona is 6 to 9 months. Frozen trigona make wonderful gifts.

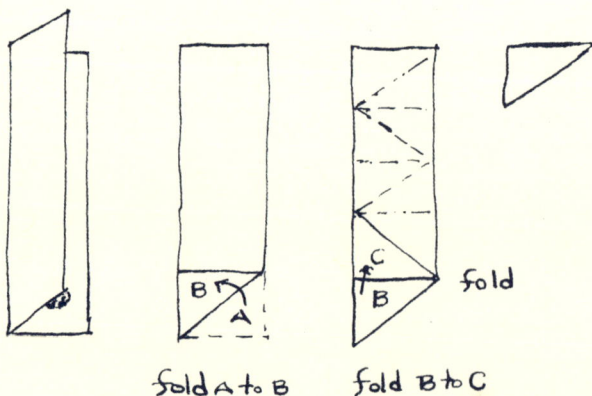

fold A to B   fold B to C

28

3. Method for preparing rolls: Flutes/Flogeres
To be used for foods and pastries, dry or creamy fillings.

Large rolls:
Start with a whole sheet of filo, brush entire surface with melted butter. Fold in half and brush with butter; place a heaping tablespoonful of filling about an inch from the bottom edge,and spread (as shown in drawing). Fold bottom edge up over filling, and brush with butter. Fold sides inward and brush with butter. Finish by rolling up from the bottom, brush the seam with butter, and place seam side down in pan; then brush top with butter. Approximate size when finished: 6" long.

Small or bite-size rolls:
Cut filo in half crosswise and use the same directions as for large rolls. Approximate size when finished: 3" long.

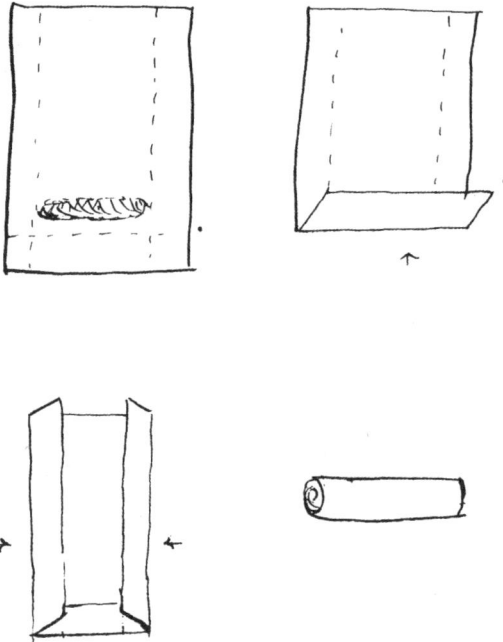

BREAD: Braided Method.

From prepared dough, take a one pound portion, and cover remaining dough. Divide one-pound portion into 3 equal pieces. Oil hands, roll each piece into a long rope. When all three are about the same length, begin braid by pressing all three together at one end. Make braid (see drawing); press ends to seal. This is the basis for several types of loaves:

(1) Prepared loaf may be placed in a greased or floured loaf pan and baked;
(2) Braid may be placed on a greased or floured cookie sheet and baked; or
(3) Braid may be formed into a "kouloura" (circle) and baked on a cookie sheet or in a round pan larger than the braid itself.

KOULOURA: Traditional Easter Bread shape. This shape is popular for other breads year-round. A kouloura is characterized by an open space in the center of the bread and achieved by methods 2 and 3 above or by putting braid in a tube pan.

KOULOURA WITH EGGS: Traditional for Easter. Follow the directions for braiding and place into a round pan larger than the braid. Slightly separate the braided dough and place a dyed egg upright into the open space between braids; place one egg upright in the center. As bread rises, the eggs will be pushed upward and the center egg will be enclosed. Number of eggs used will be determined by size of kouloura and individual taste. Hard boiled eggs are traditionally dyed a deep red.

DECORATIONS: Other traditional decorations are used for holiday breads. It is impossible to depict all the methods of decorations used. They are as varied as the geographic locations, and they differ from family to family. The methods described here are some widely used in our parish.

Byzantine Cross: Used at Easter, Christmas and decoration for Artos. Before dividing and placing prepared dough into pans, set aside an amount to be used for decoration. The size of pan and size of cross is an individual thing determined at time of baking; therefore, after dough is in the pans, take a portion of the dough which has been set aside and roll it into a rope. The thickness of the rope should correspond to the size of the loaf. (Remember that it will double in size.) Cut the rope so that it extends about 2" over the pan on both sides.

With a sharp knife or kitchen shears, make a 2" or 3" split in each end of the rope. Separate the cut ends and curl as shown in the drawing. Repeat process with another rope to form the other arm of the cross, laying it over the first arm. Another variation is to form the letters "alpha" and "omega" which may be made large and used alone or made small and used with the large cross. For Easter decorations, push red dyed Easter eggs firmly into the dough and criss-cross small ropes of dough over them to form small crosses and garnish all around with nut halves and/or Jordan almonds.

Clipping: With clean kitchen shears or scissors, clip the dough along the ridge of the cross or letter decorations or symbols in the surface of the dough. Depth and spacing of the clipping will determine prominence of decoration after baking.

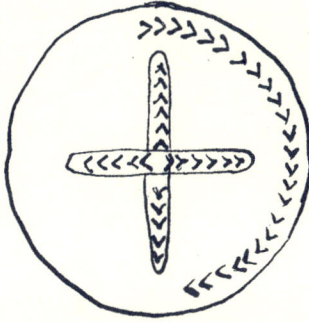

FILLED BRAID: After one pound portion has been divided into equal parts, take one portion and roll on a floured surface into a rectangle; then spread filling over it to approximately one inch from the edges. Begin rolling, jelly roll fashion. When roll is complete, pinch ends and along edge to close. When all three portions are filled, braid them together loosely (see drawing). Place on greased cookie sheet or in greased pans and bake according to recipe.

Method 1.

Method 2. In which braid is started at center and worked out to ends. This bread will be thicker in center when baked.

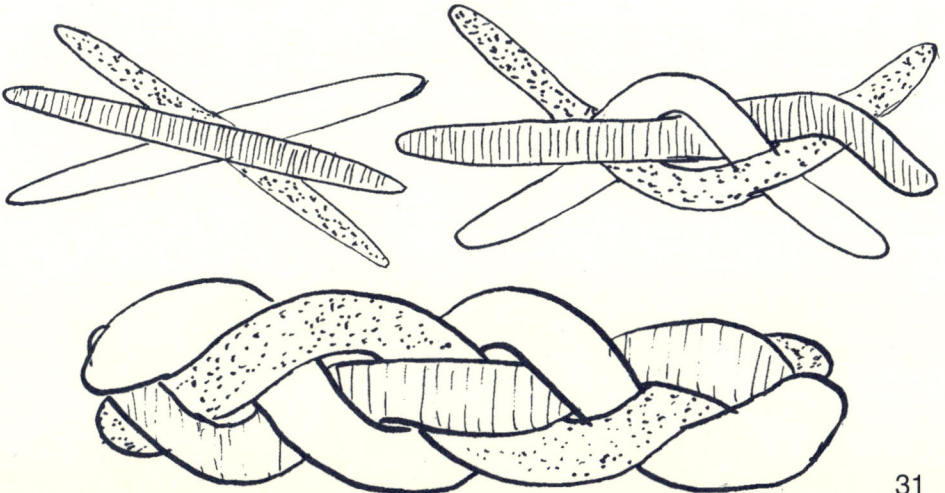

EASTER EGGS

THE RED EASTER EGG–Greek. The tradition of the Easter Egg was originated when Mary Magdalene went to visit the Emperor of the Roman Empire after the Ascension of Christ. She greeted the Emperor with, "Christ is Risen! Christos Anesti!" and gave him a red egg. The egg symbolizes future life. To us Christians, the egg represents the sealed tomb of Christ. The eggs are dyed red on Holy Thursday since that was the day Christ was crucified. The color red represents His precious blood which was shed for the salvation of mankind. The red eggs are distributed to the congregation at the end of the Easter Sunday Divine Liturgy. The family members each take turns striking each other's egg (representing the seal of the tomb is broken), and proclaiming, "Christ is Risen! Truly He is Risen!" "Christos Anesti! Alithos Anesti!"

PYSANKY–Carpatho-Russian/Ukrainian. Among Ukrainians there is a belief that the fate of the world depends upon pysanky. As long as egg-decorating continues, the world will exist. Should the custom cease, evil, in the guise of an ancient, vicious monster chained to a huge cliff, will encompass the world and destroy it. Each year the monster's servants encircle the globe, keeping a record of the number of pysanky made. When there are few, the monster's chains loosen, and evil flows through the world. When there are many, the monster's chains hold taut, allowing love to conquer evil.

SURMA–Easter Egg Legend

ANGIE'S EASTER EGGS   GREEK

Eggs
Greek Red Dye
Italian parsley (flat leaf)
Nylon mesh
Vegetable oil
Soft cloth or paper towels

Place parsley leaf on egg, wrap with nylon mesh (cut up nylon stockings), and tie with thread. Place wrapped eggs in a deep pot; fill the pot with cold water to cover eggs; let stand about 30 minutes or until eggs stop making bubbles. Dilute dye according to directions on package and add to eggs*; boil according to package instructions. Remove eggs from dye with slotted spoon; allow to cool enough to handle and remove wrappings and leaves; polish each egg with oil on a soft cloth or paper towel; wipe thoroughly with dry cloth. Leaf pattern will show in a soft pink color.

*Most dyes need the addition of vinegar to the solution to bring out the true depth of the red color. (Package of dye will give the number of eggs it will color.)

Mrs. Nicholas Kolopanas (Angie)

APPETIZERS

BABA GA-NOOJ

LEBANESE

Eggplant Appetizer

Temperature: 300°
Yield: 6-8 servings

1 large eggplant
3 Tbsp. sesame paste
1 Tbsp. olive oil
2 lemons, juice of
1/2 tsp. salt
1/2 clove garlic
Parsley for garnish

Step 1. Cut stem from eggplant; do not peel. Place eggplant on baking pan, place in 300° oven; bake until tender. (30-45 minutes)

Step 2. Cut skin and scoop out pulp. Let cool.

Step 3. Mix sesame paste with 1 Tbsp. cold water, stir well; add oil, lemon juice, salt and garlic. Mix this with the egglant pulp, stirring well. Chill. Serve with crackers or chips.

Minnie Zambie
West Helena, Arkansas

DOLMATHAKIA

GREEK

Stuffed Grapevine Leaves

Yield: Approximately 50 "little finger" size rolls

4 cups onions, chopped
1 cup olive oil or vegetable oil
1 cup rice, raw
1 cup water
2 tsp. dried dill, crushed
2 tsp. dried mint, crushed
1 cup parsley, finely snipped
1 tsp. salt
Dash of pepper
1 16-ounce jar grapevine
 leaves
3 cups boiling water, divided
1/4 cup lemon juice

Step 1. Cook onions in oil until soft. Add rice and 1 cup water. Cook 8 minutes. Add dill, mint, parsley, salt, and pepper. Cook 4 minutes. Let cool for 5 minutes.

Step 2. Spoon 1 teaspoonful of this filling near the stem end of a grape leaf with wrong side of leaf up and shiny side down. Fold sides in, then roll up loosely.

Step 3. Layer closely in a heavy dutch oven. Add 2 cups boiling water and lemon juice. Place a Pyrex dish, or heavy saucer, (upside down) directly on top of rolls to keep rolls intact while cooking.

Step 4. Cover and simmer for 1 hour or until rice is done. Add more boiling water if needed.

Step 5. When done, remove dish and allow rolls to come to room temperature in the pot. Sprinkle with more lemon juice.

Step 6. Remove rolls to platter and garnish with lemon wedges. Serve as a first course or as an hors d'oeuvre. May be served with plain yogurt.

Mrs. Raymond Guidi (Sophia)

KEFTETHAKIA

GREEK

Cocktail Meatballs

Yield: 30-40

1 pound ground beef or lamb
3 slices bread, trimmed and
  soft soaked
1 egg
1 medium onion, chopped
2 Tbsp. parsley, chopped
1/8 tsp. garlic powder (or 1
  minced clove of garlic)
1/2 tsp. oregano
Salt and pepper to taste

Step 1. Combine meat, bread, egg, seasonings and mix well. Add water if necessary to soften mixture.

Step 2. Shape into small balls. For extra flavor, moisten hands with wine before shaping balls.

Step 3. Lightly dredge meatballs in flour and fry in vegetable oil. If desired, they may be baked in over at 350° until brown.

Variations: Add 2 Tbsp. Parmesan cheese or a dash of cinnamon, or 1/4 tsp. mint to meat mixture for additional flavor.

Grecian Gourmet

KREATOPETAKIA

GREEK

Meat Triangles

Temperature: 325°
Yield: Approximately 60 pieces

1 pound ground beef
1 pound ground lamb
1/8 tsp. pepper
1 to 1-1/2 tsp. salt
1/8 tsp. cinnamon
1/8 tsp. ground cloves
1/8 tsp. nutmeg
1 large onion, chopped
1 Tbsp. olive oil
1 bell pepper, finely chopped
2 Tbsp. parsley,
  finely chopped
1 6-ounce can tomato paste
1 pound filo
3/4 cup melted butter

Step 1. Sauté onion and bell pepper in olive oil. Add parsley and sauté 1 minute. Add ground lamb and ground beef. Brown lightly and drain off all fat.

Step 2. Add salt, pepper, and spices and cook slightly. Add tomato paste and mix well.

Step 3. Cut filo into 2" strips. Using 2 strips, brush each with butter and place one strip on top of the other.

Step 4. Place 1 tsp. filling at the end and roll up in triangles. (See diagram in Basic Techniques Section.)

Step 5. Place on a cookie sheet and bake at 325° for 25 minutes or until golden brown.

Note: Kreatopetakia may be frozen unbaked. Baked as directed, unthawed.

Mrs. Gerry Touliatos (Olga)

MELIDZANA CAVIAR
Eggplant Canape

GREEK

Temperature: 350°
Yield: 2 cups

1 large eggplant (approx.
  2 pounds)
1/4 cup Wesson oil
1 onion, chopped fine
1/2 green pepper, chopped
  fine
1 stalk celery, chopped fine
1-1/2 tsp. Worcestershire
  sauce
Salt and pepper to taste

Step 1. Rub a small amount of oil on skin of unpeeled eggplant. Place in pan and bake at 350° for 30 minutes, until soft. Remove from oven and cool.

Step 2. Cut baked eggplant in half, scoop out pulp and mash.

Step 3. Combine onion, celery, green pepper, Worcestershire sauce and oil in pan and fry until vegetables are soft. Add eggplant pulp to mixture, season with salt and pepper and cook a few minutes more.

Step 4. Cool and refrigerate. Serve cold on buttered toast triangles.

Mrs. Charles Schneider (Katherine)
Pebble Beach, California

SAGANAKI
Fried Cheese

GREEK

Yield: 4 servings

1/2 pound Kasseri or
  Kefalotyri cheese
Flour
One stick butter
1 lemon, juice of
2 Tbsp. brandy

Step 1. Cut slices of cheese 1/2" thick.

Step 2. Dust both sides lightly with flour.

Step 3. Fry in very hot butter for 30 seconds on each side. Remove to heated serving plate.

Step 4. Heat brandy and flame; pour over cheese.

Step 5. When flame burns out squeeze lemon over all slices.

Mrs. Angelo Liollio (Tina)

SPANAKOPETAKIA

GREEK

Spinach Puffs

Temperature: 325°
Yield: Approximately 6 dozen

5 10-ounce boxes frozen
   chopped spinach
3 bunches fresh green
   onions, chopped
1 bunch fresh parsley,
   chopped
1/2 cup fresh dill, chopped or
   4 Tbsp. dry dill weed
1 pound feta cheese,
   crumbled
1/2 cup grated Parmesan
   cheese
3 Tbsp. Wesson oil
3 Tbsp. Cream of Wheat
6 eggs, beaten
1 pound butter, melted
1 pound filo

Step 1. Place frozen spinach in a colander and allow to thaw overnight.

Step 2. Squeeze as much moisture out of spinach as possible.

Step 3. Add onions, parsley, dill, cheeses, Wesson oil, Cream of Wheat, and beaten eggs. Mix well.

Step 4. Follow procedure for rolling triangles (See diagram in Basic Techniques Section.)

Step 5. Bake on cookie sheets for 20-25 minutes until golden brown.

Note: May be frozen before baking. Not necessary to thaw before baking.

Traditional Annunciation Bazaar Recipe

TARAMOSALATA

GREEK

Caviar Dip

Yield: 2 cups

Tarama, 4 ounces
1/4 cup olive oil
1/4 cup grated onion
1/2 cup Wesson oil
1/4 cup lemon juice
12-15 slices white bread,
   trimmed

Step 1. Beat tarama with olive oil until smooth and pasty.

Step 2. Add grated onion and beat well.

Step 3. Alternately, beat in Wesson oil and lemon juice, until all oil and juice have been added.

Step 4. Sprinkle bread with water to moisten (do not saturate). Add first 12 slices and beat mixture. Dip should be the consistency of mayonnaise. Beat in additional bread if dip needs to be thickened.

Mrs. James Liollio (Helen)

TOURSI

Pickled Vegetables

Bell peppers, cut lengthwise
  in quarters
Green tomatoes, quartered
Cauliflower, cut in flowerettes
Carrots, cut lengthwise
  in halves
Cabbage, cut in thin wedges

2 Tbsp. salt
2 cloves garlic
1/2 tsp. mustard seed
Cider vinegar
Water

Step 1. Fill sterlized canning jar with vegetables.

Step 2. Add spices and fill half the jar with vinegar. Add water to cover vegetables. Shake to mix and seal jar tightly.

Step 3. Set in cool place for at least two weeks or more.

Step 4. Serve chilled.

Grecian Gourmet

TIROPITAKIA

GREEK

Cheese Triangles

Temperature: 325°
Yield: Approximately 50

1 pound feta cheese
3 ounces cream cheese
8 ounces cottage cheese
3 eggs, separated
1/2 pound filo
2 sticks melted butter

Step 1. Mix all cheeses with beater. Separate eggs. Add yolks to cheese mixture, beating until well blended. Fold in stiffly beaten egg whites.

Step 2. Cut filo into 4" strips. Brush one strip lightly with melted butter. Place second strip of filo over first and brush again with melted butter.

Step 3. Place 1 tsp. of cheese mixture at one end of strip. Fold both sides over lengthwise, sealing in mixture and fold diagonally until triangle is formed, in manner of folding flag. See diagram in Basic Techniques Section.)

Step 4. Brush tops with melted butter and place on baking sheet. Bake at 325° for 20 minutes or until golden. Serve warm.

Note: May be frozen before baking and kept up to 6 months. Not necessary to thaw before baking.

Grecian Gourmet

SOUPS

AVGHOLEMONO SOUPA

GREEK

Egg-Lemon Soup

Yield: 5-6 servings

1 4-pound hen
1 medium onion, quartered
1 stalk celery
1 carrot
1 bay leaf (optional)
2 Tbsp. salt
6 to 8 whole peppercorns
1 whole clove (optional)
3/4 cup rice or Rosamarina

SAUCE:
4 eggs, separated
2 lemons, juice of or
 4 Tbsp. reconstituted
 lemon juice
2 to 3 cups broth

Step 1. Place hen in deep pot. Cover with water. Bring to a boil. Begin skimming off foam as chicken boils and continue until foaming has finished.

Step 2. Add all other ingredients except rice or Rosamarina. Bring to a boil. Cover and reduce heat. Simmer 1-1/2 to 2 hours or until hen is done.

Step 3. Remove hen from broth and set aside. Strain broth. Bring broth to boiling point again and stir in rice. Cover and cook until tender, about 20 minutes.

Step 4. Avgholemono Sauce: Beat egg whites until stiff but not dry. Add yolks and continue beating at medium speed, adding lemon juice very slowly.

Step 5. Add hot broth very slowly to egg-lemon mixture, beating constantly. Return this mixture to soup and stir constantly, over very low heat, until slightly thickened, about five minutes. Remove from heat and serve at once.

Note: Leftover soup may be stored in refrigerator and reheated over low heat.

The Cookbook Committee

FASOULATHA

GREEK

Bean Soup

Yield: 6-8 servings

1 pound dry Navy or
 Northern beans
2 quarts water
1/2 cup celery, chopped
1-1/2 cups onions, chopped
1 cup carrots, chopped
1/4 cup parsley, chopped
1 Tbsp. tomato paste
1 cup olive oil
Salt and pepper to taste

Step 1. Cover beans with water and soak overnight.

Step 2. Drain. Add 2 quarts water. Bring to a boil; lower heat. Add all other ingredients. Cover and simmer for 2 hours or until beans are very soft.

Grecian Gourmet

MAYERITSA I

Traditional Easter Soup

Yield: 12-15 servings

1 lamb tripe
1 set baby lamb intestines
1 lamb lung
1 lamb heart
1/2 lamb liver
2 lemons, juice of
3 bunches scallions
1 large onion, finely
  chopped
1/2 pound butter
1 Tbsp. salt
1 tsp. pepper
1/2 cup fresh dill or 1 Tbsp.
  dill weed
1/2 cup parsley, chopped
1/2 cup white wine
1/2 cup rice (optional)

Step 1. Wash tripe and place in bowl; squeeze juice of 1 lemon over it and let stand while you prepare intestines.

Step 2. If using intestines, turn them inside out and wash thoroughly under running water. Place in bowl and squeeze juice of 1 lemon over them and let stand for 1/2 hour. Drain and place in kettle with tripe (which has also been drained). Cover with water. Bring to a boil and simmer 15 to 30 minutes. Strain, reserving broth. When meats are cool enough to handle, chop them into pieces no larger than 1/4".

Step 3. Place washed lung, heart, and liver in kettle; barely cover with water. Add 1/2 tsp. salt; bring to boil and remove foam as it forms. Simmer for 30 minutes. Strain, reserving the broth and set meats aside to cool. Chop all meats into pieces no larger than 1/4".

Step 4. Sauté chopped onion in butter until transparent; add all chopped meats and saute until lightly browned. Add wine and broth. Bring to a boil, add scallions, dill, parsley, and salt and pepper to taste. Simmer covered for 1-1/2 hours. Check liquid and stir occasionally (should not be too thick).

Step 5. If rice is to be used, at this point add rice plus 2 cups boiling water and cook until rice is done.

Step 6. Prepare Avgholemono sauce. (See Sauce section.) Fold into soup just before serving.

Mrs. Bill Taras (Bessie)

MAYERITSA II
Easter Soup

Yield: 6 servings

2 pounds lamb liver
3 cups water
1 stick butter
8 green onions, chopped
6 cups water
1/3 cup dill, snipped
1/3 cup parsley, chopped
1/2 cup rice
Salt and pepper to taste

AVGHOLEMONO SAUCE:
5 eggs, separated
3 lemons, juice of
Hot broth from soup

Step 1. Boil liver in 3 cups water for 20 minutes. Remove from heat, strain broth and set aside. Chop liver in small pieces.

Step 2. Saute onions, dill, and parsley in butter. Add salt and pepper. Onions should be soft but not brown. Add chopped liver and cook over low heat for 5 minutes. Stir frequently.

Step 3. Add liver broth and enough water to make 2 quarts liquid. When broth comes to a boil, add rice. Reduce heat and cook until rice is tender.

Step 4. Avgholemono Sauce: Beat egg whites until stiff, but not dry. Lower speed of mixer and add egg yolks. Very slowly add lemon juice. Slowly, add as much broth from soup as possible, beating constantly.

Step 5. Return this mixture to pot, stirring slowly and constantly, about 5 minutes. Serve immediately.

Grecian Gourmet

FAKI
Lentil Soup

GREEK

Yield: 4-6 servings

1 cup lentils
5 cups water
1/2 cup olive oil
1 medium onion, chopped
1/2 cup tomato sauce
2 cloves garlic
1 tsp. salt
1/4 tsp. pepper
1 bay leaf
1 stalk celery, chopped
   (optional)
2 carrots, chopped (optional)
1/4 tsp. oregano (optional)
2 Tbsp. vinegar

Step 1. Sort and wash lentils. Put in a deep pot with water. When boiling point is reached, add all other ingredients except vinegar. Reduce heat, cover and simmer over low heat for 1 to 1-1/2 hours.

Step 2. Add vinegar. Remove garlic and bay leaf before serving. Additional olive oil and vinegar may be added when served.

Grecian Gourmet

HORTOSOUPA   GREEK-AMERICAN
Vegetable Soup

Yield: Approximately 4 quarts

Soup bone (beef or lamb)
2 pounds cubed meat (beef or lamb)
3 quarts water
2 onions, diced
2 cloves garlic, minced
2 stalks celery, diced
1 carrot, diced
1 14-ounce can whole tomatoes
1 14-ounce can tomato sauce
1 6-ounce can tomato paste
2 bay leaves
1-1/2 tsp. oregano
1 tsp. thyme
1 tsp. tarragon
1/2 tsp. basil
2 Tbsp. Worcestershire sauce
1 tsp. sugar
1-1/2 tsp. salt
1/2 tsp. pepper
2 cans VegAll*
1/2 cup Rosamarina
1 quart water

Step 1. Cover soup bone and cubed meat with 3 quarts water. Bring to a boil and boil 30 minutes.

Step 2. Add remaining ingredients to meat stock (except VegAll and Rosamarina) and simmer for 4 hours.

Step 3. Add VegAll (including liquid), Rosamarina and another quart of water. Simmer for 1 hours.

Step 4. Remove bay leaves and soup bone prior to serving.

Note: Freezes well.

*Assorted diced vegetables of your choice may be substituted. Use approximately 2 or 3 cups, depending on desired amount of vegetables in soup.

Mrs. Michael Speros (Carolyn)

PSAROSOUPA   GREEK
Fish Soup

3-4 pounds fish of your choice (or combination of red snapper, bass, shrimp, squid, etc.) cut into serving size pieces
1/2 cup parsley, chopped
2 medium yellow onions, quartered, then slivered
2 stalks celery, chopped
1/2 cup olive oil
2 cloves garlic
1 large white potato, diced
1 bay leaf
1 Tbsp. salt
6-8 black peppercorns
1 cup dry white wine (optional)

Step 1. Heat oil in large, wide bottomed pot; add chopped vegetables, garlic, and bay leaf and peppercorns, and sauté until onions are well wilted. Add fish and just enough water to barely cover fish. Add wine. Sprinkle with salt. Bring to a boil; reduce heat so that liquid is at a steady simmer. Cover pot and cook 15-20 minutes or until largest chunks of fish will flake.

Note: If whole fish is available, you may either add heads and tails with the fish or these and any seafood shells may be stewed in a separate pot and the liquid strained and added to the soup before serving.

Mrs. James Varnavas (Helen)

SQUASH SOUP

Yield: 4-6 servings

**4 or 5 medium size zucchini
  or yellow squash (or a
  combination)**
1/4 cup water
1/4 tsp. salt (optional)
2 or 3 Tbsp. butter
**Milk for desired
  consistency**
**1/2 to 1 cup Feta cheese,
  crumbled**

Step 1. Clean squash; partially peel or scrape skin; cut into pieces. Boil water, add squash (and salt); cook until tender

Step 2. Remove from heat, mash until slightly lumpy, add butter. Return to medium heat, add milk for consistency desired, heat to simmer. Remove from heat, add cheese, blend. Cover and let stand about 5 minutes to soften cheese. Serve immediately or serve cold.

May be prepared without the milk, for thick consistency, and served as a side dish.

Mrs. James (Helen) Varnavas

SALADS

DOMATOSALATA

GREEK

Tomato Salad

Yield: 4 servings

4 tomatoes, cut into small
   pieces or slices
1 large onion, sliced thin
1/2 Tbsp. salt or to taste
3 Tbsp. olive oil or salad oil
1 tsp. oregano
1 Tbsp. vinegar or to taste

Step 1. Place sliced onions, salt, olive oil, oregano, and vinegar in salad bowl. Allow to marinate for about 10 minutes.

Step 2. Add quartered tomatoes. Toss gently. Refrigerate before serving.

Mrs. James Varnavas (Helen)

HORIATIKI SALATA

GREEK

Provincial Salad

Yield: Judge quantity according to need

Tomatoes, quartered or
   sliced
Onions, thinly sliced
Cucumbers, peeled and
   cubed or round slices
Feta cheese, cubed or
   crumbled
Salt and pepper to taste
Olive oil, or salad oil
Wine vinegar

Step 1. Mix seasonings; pour over onions. Let stand at least 10 minutes.

Step 2. In salad bowl place tomatoes and cucumbers. Pour onion with seasoning over these and combine gently. Add feta cheese and serve.

Mrs. Bill K. Taras (Bessie)

MAVROMATIKA FASOLIA SALATA

GREEK

Blackeyed Pea Salad

Yield: 4 servings

1 10-ounce package
   blackeyed peas, frozen
1 small or 1/2 large onion,
   chopped
1/2 tsp. oregano
1/4 cup olive oil or salad oil
1/2 lemon, juice of
1/4 cup celery (optional
Salt and pepper to taste
Dash of garlic salt

Step 1. Cook peas according to package directions. Cool. Drain.

Step 2. Beat lemon juice and oil together. Place peas in serving bowl; add onions, oregano, salt and pepper to taste. Toss gently. Add dressing and toss again.

Mrs. Bill K. Taras (Bessie)

PANZARIA SALATA
Beet Salad

Yield: 6-8 servings

2 cans sliced beets or
  2 pounds fresh beets,
  cooked, sliced
2 onions, sliced thin
1 bay leaf
Salt and pepper to taste
1/2 cup vinegar
1/2 cup olive oil
1 or 2 garlic cloves, minced
  (optional)

Step 1. Several hours before or even early in the day, combine all ingredients in a bowl, and allow to marinate in refrigerator.

Mrs. Bill K. Taras (Bessie)

SALATA
Green Salad

Yield: 6 servings

1 small head lettuce or
  1/2 small head lettuce and
  1/2 head romaine or
  escarole, or endive
  and/or spinach
1 small cucumber, sliced
1 or 2 green onions, thinly
  sliced
Radishes
1 small green pepper or 1/2
  large green pepper
4 tender stalks of celery
Anchovies
Calamata olives
Feta cheese

DRESSING:
3/4 cup olive oil or
  3/4 cup salad oil and
  olive oil combined
1/3 cup wine vinegar
1 tsp. salt
1 clove garlic, crushed
  (optional)
1 tsp. oregano

Step 1. Combine dressing ingredients in a jar and let stand.

Step 2. Combine salad ingredients in a large bowl.

Step 3. Pour dressing over salad. Toss and sprinkle crumbled feta cheese on top. Garnish with anchovies and Calamata olives.

Mrs. James Varnavas (Helen)

SAF-SOOF
Cracked Wheat Salad

LEBANESE

Yield: 6-8 servings

1 cup fine cracked wheat
1 bunch parsley
1 bunch green onions
3 tomatoes
1 green pepper (optional)
1 head lettuce

DRESSING:
2 Tbsp. dried mint
1/2 cup olive oil
1 tsp. salt
1/2 tsp. black pepper
3 lemons, juice of

Step 1. Cover cracked wheat with water; cover and let soak in refrigerator for 1 hour.

Step 2. Cut parsley from stems and chop fine. Cut onions fine; chop tomatoes into small pieces; dice green pepper.

Step 3. Drain wheat; squeeze out water; mix with other vegetables (except lettuce); pour the dressing mix over this mixture and serve on lettuce leaves.

Minnie Zambie
West Helena, Arkansas

TABOULEH
Cracked Wheat Salad

LEBANESE

Yield: 6-8 servings

3/4 cup cracked wheat,
   uncooked (Bulgar wheat #1)
5-6 large ripe tomatoes
1-1/2 tsp. salt
1 bunch green onions or
   1 small yellow onion
4-5 large bunches curly
   parsley, discard stems
1/4 cup mint leaves
5 lemons, juice of
1 cup olive oil
1 head Romaine lettuce (use
   leaves as scoops for salad)

Step 1. Chop tomatoes, onions, parsley, and mint very fine, chopping each vegetable separately by hand to preserve each one's texture.

Step 2. Place cracked wheat in large salad bowl; add chopped tomatoes and a little salt, toss to blend.

Step 3. Gradually add chopped onion and more salt; add parsley and toss to mix thoroughly.

Step 4. Pour lemon juice and olive oil over salad; toss to combine all ingredients thoroughly.

Step 5. Taste; add more salt and olive oil, if needed. Let salad stand for about 15 minutes before serving. Toss again before serving

Mrs. Sarkis Kish (Jenny)

CHEESE DISHES

GIBANICA I

SERBIAN

Strudel and Cheese Cake Combination

Temperature: 350°
Pan Size: 9" by 14" –glass
Yield: 28 servings

4 ounces poppy seeds
1/2 cup sugar
1/4 cup milk
1-1/2 cups chopped walnuts
1/2 cup sugar
1/2 cup warm milk
 (about 110°)
6 egg yolks
2 pounds ricotta cheese,
 beaten
1 cup sugar
1/2 cup raisins
1 tsp. vanilla
1/2 tsp. salt
3 tart apples, pared
 and diced
1/2 cup sugar
1 tsp. cinnamon
3/4 pound sweet butter,
 melted
1 1-pound package filo pastry

Step 1. Mix poppy seeds, sugar, and milk in bowl and set aside.

Step 2. Mix chopped walnuts, sugar, and milk; set aside.

Step 3. Add egg yolks and sugar to cheese which has been beaten until smooth. Stir in raisins, vanilla,and salt; set aside.

Step 4. Mix apples, sugar and cinnamon together and set aside.

Step 5. Line well-buttered pan with 6 sheets filo, each brushed individually with melted butter.

Step 6. Spread the poppy seed mixture over filo. Top with 4 sheets filo, buttered as before.

Step 7. Spread with cheese filling; top with 4 sheets filo, buttered.

Step 8. Cover with chopped walnut mixture; top with 4 sheets of filo, buttered.

Step 9. cover with apple mixture.

Step 10: Trim filo around sides of pan so that they are even with top of filling. Top with remaining sheets of filo, buttered as before.

Step 11. Bake at 350° for 1 hour or until golden. Cool completely before placing in refrigerator. Then chill thoroughly before serving.

Note: Keeps well in refrigerator. May be frozen.

Ann Pekovich

LAGANA
Feta Cheese Bread Roll

GREEK

Temperature: 375°
Pan Size: 9" by 5" loaf pans
Yield: 2 loaves

1 cup milk
1/4 cup shortening
1/2 tsp. salt
2 tsp. sugar
1 package granulated yeast
1/4 cup warm water
4 cups flour, all-purpose
1 pound feta cheese,
   coarsely crumbled
1/2 pound butter, at room
   temperature

Step 1. Heat milk to scalding; add shortening, salt and sugar; set aside to cool.

Step 2. Sprinkle yeast into warm water and set aside to rise.

Step 3. Sift flour into a large bowl; make a well in the flour; pour in the yeast mixture and milk mixture; stir to make a firm dough.

Step 4. Knead on floured surface until smooth and elastic; place dough in well oiled bowl to rise until doubled in bulk. Punch down and divide into 2 equal portions.

Step 5. Divide cheese and butter each into 2 equal portions.

Step 6. On well floured surface, roll out 1 portion of dough to an 8" x 16" rectangle (approximate size); spread half of the butter on the lower half of the rectangle, sprinkle with half of the cheese. Fold down top half of dough and press down lightly all over surface; then, using hands, press dough out to about the original size and repeat butter and cheese step. Roll up as for jelly roll and place seam side down in well greased loaf pan. Butter surface to keep it from drying out. (Repeat entire step 6 for second portion of dough.)

Step 7. Set loaves in a warm place, cover with cloth and allow to rise until doubled in bulk. Bake at 375° for 15 minutes, reduce heat to 350° and bake 30 minutes or until golden brown. Allow loaves to cool at least 10-15 minutes before slicing.

Mrs. Stephen S. Lenis (Mary)

MAKARONOPETA I
Macaroni and Cheese Peta

GREEK

Temperature: 450°
Pan Size: 9" x 13"
Yield: 20 squares

6 ounces elbow macaroni
5-6 large eggs, well beaten
2-1/2 cups lukewarm milk
2-1/2 sticks butter, melted
Salt to taste
1 cup feta cheese, crumbled
1/2 cup cottage cheese
1/2 cup grated Parmesan
cheese
1 pound package filo leaves

Step 1. Cook elbow macaroni in boiling salted water until almost done. Drain well.

Step 2. Beat eggs well, add milk, and 1/2 cup melted butter.

Step 3. Mix macaroni with cheeses and stir lightly to mix. Add to eggs and milk. Salt to taste. Stir well.

Step 4. Carefully line 9" x 13" pan (which has been greased with melted butter) with 8 sheets filo, brush each with melted butter. Pour mixture into pan, top with additional 8 sheets filo and brush each with butter.* Sprinkle with water or milk.

Step 5. Bake at 450° for 10 minutes, then lower to 350° for 30 minutes.

*Refer to Basic Techniques section.

Mrs. Bill Taras (Bessie)

GIBANICA II
Cheese Peta

SERBIAN

Temperature: 325°
Pan Size: 13" x 9" x 2"
Yield: 8-10 servings

1 pound feta cheese,
chopped
1 pound cottage cheese,
small curd
6 eggs, beaten
1/2 cup carbonated water
1 pound filo (strudel dough)
1/2 pound butter, melted

Step 1. Heat oven to 325°. Mix feta and cottage cheese, eggs, and water in large bowl.

Step 2. Cover bottom of butter baking dish 13" x 9" x 2" with two filo sheets. Pour 2 Tbsp. melted butter over filo. Spread about 6 large spoonfuls of cheese mixture on top.

Step 3. Repeat the dough, butter and cheese layers until two sheets of dough are left. Add last two sheets of dough and pour remaining butter over it. Bake in 325° oven for about one hour. Cut in squares. Serve warm.

Mrs. George Cavic (Mileva)
Chesterfield, Missouri

MAKARONOPETA II
Macaroni and Cheese Peta

GREEK

Temperature: 350°
Pan Size: 9" x 13"
Yield: 20 medium size servings

8 ounces elbow macaroni,
  cooked in salted water and
  drained
6 eggs, beaten
3 cups milk
1/2 pound feta cheese,
  crumbled
1/2 cup grated Parmesan
  cheese
2 sticks butter (1 stick for
  filling and 1 stick for filo)
1/2 pound filo (approximately)

Step 1. Melt 1 stick butter. Brush bottom and sides of pan generously with butter. Line pan with filo sheets, covering bottom and sides, brushing each filo with melted butter. Use 8 or 9 sheets of filo.

Step 2. Melt second stick butter and combine with all other ingredients; taste and salt if necessary.

Step 3. Pour macaroni mixture carefully into prepared pan.

Step 4. Cover with 8 or 9 sheets of filo, again brushing each layer with melted butter. Sprinkle top lightly with milk. Bake at 350° for 40 to 50 minutes. Cut into squares. Serve hot or cold.

Mrs. Charles J. Vergos (Tasia)

TIROPETA
Cheese Peta

GREEK

Temperature: 450°
Pan Size: 11" x 14" X 2"
Yield: 40 squares

6 eggs, separated
1/2 pound feta cheese
3 ounces cream cheese
8 ounces large curd cottage
  cheese
1 pound filo sheets
1-1/2 sticks butter, melted

Step 1. Beat egg yolks; add feta cheese, cream cheese, and cottage cheese; blend well.

Step 2. Beat egg whites until stiff but not dry. Fold into cheese mixture.

Step 3. Line pan with 8 filo sheets, brush with melted butter between each layer. Pour filling in pan and cover with 8 more sheets, brush between each sheet with butter.

Step 4. Bake in 450° oven for 15 to 20 minutes until filo begins to turn light golden color and puffs in the center. Reduce oven to 350° and bake 30 minutes longer until golden brown.

Step 5. Let peta stand 15 to 20 minutes before cutting.

Grecian Gourmet

TIROPSOMO

GREEK

Cheese Bread

This cheese bread is a favorite snack (or an addition to lunch) of the ladies of the Annunciation Church during the bread baking workshops for the annual bazaar. The idea stems from the village life of Greece when busy housewives used part of the dough being prepared for the day's meals as a tide-me-over until dinner. Tiropsomo can be a quick meal on a busy baking day, a side dish, or the bread for a light meal.

Temperature: 350°

Plain yeast bread dough
Feta cheese, crumbled
Soft butter

Step 1. Divide dough into 2 portions. With rolling pin, roll out each one (round or square) as thin as it will stretch. Brush with melted butter, sprinkle feta cheese evenly over 1 portion; dot generously with butter.

Step 2. Top with second portion of dough; seal by firmly pinching edges together. Place bread on a buttered cookie sheet; with your fingers, make depressions in the dough and drizzle melted butter over entire surface; set in a warm place to rise (about 45 minutes to an hour). Bake for 30 minutes or until golden brown. Serve hot.

Mrs. George Karkatsugas (Agori)

EASY TIROPETA

GREEK

Temperature: 350°
Pan Size: 9" x 13"

1/2 pound filo
1-1/2 sticks butter for filo,
  melted
1 cup feta cheese,
  crumbled
1 cup low fat cottage
  cheese
7 eggs
2 cups milk (low fat)
8 Tbsp. flour
5 Tbsp. butter or
  margarine, melted
Freshly ground pepper

Step 1. Brush 9" x 13" pan with butter, then layer pan with 6 sheets filo after buttering each sheet.

Step 2. Combine all other ingredients in blender and blend well. Then pour mixture into prepared pan.

Step 3. Layer 6 more sheets of filo, buttering each sheet. Sprinkle cold water on top

Step 4. Bake for approximately 45 minutes. Peta will rise and turn a golden brown. Delicious!

Step 5. Cut into squares and serve.

Helen A. Knight

PASCHA RUSSIAN
Traditional Easter Dessert

*Pan Size: Clay flower pot (with hole in bottom), approximately 10" deep x 7" across
or Pascha mold
Yield: 25-30 servings*

1 pound sweet butter
7 egg yolks
2 cups sugar
**2 pounds dry cottage cheese,
  drained until dry**
1/2 pint whipping cream
**1 tsp. vanilla or
  almond extract**
1/2 cup ground almonds
Cheese cloth

Step 1. Beat egg yolks until thick and lemon colored. Add sugar gradually and beat well. Cream butter; beat in sugar and yolks. Sieve the cottage cheese, making it very fine in consistency. Add to butter mixture gradually and blend thoroughly. Whip cream, then fold with vanilla and ground almonds, into cheese mixture.

Step 2. Have wooden Pascha mold or flower pot lined with doubled cheese cloth, extending ends over the sides slightly. Pour mixture into mold. Cover with ends of cloth, and place a weight on top. Place mold on rack set in plate in refrigerator and allow to drain for 2 days. Unmold and remove cloth carefully. Decorate with almonds, cherries, etc. Pascha can be made in different fruit flavors, such as maraschino cherries, lemon, or prune by adding the chopped fruits or grated rind and flavorings to the cheese. Decorate with the letters XB–the Easter greeting "Christos Voskres," which means "Christ is Risen."

Mrs. George Ostrosky (Helen)

55

PIROSHKI

Stuffed Dumplings

Yield: 5 dozen

PASTRY:
1 large potato, cooked and
  sieved (about 1 cup)
1-1/2 cups lukewarm water
4 eggs, beaten
1 Tbsp. sour cream
2 Tbsp. melted Crisco
6 cups flour, sifted
1 cup instant dry milk
1/4 tsp. salt
2 cups extra flour, sifted
Oil for frying

FILLING:
3 pounds potatoes, peeled
  and boiled
1/2 pound sharp cheese,
  coarsely shredded
1 tsp. salt
1/4 tsp. pepper, or more
  to taste
5 Tbsp. margarine
1 large onion, chopped
  coarsely

Step 1. Pastry: Mix together first 5 ingredients. Add 6 cups flour, dry milk, and salt. If needed, add 2 extra cups flour, a little at a time, until dough no longer sticks to hands. Separate dough into 5 balls. Let sit on a board, covered, with dry cloth.

Step 2. Filling: Drain and mash potatoes with cheese. Brown onions in margarine. Add to potatoes, along with seasonings. Cool.

Step 3. Roll out dough about 1/4 inch thick, 1 ball at a time. Cut the dough with a heavy water glass about 3 inches wide, so that each piroshki will be the same size. Put a heaping teaspoonful of potato mixture on each round of dough. Fold over, press the edges together, and lay on a cloth until all piroshki are made.

Step 4. Fry in deep, hot oil (450°) a few at a time, until light brown. Takes just a few minutes.

Serving suggestion: You may smother with extra fried onions and melted margarine, or eat as is. Serve with borscht or dried mushroom soup, as main dish or vegetable.

Note: May be frozen and warmed in oven.

Mrs. Mary Kinn Daduk
Coaldale, Pennsylvania

SEAFOOD

GARIDES TOURKOLIMANO GREEK
Shrimp Tourkolimano

Yield: 4 servings

1-1/2 pounds raw shrimp, shelled and deveined
2 Tbsp. olive oil
3 medium sized tomatoes, peeled and chopped
1 cup green onions, chopped
2 cloves garlic, minced
1 Tbsp. brandy
1 Tbsp. red wine
1/2 tsp. oregano
Salt and pepper to taste
1/2 pound feta cheese, crumbled

Step 1. Place olive oil in hot skillet and add shrimp. Stir until pink. Remove shrimp and put in 1-1/2 quart casserole dish.

Step 2. In frying pan add onions, garlic and tomatoes. Cook 6 or 7 minutes; add salt, oregano, pepper, and liquids during this time.

Step 3. Pour ingredients from Step 2 over shrimp, adding feta cheese, and heat in oven about 20 to 25 minutes. Serve over hot rice.

Mrs. Pete J. Vergos (Helen)

GARIDES SOUVLAKIA GREEK
Skewered Shrimp

Yield: 4 servings

24 large shrimp, shelled and deveined
2 lemons, juice of
3 cloves garlic, minced
3 Tbsp. parsley, chopped
2 Tbsp. oregano
1/2 cup melted butter
1/4 cup white wine
Salt and pepper

Step 1. Place all ingredients in a bowl, mix well, and marinate for about 1 hour.

Step 2. Skewer marinated shrimp (6 to a skewer).

Step 3. Place on a broiler rack, with pan underneath to catch drippings. Pour marinade over shrimp; broil under hot fire, turning and basting until golden brown on all sides, about 10 to 15 minutes.

Step 4. Remove shrimp from skewers. Place on serving dishes and pour pan juices over them. Serve immediately with lemon wedges. Serve with a rice pilaf, sliced tomatoes, feta cheese, and chilled white wine.

Mrs. Angelina P. Kolopanas

GARIDES PILAF
Shrimp with Rice Pilaf

GREEK

Yield: 6-8 servings

1 large onion, chopped
1/2 cup oil or butter
1-1/2 cups long grain rice
2 pounds shrimp, shelled
3 cups boiling water
1 tsp. parsley, chopped
Salt and pepper to taste
1 8-ounce can tomato sauce

Step 1. Sauté onion in oil or butter until soft. Add rice and shrimp and sauté 2 to 3 minutes.

Step 2. Add water, parsley, salt, pepper and stir. Remove shrimp with slotted spoon. Simmer for 30 minutes until rice is tender.

Step 3. Return shrimp and heat thoroughly.

Grecian Gourmet

KALAMARAKIA
Sautéed Squid

GREEK

Yield: 12 servings

1 5-pound box frozen squid
  (thawed)
1 cup flour
1-1/2 tsp. salt
1/8 tsp. freshly ground
  pepper
1/8 tsp. garlic powder
1/2 cup olive oil
1/2 stick butter
1/4 cup dry white wine
2 lemons, juice of

Step 1. Wash squid thoroughly and pull out the soft backbone and ink sac from each. Remove black membrane covering squid.

Step 2. Combine flour, salt, pepper, and garlic powder.

Step 3. Heat oil and butter in heavy frying pan until hot.

Step 4. Coat each squid with seasoned flour. Leave squid whole if very small, otherwise, cut into bite-size pieces.

Step 5. Sauté over medium high heat until golden brown on both sides. Remove to heated serving platter.

Step 6. Reserve oil from pan; scrape and remove any burned particles from pan; reheat oil over high heat. Add wine and lemon juice, scrape all browned juices from pan and quickly bring to a boil; pour over squid. Serve with hot, crusty bread to soak up juices.

Mrs. Angelo D. Liollio (Tina)

KALAMARAKIA YEMISTA
Stuffed Squid

Pan Size: Large covered skillet
Yield: 6-8 servings

3 pound box of frozen squid, or 12 fresh squid
1/2 cup olive oil
1/4 cup wine or wine vinegar
2 large onions, chopped
2 cloves garlic, minced, or 1 tsp. garlic powder
2 to 3 Tbsp. raisins, or currants (optional)
1/2 to 3/4 cup rice
Salt and pepper to taste
2 tsp. tomato sauce or paste
1/4 cup parsley, chopped
1-1/2 cups boiling water
1/2 cup wine

Step 1. Have squid cleaned at market or discard celluloid backbone and ink sac. Chop tentacles and set aside. Place squid in bowl and sprinkle with wine or wine vinegar.

Step 2. In 1/2 cup oil sauté onions and garlic until transparent. Add chopped tentacles, cover and simmer until they turn white in color. Add rice, salt and pepper and tomato sauce and parsley. Cook 5 minutes and set aside to cool.

Step 3. When mixture is cool enough to handle, stuff each squid, using a teaspoon. Do not over stuff. Place Kalamaria (squid) sides touching in oiled skillet. (Squid opening may be held closed with toothpick.)

Step 4. Sprinkle Kalamaria with remaining oil, crumbled bay leaf, wine, salt and pepper. Cover and simmer for 30-35 minutes. Add more boiling water as liquid is absorbed so there will be enough sauce to spoon over squid when served.

Mrs. Jerre Duzane (Madeline)

MARITHES
Fried Smelts

Yield: 6 servings

1 pound smelts
1 cup flour
1 cup cornmeal
1 tsp. salt
1/4 tsp. pepper
1/2 tsp. garlic powder
1/2 tsp. oregano
Wesson oil

Step 1. Mix flour, cornmeal, and seasonings together.

Step 2. Dust smelts with flour mixture and fry in hot oil (about 350° on electric frying pan) until golden.

Step 3. Remove and drain on paper towels.

Note: One pound of cleaned baby squid may be used in place of smelts, adding optional seasoning of 1 tsp. Lawry's seasoned salt.

Ms. Lynda Liollio

PSARI MARINATO
Marinated Fish

GREEK

Yield: 6 servings

1 3-pound red snapper,
   filleted
Salt and pepper to taste
Oil for frying
1 Tbsp. flour
3 cloves garlic, minced
1 bay leaf
Pinch of rosemary leaves
1 14-ounce can whole
   tomatoes
1/4 cup vinegar

Step 1. Season fish with salt and pepper. Roll in flour and fry in 1" hot oil until golden brown. Remove from pan and place on serving platter. Keep warm.

Step 2. Blend flour in drippings. Reduce heat. Add garlic, bay leaf, and rosemary and slowly stir in tomatoes and vinegar. Simmer for 10 minutes until slightly thickened.

Step 3. Pour sauce over fish and serve.

Grecian Gourmet

PSARI MAYONEZA I
Chilled Snapper with Mayonnaise Sauce

GREEK

Yield: 6 servings

1 whole red snapper
   (3-4 pounds)
3 whole carrots
2 onions, quartered
1 potato, quartered

2 stalks celery
1 bay leaf
Salt and pepper to taste

SAUCE:
2 egg yolks
1/2 tsp. salt
1 tsp. prepared mustard
2 cups salad oil
6 Tbsp. lemon juice
3 Tbsp. vinegar

Step 1. Clean fish and tie in a cheesecloth, so that fish will not fall apart. Add carrots, onions, celery, salt and pepper. Add enough water to cover fish and vegetables. Simmer fish 25 minutes.

Step 2. Remove fish from stock and place on platter. When cool, split fish and bone carefully. Remove skin. Form in shape of fish and place in refrigerator.

Step 3. Sauce: Beat egg yolks, salt, and mustard together. Beat well and add oil very slowly and alternately with lemon juice and vinegar. Beat until thick.

Step 4. Assembling: Spread top and sides of fish with mayoneza sauce. Garnish with sliced carrots, black olives (for eyes), parsley (for fins), and lemon wedges around platter.

Mrs. George Cotros (Katina)

61

PSARI MAYONEZA II

GREEK

Red Snapper with Mayonnaise Sauce

Yield: 6 servings

1 3-4 pound red snapper
4 egg yolks
1 tsp. dry mustard
(or more to taste)
1 lemon, juice of
1 cup salad oil or
1/4 cup olive oil plus
3/4 cup salad oil
Salt to taste

GARNISH:
2 black olives
Bell pepper strips
Paprika
1 hard-boiled egg
Parsley
Tail of snapper

Step 1. Cut tail off of the snapper, wrap, and place in refrigerator. Simmer snapper until tender in salted water to cover. After cooking, cool fish in broth, drain, and reserve 1/2 cup broth.

Step 2. Remove skin and bones. Arrange fish meat on large platter in the shape of a fish. Place the tail in appropriate place to complete shape of fish. Chill well; spoon a few teaspoons reserved fish broth over the meat to moisten.

Step 3. Mayoneza: Beat egg yolks. Mix mustard with lemon juice; add alternately to yolks with oil; add salt to taste. Cook in top of double boiler until thick, stirring constantly. Allow to cool. Pour mayoneza carefully over chilled fish using a large spoon. Cover all the fish except the end of the tail. Decorate with black olives for eyes and bell pepper strips for backbone. Garnish platter with hard-boiled egg slices and parsley. Sprinkle with paprika for color. Chill several hours before serving.

Mrs. Gregory Bacopulos (Pat)

PSARI PLAKI I

GREEK

Baked Red Snapper with Vegetables

Temperature: 350°
Yield: 4 servings

2 pounds red snapper
Salt and pepper to taste
Oregano
Accent
1 lemon, juice of
2 bunches green onions,
chopped
6 cloves garlic, chopped
3/4 cup parsley, chopped
1/2 cup oil
1 16-ounce can whole
tomatoes, chopped
1 tsp. dill weed

Step 1. Place fish in a baking pan and sprinkle with salt, pepper, oregano, Accent, and lemon juice.

Step 2. In a large skillet, sauté onions, garlic, and parsley in oil. Add chopped tomatoes. Cook until onions are soft. Add dill.

Step 3. Pour this mixture over fish and bake for 45 minutes or until fish is done.

Mrs. Kosta N. Taras (Loretta)

PSARI PLAKI II

GREEK

Baked Fish with Vegetables

Temperature: 350°
Pan Size: 9" x 13"
Yield: 6 servings

**3 pounds cod or haddock
  fillets
Salt and pepper
1 lemon, juice of**

**SAUCE:
5 Tbsp. olive or vegetable oil
1 large onion, chopped
2 bunches green onions,
  chopped
2 cloves garlic, minced
1 cup canned tomatoes
1 8-ounce can tomato sauce
1 cup parsley, chopped
1 bell pepper, chopped
4 stalks celery,
  finely chopped
1 tsp. salt
1/4 tsp. pepper
1/2 cup white wine (optional)**

Step 1. Season fish with salt, pepper and juice of lemon. Let stand.

Step 2. Sauce: Sauté onions in oil until soft; add garlic, tomatoes, parsley, bell pepper, celery, and salt and pepper. Cook 10 minutes. Pour half of sauce in baking dish; place fish on top and pour wine over fish. Cover with remaining sauce.

Step 3. Bake in oven at 350° for 45 minutes, basting often. Serve warm or cold.

Mrs. Nota Kolopanas

PSARI PLAKI III

GREEK

Fish with Vegetables

Temperature: 300°
Yield: 6 servings

**1 3-pound red snapper
1/2 cup olive oil
1 large onion, chopped
1 cup tomato sauce
1/2 cup water
1 bay leaf
2 Tbsp. fresh parsley
1 cup carrots, chopped
1 cup celery, chopped
1 lemon, juice of
1 to 2 cloves garlic, minced
Salt and pepper to taste**

Step 1. Sauté onions in oil and cook until soft. Add tomato sauce and other ingredients and simmer for 15 minutes. Remove bay leaf.

Step 2. Place snapper, which has been seasoned with salt, pepper, and lemon juice in foil. Pour sauce over fish. (Have foil large enough to fold over, so sauce will be sealed in).

Step 3. Bake for 45 minutes.

Grecian Gourmet

PLAKI IV
Baked Fish

GREEK

Temperature: 350°
Pan Size: 9" x 12" x 2"
Yield: 6-8 servings

1 medium onion, sliced
1 clove garlic, minced
2 medium tomatoes, sliced
1 cup parsley, chopped
1/2 cup margarine
2 pounds fish fillets; frozen
 may be used—thawed
1/2 tsp. salt
1/2 tsp. oregano
1/4 tsp. pepper
1/2 cup bread crumbs

Step 1. In large skillet sauté onion, garlic, tomatoes, and parsley in 1/4 cup margarine. Set aside.

Step 2. Arrange fillets in an oblong baking dish. Sprinkle with salt, oregano, and pepper.

Step 3. Arrange sautéed mixture over fillets; sprinkle bread crumbs evenly over all. Dot with remaining margarine. Cover and bake at 350° for 35-40 minutes, or until fillets are fork tender.

George L. Koleas

TARAMA KEFTETHES
Caviar Cakes

GREEK

Yield: 2 dozen patties

1 7-ounce jar Tarama
4 medium boiled potatoes
1/4 cup parsley, chopped
1 tsp. fresh mint or dill
 (optional)
2 Tbsp. scallions or
 green onions, chopped
Flour
Oil for frying
Salt and pepper to taste

Step 1. Place Tarama in bowl and mix with electric mixer to a thin paste.

Step 2. Mash potatoes and add to Tarama. Blend well.

Step 3. Add scallions, parsley, mint or dill, and salt and pepper.

Step 4. Form into 3" patties. Dust with flour and fry in hot oil until golden brown.

Grecian Gourmet

POULTRY

KOTOPETAKIA AVGHOLEMONO   GREEK
Chicken Rolls with Egg-Lemon Sauce

Temperature: 375°
Pan Size: 2–9" x 13"
Yield: 2 dozen, approximately

1 broiler-fryer chicken
1 medium onion, quartered
1 carrot
2 stalks celery
2 Tbsp. salt
10 peppercorns (whole black
  pepper)
3 sticks butter

FILLING:
1 medium onion, chopped
1 stalk celery, chopped
1/4 cup grated Parmesan
  cheese
1 Tbsp. butter
2 Tbsp. flour
2 Tbsp. butter
1 cup chicken broth
1/2 cup milk
2 eggs, well beaten
Salt and pepper to taste
1/4 tsp. nutmeg, ground
1 pound filo
Reserved chicken

SAUCE:
4 eggs
2 lemons, juice of
1 Tbsp. cornstarch
2 cups hot chicken broth

Step 1. In a deep pot, cover chicken with water. Bring to a boil and skim off foam as it forms until foaming stops. Add onion, carrot, celery, salt and peppercorns. Cover and boil until tender, about 1 to 1-1/2 hours. Turn off heat and allow chicken to cool in broth. When cooled, bone the chicken and chop the meat coarsely and reserve. Strain broth and reserve.

Step 2. In a saucepan, melt 3 sticks butter and keep warm. Brush two 9" x 13" baking pans with melted butter. Set aside. Sauté onion and celery in 1 tablespoon butter until tender. Set aside.

Step 3. FILLING: In a saucepan, melt 2 tablespoons butter; add 2 tablespoons flour. Remove from heat and add chicken broth and milk slowly, stirring constantly. Return to heat and cook over medium heat until sauce thickens. Add half of cream sauce to beaten eggs and stir egg mixture back into cream sauce, stirring quickly. Cook about 1 minute. Remove from heat and stir in Parmesan cheese, salt, pepper, and nutmeg. Add chicken, onion and celery and mix well.

Step 4. Prepare pastry leaves by taking one sheet at a time. Lay flat; brush lightly and carefully with butter. Fold sheet in half and again brush lightly with butter. Place 1 heaping tablespoon filling at long end of sheet, roll over once, then fold in sides, brushing sides with butter. Roll completely; brush seam with butter to seal and place, seam down, in pan. Brush top with butter. Continue this process until all filling is used.

Note: At this point, pans may be covered with aluminum foil and refrigerated if used the same day or frozen for later use.

Continued...

...continued from
previous page

Step 5. Bake for 30 minutes in preheated oven, reducing temperature to 350° if browning too quickly.

Step 6. Sauce: Beat eggs whites until stiff; reduce mixer speed to medium and add egg yolks; then slowly add lemon juice. Gradually beat in hot broth to which corn starch has been diluted. Beat 1 minute. Pour mixture into saucepan, place over medium-low heat, and stir until thickened.

To serve, ladle a little sauce over each roll. This recipe may be served for luncheon or dinner as a main dish. Suggested accompaniment is a Greek green salad and homemade bread or rolls.

Variation: Follow basic technique on page 26 using 10 fila in bottom of pan. Pour in filling and add 10 fila for top.

Mrs. Angelo D. Liollio (Tina)

KOTA ME BAMYES GREEK
Chicken with Okra

Yield: 6 servings

**2 pounds fresh okra or 2
    packages frozen (thawed)
1-1/2 lemons, juice of
1 2-1/2 pound fryer, cut into
    serving pieces
4 Tbsp. butter
1 large onion, chopped
1/4 cup vegetable oil
1 cup whole tomatoes
1 cup tomato sauce
2 cups water
Salt and pepper**

Step 1. Wash okra carefully; trim the stems. Dip stem ends in salt; place in deep bowl. Sprinkle lemon juice over all; let stand.

Step 2. Brown chicken and onion in butter.

Step 3. In separate pan, brown rinsed and drained okra in vegetable oil. Set okra aside.

Step 4. Add tomatoes, tomato sauce, and water to browned chicken and onions. Cook slowly for 45 minutes.

Step 5. Add browned okra. Cook slowly for 30 minutes, shaking saucepan occasionally to prevent scorching. Season to taste.

Variation: Lamb, cut into 2" pieces, may be used in place of chicken.

Mrs. Angie K. Argol

KOTA KAPAMA I GREEK
Chicken in Tomato Sauce with Spaghetti

Yield: 6 servings

1 2-1/2 pound frying chicken,
  cut in serving pieces
Salt
Freshly ground pepper
Garlic salt
1/2 stick butter
2 medium white onions,
  chopped
2 to 3 cloves garlic, minced
1 pound fresh mushroom
  buttons and stems
1 15-ounce can tomato puree
1 7-ounce can tomato paste
1 large cinnamon stick
1/4 cup sugar or to taste
1/4 cup cooking sherry
1 pound Vermicelli or thin
  spaghetti
1 cup grated Parmesan or
  Mizithra cheese
1 stick butter

Step 1. Generously sprinkle chicken pieces with salt, pepper, and garlic salt to taste.

Step 2. In a dutch oven or heavy, deep pot, melt butter over medium heat and brown chicken on all sides.

Step 3. Add onions, garlic, and mushrooms to chicken and saute until onions are transparent.

Step 4. Add tomato puree, paste, and cinnamon stick to chicken. Cover, and simmer over low heat for 20 minutes.

Step 5. Uncover and add sugar and cooking sherry. Simmer over low heat, uncovered for an additional 15 minutes.

Step 6. At this point you may refrigerate and serve the next day by reheating, covered.

Step 7. Preparing the spaghetti: Cook spaghetti according to package directions. Drain and rinse under hot running water to remove some starchiness.

Step 8. Sprinkle large platter generously with grated cheese. Layer with spaghetti and cheese alternately.

Step 9. Brown butter in frying pan and pour over spaghetti. If desired, sprinkle top with cinnamon.

Step 10. Ladle some of sauce over top of spaghetti.

Suggested Accompaniment: Any oil and vinegar salad.

Mrs. Dimitri Taras (Mary Katherine)

KOTA KAPAMA II

Chicken in Tomato Sauce

Yield: 6 servings

3 to 4 pounds chicken pieces
1 stick butter
1 medium onion, chopped
2 cloves garlic, minced
Salt and pepper to taste
1 tsp. sugar (optional)
1 stick cinnamon or
  1/8 tsp. ground cinnamon
2 whole cloves (optional)
1/4 cup wine
1 bay leaf (optional)
1 4-ounce can tomato paste
1 8-ounce can whole
  tomatoes
1 cup water

Step 1. In a skillet, brown chicken in butter on both sides. Remove from skillet, place in heavy saucepan, and set aside.

Step 2. Sauté onions and garlic in same pan over medium heat, until transparent. Add salt, pepper, sugar, cinnamon, cloves, wine, bay leaf, tomato paste, whole tomatoes and water. Bring to a boil and pour over chicken. Allow to simmer approximately 1 hour or until chicken is done.

Note: This stewed chicken is good over macaroni, spaghetti, or rice. May be topped with yogurt or sour cream when using rice.

For variation (as a main dish), add green peas, artichokes, or okra to chicken when it is half-way cooked. (Okra should be lightly braised in salad oil and drained well before adding to chicken.)

Grecian Gourmet

KOTA ANGINARES KE MANITARIA GREEK

Chicken with Artichokes and Mushrooms

Temperature: 350°
Yield: 6 servings

6 chicken breasts
  (or quarters)
2 cans artichokes, drained,
  reserve liquid
2 small jars mushrooms,
  drained
1 3-ounce can tomato paste
1/3 cup white wine
1 stick butter
1/4 to 1/2 tsp. oregano
1/2 tsp. Worcestershire sauce
Salt to taste
Pepper to taste
Lawry's salt to taste

Step 1. Combine salt, pepper, and Lawry's salt and sprinkle over chicken, dot with butter and broil until brown. Remove from broiler; arrange artichokes and mushrooms around chicken.

Step 2. Dilute tomato paste in juice of artichokes, 1/3 cup wine, and Worcestershire sauce. Pour over broiled chicken. Sprinkle with oregano and bake at 350° for 45 minutes. Serve with rice or noodles.

Mrs. Michael Scaljohn (Vicky)

KOTA MELANAISE

Chicken with Melanaise Sauce

Yield: 6 servings

1 4-pound chicken
3-1/2 quarts water
3 stalks celery
Salt to taste
1/4 pound butter
2 cups rice
5 cups reserved broth

SAUCE MELANAISE:
1/2 cup butter
1/2 cup flour
4 cups reserved broth
Salt to taste
3 egg yolks
2 Tbsp. lemon juice
2 Tbsp. grated Parmesan
cheese
Pepper to taste

Step 1. Place chicken in a deep pot and add water. Bring to a boil, skim off foam, and add celery and salt. Cover and simmer until chicken is tender (approximately 1 to 1-1/2 hours). Remove chicken to platter and strain broth. Carve chicken into serving pieces and keep warm while preparing rice and sauce.

Step 2. Soak rice in salted water for 20 minutes and drain.

Step 3. Melt 1/4 pound butter in a deep pan over medium heat and add rice. Stir for 5 minutes. Add 5 cups reserved broth and bring to a boil. Reduce heat; cover and cook until rice is tender and broth is absorbed. Set aside and prepare sauce.

Step 4. Preparing sauce: Melt butter; blend in flour, stirring constantly (preferably with a wooden spoon). Gradually add reserved broth and continue cooking until smooth and thick. Add salt and pepper to taste. Reduce heat.

Step 5. Beat egg yolks and stir in lemon juice. Add egg mixture to sauce; then add grated cheese.

Step 6. When sauce is ready, pack rice in buttered ring mold. Turn onto heated platter, fill center with chicken pieces and pour sauce over rice and chicken.

Mrs. Katina Cotros

KOTA PILAF
Chicken Pilaf
GREEK

Yield: 4 servings

1 stewing hen or fryer
   (3 to 4 pounds)
3 Tbsp. butter
1 cup onion, chopped
2 cloves garlic
2 Tbsp. tomato paste mixed
   with 2 cups water or
   1 14-1/2 ounce can
   whole tomatoes
1 stick cinnamon
4 cups water
1 cup rice
Salt and pepper to taste

Step 1. Cut chicken into serving pieces. Sauté in butter with onions and garlic until golden brown, stirring occasionally. Add salt and pepper.

Step 2. Dilute tomato paste with water, or use canned tomatoes. Add to chicken.

Step 3. Add 4 cups of water and stick of cinnamon. Bring to a boil. Reduce heat and simmer until chicken is tender. Add rice and cook until rice is done.

Grecian Gourmet

KOTA RIGANATO
Chicken with Oregano
GREEK

Temperature: 350°
Yield: 4 servings

1 fryer chicken
1 lemon, juice of
1 clove garlic, minced
1 tsp. oregano
4 Tbsp. olive oil
1/2 stick butter
Salt and pepper to taste

Step 1. Season chicken with salt and pepper, lemon juice, oregano, garlic, and oil. Dot with butter.

Step 2. Bake at 350° until golden brown (approximately 1-1/2 hours), basting frequently.

Note: Marinate overnight for richer flavor.

Annunciation Bazaar Recipe

SIKOTAKIA
Fried Chicken Livers

Yield: 6 to 8 servings

1 pound chicken livers
1/2 cup olive oil or cooking oil
1 or 2 lemons, juice of
Salt and pepper to taste
Oregano

Step 1. Rinse livers thoroughly. Drain, place on paper toweling to absorb excess moisture.

Step 2. Prick livers slightly with fork. (This prevents spattering during frying.) Season with salt and pepper to taste.

Step 3. Heat oil in heavy skillet. When oil is hot, add livers and fry on both sides until well done. Remove livers from pan and place in warm serving dish; sprinkle with lemon juice and oregano. Serve immediately.

These may be served over cooked rice or as appetizers.

Mr. Gus Vantis
Miami Beach, Florida

PAN BROILED CHICKEN
GREEK

Pan Size: 12" Frying Pan
Yield: 4 servings

1 2-pound fryer
1 large white potato
2 lemons, juice of
Pure garlic powder
Salt
Pepper
Oregano (if desired)
1/2 stick butter
2 medium onions, finely
** chopped**

Step 1. Cut chicken into quarters; and slice potato into 1/2" round slices.

Step 2. Cover both sides of chicken and potatoes with lemon juice and season well with garlic powder, salt, and pepper.

Step 3. Melt butter in frying pan (which has been sprayed with Pam) and then add onions.

Step 4. Place chicken and potatoes in pan with onions.

Step 5. Cook slowly uncovered until brown on both sides, turning often to avoid sticking; then cover pan and continue cooking until chicken is done.

Mrs. Jerry Skefos (Katherine)

MEATS/MEAT COMBINATIONS

ARNI FRICASSEE

Lamb in Egg-Lemon Sauce

Yield: 6 servings

2 pounds lamb shoulder
1/2 stick butter
1 tsp. dry dill weed or
  1 Tbsp. fresh dill
6 bunches scallions,
  chopped
Salt and pepper to taste
1-1/2 cups water

Step 1. Trim excess fat from meat and cut into stew pieces. Place in a deep saucepan over high heat. Add butter and seasonings. Brown meat well until juices are absorbed.

Step 2. Add green onions and dill; cover and cook over low heat until onions are soft.

Step 3. Add water and continue cooking slowly for 1-1/2 to 2 hours or until meat is done.

Serve with avgholemono sauce. (See recipe in Sauce section.)

Traditional Recipe

ARNI ME SPANAKI

GREEK

Lamb with Spinach

Yield: 6-8 servings

2 pounds lamb, cubed
2 pounds fresh spinach
1/2 stick butter
2 large onions, chopped
1 14-ounce can whole
  tomatoes
1-1/2 cups water
1 Tbsp. fresh dill or
  1 tsp. dry dill weed
1/2 cup parsley, chopped
Salt and pepper

Step 1. Braise meat in large saucepan, browning on all sides. Add butter and onions and brown.

Step 2. Add tomatoes, salt, pepper, and 1 cup hot water. Bring to a boil, cover and simmer for 1 hour or until meat is tender.

Step 3. In the meantime, wash and drain spinach thoroughly. Add to meat. Add dill and parsley. Cover and continue cooking until spinach is tender.

Good accompaniments are mashed potatoes or rice and crusty bread.

Traditional Recipe

ARNI PSITO
Roast Lamb

GREEK

Temperature: 400° for 30 minutes, then 350°
Yield: 10 to 12 servings

**5 to 6-pound leg or
  shoulder of lamb
2 to 3 cloves garlic,
  finely sliced
Salt and pepper to taste
1 lemon, juice of
1 Tbsp. oregano
Butter**

Step 1. Slit meat in several places and insert slices of garlic, or rub meat with finely minced garlic.

Step 2. Rub meat with lemon juice and oregano. Salt and pepper meat well.

Step 3. Place meat in roasting pan, add a little water, and dot with butter (if desired).

Step 4. Bake in 400° oven for 30 minutes, then lower heat to 350° and roast to desired doneness.

Traditional Recipe

KEFTETHES
Meatballs

GREEK

Yield: 12-16

**1 pound ground beef
1/2 cup dry bread crumbs
  or 2 slices of bread
  soaked in milk or water
2 cloves garlic,
  finely chopped
1/4 cup parsley, chopped or
  1 Tbsp. dried mint leaves
  or 2 Tbsp. fresh mint,
  snipped
1 egg, beaten
1 large onion, chopped
1/4 cup grated Romano or
  Parmesan cheese
2 tsp. salt
1/4 tsp. pepper**

Step 1. Mix all ingredients together. Be sure mixture is soft; add a little water if necessary.

Step 2. Shape into round balls and roll lightly in flour.

Step 3. Fry in hot olive oil or butter, or a combination of both.

May be broiled at 500° or baked at 350° until brown (approximately 20 minutes).

Grecian Gourmet

ARNI TIS SOUFLAS
GREEK
Whole Lamb Barbecued on a Spit

1 8-foot oak skewer (spit),
with handle on one end
and sharpened to a point
at the other end
1 whole lamb,
30 to 40 pounds
Olive oil
Salt and pepper

BASTING SAUCE:
4 ounces salt
2 ounces ground black
pepper
1 clove garlic, minced
3 lemons, juice of
1 pound margarine
1 pint wine vinegar

Charcoal
Sand
Brackets

Step 1. Lamb should be whole with unsplit breast bone.

Step 2. Wipe cavity and outside of lamb with a damp cloth.

Step 3. Rub cavity of carcass with oil; season generously with salt and pepper.

Step 4. Make deep slits in legs and shoulders and stuff with garlic.

Step 5. Skewer carcass, starting at back and coming through the cavity of the neck. Wire carcass to spit at the head, shoulders, and at the point of the rack at the legs. Bring forelegs forward and wire to skewer; pull hind legs back and wire them to skewer.

Note: Steps 1 through 5 may be done the day before and refrigerated.

Step 6. Fire may be laid on ground or concrete by putting down a thick layer of sand first, then place charcoal. Fire coals and let burn to white hot; arrange coals so that they are heaped under shoulder and leg areas of the carcass; thin layer of coals under the center, less meaty, area of the lamb which will over-cook or burn over high heat.

Step 7. When coals are ready, place spit in brackets. Turn fast at first, for 2 hours. Continue turning for about 6 hours. Baste frequently; during the last hour turn very slowly.

Step 8. Check degree of doneness by inserting knife into thick part of shoulder and leg; if juices run clear, it is done.

Step 9. To remove from spit: Cut and remove wires; using cleaver or meat saw, divide meat into portions.

Mr. Charles J. Vergos

BREEZOLES TIS SKARAS

GREEK

Charcoal Broiled Lamb Chops

Yield: 4 servings

8 lamb chops
Salt and pepper to taste
1/4 cup vegetable oil
2 cloves garlic, minced
1 lemon, juice of
1/2 tsp. oregano

Step 1. Prepare charcoal for grilling.

Step 2. Salt and pepper lamb chops. Mix remaining ingredients and brush chops with some of this mixture, reserving half for basting.

Step 3. When coals have turned white, place chops on grill. Cook to desired doneness on each side, basting often.

Step 4. Remove to warm platter and serve

Mr. Bill K. Taras

CEVAPCICI

SERBIAN

Serbian Sausage

Yield: Approximately 20

1 pound beef, ground fine
1/2 pound pork, ground fine
1/2 pound lamb, ground fine
1 tsp. paprika
1 tsp. black pepper
2 tsp. salt
4 cloves garlic, chopped
1 tsp. baking soda

Step 1. Mix all ingredients well with hands.

Step 2. Shape the mixture into small cylinders, 1" in diameter and 2" long.

Step 3. Broil on a charcoal grill about 8 minutes on each side or until well done. Serve with finely chopped onions.

Mrs. George Cavic (Mileva)
Chesterfield, Missouri

BEEF STROGANOFF

RUSSIAN

Yield: 4-5 servings

2 pounds top sirloin
1/4 pound butter
1 large onion, sliced
1 small can mushrooms
1-1/2 tsp. salt
Garlic salt to taste
1 can beef bouillon
1/2 cup sour cream

Step 1. Cut beef in paper thin strips; then sauté in butter. Remove beef to bowl. Then sauté onion, and add to beef. Sauté mushrooms, and combine with beef and onions.

Step 2. Add seasonings and bouillon. Simmer 30 minutes. Add sour cream, a little at a time, beating with spoon as you add. Serve over your favorite noodles.

Mrs. George Ostrosky (Helen)

KIBBIE

Yield: 8 servings

1-1/4 cups fine cracked wheat (bulgar)
1 medium onion, ground or grated fine
1 Tbsp. salt
1/2 tsp. black pepper
Dash of cinnamon
Dash of red pepper
1 pound very lean ground round or ground leg of lamb

Step 1. Rinse wheat in cold water. Drain. Then cover wheat with cold water and allow to soak at least 30 minutes or until it swells.

Step 2. Mix remaining ingredients well.

Step 3. Squeeze water out of wheat and add to meat mixture, a little at a time. Dip hands frequently into a bowl of ice water while mixing to aid in mixture sticking together. Adjust seasonings to taste.

Note: This may be eaten as is with a little olive oil, melted butter or Kibbie stuffing (hashwa, see p. 80) on top.

Mrs. George Abraham (Katherine)

BAKED KIBBIE

Temperature: 350°
Pan Size: 9" x 13" x 2"
Yield: 8 -10 servings

Kibbie, using 2 to 2-1/2 pounds of meat
Hashwa
Oil
Butter

Step 1. Grease pan with small amount of oil. Using half of the Kibbie mixture, put a little at a time in the bottom of the pan so that the layer is smooth and even.

Step 2. Cover the Kibbie layer with hashwa (not too thick) and press the hashwa (see p. 80) into the bottom layer slightly.

Step 3. Using the other half of Kibbie, flatten small portions of Kibbie and place over hashwa, being careful not to disturb the bottom layer. Smooth with hands.

Step 4. Cut into squares, dot with butter, and bake for 1 hour until browned.

Note: Be sure to dip hands in ice water when working with Kibbie.

Mrs. George Abraham (Katherine)

FRIED KIBBIE   **LEBANESE**

Yield: 8-10 servings

Kibbie
Hashwa
Cooking oil

Step 1. Prepare preceeding recipes for Kibbie and hashwa.

Step 2. For plain fried Kibbie: Shape into hamburger sized patties or football shaped patties and fry in 1" of hot oil until deep golden brown on all sides.

Variation: For Kibbie stuffed with hashwa:

Step 1. Shape Kibbie into flat patties. Place 1-2 tsp. hashwa in the center. Cover with another Kibbie patty. Seal and smooth edges. Fry until deep golden brown.

Note: Be sure to dip hands in ice water while working with Kibbie.

Mrs. George Abraham (Katherine)

KOTLETY   **RUSSIAN**
Baked Meat Cutlets

Temperature: 350°
Pan Size: Wire rack on ccokie sheet lined with foil.
Yield: 10-12 cutlets

6 slices white bread, toasted
2 pounds ground sirloin
2 tsp. salt
1 cup onion, finely chopped
1 can beef bouillon
Bread crumbs

SAUCE:
2 Tbsp. butter
2 Tbsp. flour
2 cups hot bouillon
1 cup sour cream
Salt to taste

Step 1. Dip toast in water, and squeeze out excess.

Step 2. Mix toast with all ingredients except bread crumbs.

Step 3. Shape into balls; then flatten to look like oval cutlets. Roll in bread crumbs.

Step 4. Place on rack. Bake for 1/2 hour, turn, and bake another 1/2 hour.

Step 5. Sauce: Melt butter in pan. Stir in flour and cook for 2 minutes. Add bouillon and blend. Remove from heat, stir into sour cream. Return to stove and heat gently; season to taste. Simmer a few minutes. Serve over cutlets.

Mrs. George Ostrosky (Helen)

HASHWA
Kibbie Stuffing

LEBANESE

Yield: 8 servings

1/2 cup pine nuts
2 Tbsp. butter
1 pound coarsely ground leg
  of lamb
2 small onions, finely
  chopped
1/4 tsp. pepper
1/4 tsp. cinnamon
2 tsp. salt

Step 1. Brown pine nuts in butter to a golden color. Set aside.

Step 2. Brown meat and onions together. Add seasonings and cook until meat is well browned. Add pine nuts and cook for 5 minutes over low flame. Adjust seasonings to taste.

Mrs. George Abraham (Katherine)

KOLBASA
Sausage

RUSSIAN

Yield: 4 servings per pound

8 pounds lean pork
  (Butts)
2 pounds ground beef
3-1/2 Tbsp. salt
1-1/2 Tbsp. pepper
1 tsp. dried sage
6 cloves garlic, crushed
Garlic salt to taste
1-1/2 cups water
1 container pork casings,
  washed as needed

Step 1. Trim excess fat from pork, leaving just a little fat so that the sausage will not be too dry or too greasy. Put meat through meat grinder, using coarse grind.

Step 2. Place pork in a large container. Add beef to pork, then add seasoning to the meat, and mix well, using just enough water to moisten.

Step 3. Using stuffer attachment for grinder, stuff pork casings with meat and tie ends with a heavy string.

Step 4. Refrigerate for 24 hours to allow flavors to blend.

Step 5. Simmer sausage in very little water for 50 minutes, browning lightly. May be baked in the oven, if preferred.

Optional: To smoke sausage, place in smoker for at least 12 hours. (Not recommended in hot weather). Smoked sausage should be cooked for only 1/2 hour. May also be served cold as an appetizer, sliced thin. Especially good with horseradish and rye bread rounds.

George Ostrosky

LOOB–YEE IB LAHM
LEBANESE
Lamb and String Bean Stew

Yield: 8-10 servings

1-1/2 pounds lamb, cubed
1 large onion, chopped
2 cloves garlic, cut up
1 14-ounce can tomatoes
2 8-ounce cans tomato sauce
1 tsp. salt
1/4 tsp. pepper
2 pounds fresh string beans
or 3 cans string beans,
drained

Step 1. In large pot brown lamb cubes and then add onions and garlic. Sauté until tender but do not brown.

Step 2. Add tomatoes and tomato sauce, salt and pepper; add beans.

Step 3. Cover and cook until meat is done and beans are tender. (Fresh beans take longer to cook.) Serve over cooked rice.

Minnie Zambie
West Helena, Arkansas

NEFRA KRASATA
GREEK
Bill's Lamb Kidneys

Yield: 2 servings

6 lamb kidneys
2 Tbsp. butter
2 Tbsp. olive oil
1 tsp. salt
1/8 tsp. pepper
Garlic powder to taste
Flour
1 lemon
1/4 cup red wine

Step 1. Split kidneys and remove membrane leaving a little fat.

Step 2. Salt and pepper kidneys and sprinkle with garlic powder. Dust lightly with flour.

Step 3. Heat butter and oil over medium heat and fry kidneys on both sides. Cover and steam for 15 minutes.

Step 4. Squeeze lemon over kidneys and add wine. Remove kidneys to heated platter. Scrape drippings from pan and pour over kidneys.

Suggested Accompaniments: Serve kidneys with boiled greens and mashed potatoes or rice; or, for brunch, with scrambled eggs.

Bill K. Taras

SIKOTAKI

GREEK

Grecian Style Calf's Liver

Yield: 4 servings

1 pound calf liver
Flour
3 Tbsp. butter
1 Tbsp. olive oil
1 lemon, juice of
2 Tbsp. wine
Oregano
Salt to taste

Step 1. Flour liver lightly. Heat butter and oil until hot. Quickly fry on both sides. Remove to warm platter.

Step 2. Add lemon juice to hot drippings and add wine. Pour over liver, salt to taste, and sprinkle with crushed oregano leaves.

Jim's Place East Restaurant

SOUTSOUKAKIA

GREEK

Meatballs in Tomato Sauce

Yield: 4 servings

1 pound ground beef
1 large onion, chopped
3/4 stick butter
Dash of cinnamon
2 cloves garlic, minced
1/2 cup toasted
 bread crumbs
1/2 cup parsley, chopped
1 egg, beaten
2 cups tomato sauce
1 can beef bouillon
Salt and pepper to taste
Sherry wine (optional)

Step 1. Sauté onions with 1/4 stick butter.

Step 2. Add to meat along with cinnamon, garlic, bread crumbs, parsley, and egg.

Step 3. Using a tablespoon, form mixture into egg-shaped rolls.

Step 4. Flour meatballs lightly, *or* moisten hands with sherry while shaping meatballs.

Step 5. Fry in 1/2 stick butter until browned; remove to a deep saucepan.

Step 6. Pour off all but 1 tablespoon grease and add tomato sauce, scraping pan to loosen drippings. Add bouillon; bring to a boil. Pour sauce over meatballs. Simmer over low heat until sauce has thickened, about 45 minutes.

Serve over rice or noodles.

Grecian Gourmet

SOUVLAKIA I

GREEK

Shish-Ka-Bob

Yield: 4 servings

1 cup cooking sherry
1/2 cup wine vinegar
1/2 cup olive oil
2/3 tsp. oregano
2 or 3 cloves garlic, chopped
1/2 tsp. salt
1/8 tsp. pepper
1 to 1-1/2 pounds beef,
  cubed

PILAF:
1 stick butter
1 cup rice, uncooked
  (Uncle Ben's)
2-1/2 cups hot broth

Step 1. Mix first seven ingredients and pour over cubed beef. Marinate overnight.

Step 2. Remove meat from marinade; drain on paper towels (reserve the marinade).

Step 3. Skewer meat and cook over *hot* charcoal fire (or oven-broil), basting occasionally with marinade. Serve with Pilaf.

Step 4. Pilaf: Melt butter over medium heat, add rice, stirring constantly until rice is lightly browned. Add hot broth while stirring, until rice is at full boil. Cover, reduce heat to low, and simmer until tender. Add salt to taste.

Mrs. Pete J. Vergos (Helen)

SOUVLAKIA II

GREEK

Shish-Ka-Bob

Yield: 8 servings

2 pounds lamb or beef
2 cloves garlic, minced
1 cup Burgundy wine
1/2 cup salad oil
1 lemon, juice of
2 tsp. oregano
3 tomatoes (optional)
2 onions (optional)
4 strips bacon (optional)
2 bell peppers (optional)
1 can whole mushroom
  buttons or use fresh
  (optional)
Salt and pepper to taste

Step 1. Cut meat into 1-1/2" cubes.

Step 2. Place meat in large plastic or stainless steel bowl and add garlic, oil, wine, lemon juice, salt, pepper, and oregano and mix well. Cover and refrigerate overnight to marinate.

Step 3. Quarter onions and tomatoes; cube peppers and bacon.

Step 4. Skewer marinated meat alternating it with whichever optional ingredients are preferred.

Step 5. Charcoal over hot coals or broil in oven to desired doneness.

Grecian Gourmet

YOUVETSI
Oven Stew

Temperature: 375°
Yield: 8 servings

3 pounds lamb shoulder or lamb chops
1 large onion, chopped
2 cups hot water
1/2 stick cinnamon
1 14-ounce can tomatoes
4 Tbsp. tomato paste
1 pinch sugar (optional)
2 cups rosamarina or orzo
Salt and pepper
1 cup grated Romano or Parmesan cheese (optional)

Step 1. Preheat oven to 375°.

Step 2. Rub meat with salt and pepper.

Step 3. Place in roasting pan and bake until meat begins to brown.

Step 4. Remove from oven and lower temperature to 350°.

Step 5. Add onions, cinnamon stick, tomatoes, tomato paste, 2 cups water, and sugar to meat.

Step 6. Bake until meat is tender.

Step 7. When meat is completely cooked, remove from pan; set aside and keep warm.

Step 8. Add 6 cups hot water to pan and add rosamarina or orzo. Cover and bake 35 minutes or until rosamarina or orzo is cooked. Stir occasionally.

Note: Grated cheese may be sprinkled over this when served.

Grecian Gourmet

PSITO KREAS
Roasted Meat

LAMB, PORK OR BEEF: Wipe surface of meat with damp paper towel. Make several deep slits into the meat (particularly into pockets of fat) and insert slivers of garlic. Rub entire surface of meat with black pepper (preferably freshly cracked or ground). Place meat on rack in roasting pan, fat side up, and roast at proper temperature until meat is cooked to doneness you prefer. About 15 to 30 minutes before cooking is finished, remove pan from oven and drain off fat which has collected. Pour about one cup of water into the pan, *not over the meat*. Squeeze lemon juice over meat, sprinkle with salt and crushed oregano leaves (omit oregano for beef roast and baste with red wine). Return roast to oven to finish cooking. Remove meat to serving platter. Loosen all browned, crusted juices from pan, add water or wine to reconstitute, pour into saucepan for reheat, if necessary, and serve as a sauce over the meat slices.

STEFATHO

Stew

Yield: 6-8 servings

3 pounds meat – beef, veal,
   rabbit or venison
2 pounds whole small
   onions
2 onions, chopped
1 can whole tomatoes
1/2 cup olive oil
1/4 cup vinegar
1/4 cup Burgundy wine
3 cloves garlic
1 bay leaf
8 whole cloves
2 Tbsp. pickling spice
Salt and pepper

Step 1. Tie mixed spices and whole cloves in cheesecloth.

Step 2. Brown meat (cut into serving pieces) in 1/4 cup oil. Then add chopped onions and brown.

Step 3. Peel whole onions and brown in remaining oil and add to meat.

Step 4. Add tomatoes and other ingredients, along with spices in cheesecloth and cover tightly.

Step 5. Cook until meat is tender.

Step 6. Remove cheesecloth bag just before serving.

Grecian Gourmet

YOUVARELAKIA

Meatballs in Egg-Lemon Sauce

Yield: 4 servings

1 pound ground beef or
   lamb
1 egg
2 small onions, chopped
   fine
1/2 stick butter
Salt and pepper
1/4 cup chopped parsley or
   1 Tbsp. dried mint
1/4 cup rice
3-1/4 cups broth
Avgholemono sauce

Step 1. Mix meat, egg, onions, parsley or mint, rice, salt and pepper, and 1/4 cup broth, keeping a soft consistency.

Step 2. Shape into tiny balls.

Step 3. Drop into 3 cups boiling broth, to which butter has been added.

Step 4. Cover and cook over moderate heat for about 30 minutes.

Step 5. Prepare Avgholemono Sauce (see recipe in Sauce section).

Step 6. Pour over meat as directed.

Grecian Gourmet

DOLMATHES

Stuffed Cabbage Leaves

Yield: 6 servings

1 medium head cabbage
1 pound ground beef
1 egg
2 small onions, finely
 chopped
1 tsp. salt
1/4 tsp. pepper
1-1/4 cup water or beef stock
1/2 tsp. dry mint leaves
1/4 cup chopped parsley
1/4 cup rice
2 Tbsp. butter
Avgholemono Sauce

Step 1. Core cabbage and separate leaves; blanch a few at a time and allow to cool. Pare heavy veins.

Step 2. Combine all other ingredients except butter and mix well. Soften mixture with 1/4 cup water or stock.

Step 3. Place 1 tablespoon mixture in each leaf, fold in sides and roll (see Basic Technique section).

Step 4. Arrange dolmathes in deep saucepan in layers. Add butter and remaining water or stock. Cover with a heavy plate to keep rolls from opening as they cook. Cover and cook slowly for about one hour.

Step 5. Prepare Avgholemono Sauce (see Sauce section) using stock from dolmathes. Ladle over each serving.

Grecian Gourmet

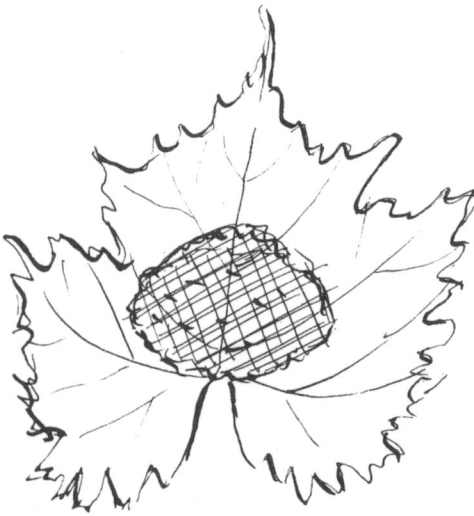

DOLMATHAKIA ME AVGHOLEMONO   GREEK
Stuffed Grapevine Leaves with Egg-Lemon Sauce

Yield: 6-8 servings

1/4 cup olive oil
1-1/2 pounds chopped meat
1 large onion, chopped
1 cup raw rice
Salt and pepper to taste
1/2 Tbsp. dried mint leaves
1 cup water
1 pound jar grapevine leaves
1 bouillon cube
1 Tbsp. butter

SAUCE:
3 eggs, beaten well
1 lemon, juice of

Step 1. Sauté onions in olive oil. Combine meat, onions, rice, seasonings, and dried mint. Add water and mix well.

Step 2. Drain brine from jar of grapevine leaves, remove leaves, and wash well with clear water. Put heaping tablespoon. of meat and rice mixture in center of each leaf, and roll tightly, folding sides over and rolling toward point of leaf.

Step 3. Place torn leaves in greased pan. Arrange rolls in layers. Dissolve bouillon cube in enough water to cover rolls. Carefully pour broth over rolls and dot with butter. Cover pan, and steam over low heat for 1 hour. If dry when cooking time is up, add water and simmer for a few more minutes.

Step 4. Sauce: Add lemon juice to beaten eggs, and beat well again. Add some of the hot liquid from casserole; then pour mixture over the dolmathakia. Serve at once.

Note: If necessary to reheat, leave uncovered while warming over low heat so egg sauce will not curdle.

Mrs. Nicholas Rokas (Sonia)

Cabbage or lettuce leaves may be used: follow the same principle dictated in the recipe.

MEAT DRESSING

Temperature: 350°
Pan Size: 2 1-1/2 quart casseroles, 4" deep
Yield: 15 servings

3 sticks butter
4 pounds ground chuck
2 large onions, chopped
1/2 bunch parsley,
   chopped
1 bunch celery, chopped
2 cups chicken broth
3 sweet potatoes, boiled
   and chopped
1/2 pound chestnuts,
   boiled, peeled, and cut
   into small pieces
1 pound pecans, chopped
Salt, pepper, cinnamon
   to taste
1 loaf Vienna bread, sliced
   and toasted
1 quart milk
3 eggs, beaten

Step 1. Melt 1-1/2 sticks butter in large heavy kettle. Add meat and keep stirring until browned.

Step 2. In separate pan or large skillet, melt 1-1/2 sticks butter, add chopped onions and brown. Add to meat.

Step 3. Add parsley, celery and broth. Cook until celery is done.

Step 4. Add sweet potatoes, chestnuts, and pecans. Season with salt, pepper and cinnamon to taste.

Step 5. When meat has cooked well, removed from heat. Let cool.

Step 6. In separate bowl, break up toasted bread and add milk. When it has soaked thoroughly, add to meat mixture.

Step 7. When mixture has cooled, add beaten eggs.

Step 8. Turn into buttered casseroles, and bake for 1 hour.

Mrs. John Touliatos (Voula)

BAKED ORZO

Temperature: 350°
Pan Size: Roasting pan

2 cups liquid - wine/broth
   (use drippings from
   bottom of pan after
   roasting a leg of lamb)
1 cup orzo (rosamarina)
1 14-1/2-ounce can stewed
   tomatoes

A favorite side dish served with roast lamb.

Step 1. Remove roasted lamb from pan. Add liquid to pan. Mix and cook on stove top until boiling.

Step 2. Add stewed tomatoes. Cook 2-3 minutes more. Add orzo.

Step 3. Bake at 350°, stirring often until orzo is tender.

Alethea Skefos

MOUSAKA I
Eggplant Casserole

GREEK

Temperature: 350°
Pan Size: 11" x 15" x 2"
Yield: 24-28 servings

**2 pounds ground beef
  (very lean)
1 cup chopped onion
1 clove garlic, finely chopped
1/2 stick butter
1-1/2 tsp. salt
1 tsp. black pepper
1 cinnamon stick
1 bay leaf
1/4 cup chopped parsley
1 8-ounce can tomato sauce
1 cup water
3 eggs
2 large eggplants (fried
  potato slices may be
  combined with eggplant)
1 cup grated Parmesan
  cheese**

**CREMA SAUCE:
3 cups milk
6 Tbsp. butter
6 Tbsp. flour
6 eggs, beaten
1/4 cup grated Parmesan
  cheese
1/2 tsp. salt
1/4 tsp. pepper**

Step 1. Brown meat with onion, garlic, butter, salt, pepper, cinnamon stick, and bay leaf. Add parsley, tomato sauce, and water; simmer until meat is done and mixture thickens (about 30 minutes). Set aside to cool. When meat has cooled, remove cinnamon stick and bay leaf. Add 3 beaten eggs to mixture.

Step 2. Slice eggplants into round 1/2 inch thick slices. Soak for 15 minutes in salted water. Drain thoroughly and blot with paper towel. Fry slices in hot vegetable oil until light brown. Drain on paper towel. (Hint: Cover several sheets of newspaper with paper towel, lay eggplant slices in single layer, cover with more paper towel, blot.)

Step 3. Crema Sauce: Heat 2 cups milk to scalding, add butter, remove from heat. Blend flour into 1 cup cold milk. Stir cold mixture into hot mixture. Return to heat, stirring constantly until thickened. Remove from heat and add eggs, cheese, salt, and pepper.

Step 4. Sprinkle bottom of baking pan with 1/4 of cheese; place a layer of eggplant, sprinkle with 1/4 of cheese; place meat sauce, cover with layer of eggplant, sprinkle with 1/4 of cheese; top with Crema Sauce and sprinkle with remaining 1/4 of cheese; and bake until golden brown.

Mrs. K. N. Taras (Loretta)

MOUSAKA II

GREEK

Eggplant-Meat Casserole

Temperature: 400°
Pan Size: 9" x 12" x 2-1/2"
Yield: 6 servings

1 eggplant (about 1-1/2 pounds)
1/4 cup olive oil or cooking oil
6 Tbsp. butter or oleo
1 cup finely chopped onion
1 tsp. finely chopped garlic
1-1/2 pounds lean ground lamb or beef
1/8 tsp. ground cinnamon
1/2 cup crushed tomatoes, fresh or canned
1/4 cup tomato paste
1/4 cup dry red wine
1/4 cup chopped parsley
3 Tbsp. flour
2 cups milk
2 eggs, lightly beaten
1/8 tsp. ground nutmeg
1 cup ricotta cheese or cottage cheese
1/4 cup freshly grated Parmesan cheese

Step 1. Preheat oven to 400°. Peel eggplant; cut it into 5 or 6 slices. Sprinkle with salt and pepper. Heat half the oil and cook eggplant slices, a few at a time, until golden brown on both sides. Remove from pan; drain on absorbent paper toweling. Add more oil as necesary to prevent burning. Set eggplant aside.

Step 2. Heat 2 tablespoons butter in a heavy skillet and add the onion. Cook, stirring, until transparent. Add the garlic and meat; cook, stirring until meat begins to brown. Add cinnamon, salt, and pepper; stir. Blend the tomatoes and tomato paste; then add wine and parsley. Let simmer until most of the wine is evaporated.

Step 3. Heat 3 tablespoons of butter or oleo in saucepan and add the flour, salt and pepper, stirring with a wire whisk. When blended and smooth, add the milk, stirring rapidly with the whisk. Cook, stirring often, about 5 minutes.

Step 4. Beat eggs with a whisk and add nutmeg and ricotta or cottage cheese. Beat to blend well.

Step 5. Add the cheese mixture to the white sauce. Beat well without cooking.

Step 6. Butter a rectangular baking dish, 9" x 12" x 2-1/2", with the remaining butter. Add a layer of eggplant slices and spoon the meat mixture over this. Sprinkle with half of the Parmesan cheese. Add the cheese sauce and smooth over meat mixture. Sprinkle with remaining Parmesan cheese. Bake approximately 30 minutes.

Mrs. George Vafinis (Vangie)
Tuscumbia, Alabama

PAPOUTSAKIA ZUCCHINI

GREEK

Stuffed Zucchini

Temperature: 350°
Yield: 4 servings

4 medium zucchini
5 Tbsp. butter
1 small onion, chopped
1/4 pound ground beef
1 clove garlic, minced
1 tsp. tomato paste or
  2 tomatoes, peeled and
  chopped
Dash of cinnamon
2 Tbsp. chopped parsley
Salt and pepper to taste
Parmesan cheese

BECHAMEL SAUCE:
2 cups milk
3 Tbsp. flour
2 Tbsp. butter
2 Tbsp. grated Parmesan
  cheese
1/4 tsp. ground nutmeg

Step 1. Wash zucchini and blanch for 5 minutes in boiling salted water. Drain. Slice in half lengthwise and scoop out centers. (Reserve pulp.) Arrange in shallow baking dish and set aside.

Step 2. Brown meat in 3 tablespoons of the butter. Add onions, garlic, tomato paste or tomatoes, cinnamon, parsley, and half of pulp. Add salt and pepper and cook for 10 minutes until liquid is absorbed.

Step 3. Bechamel Sauce: Melt butter in saucepan. Gradually stir in flour. Remove from heat and slowly add milk. Continue to stir over medium heat until mixture thickens and begins to boil. Add cheese, salt, and nutmeg, blending until smooth.

Step 4. Fill squash halves with meat mixture and cover each half thickly with Bechamel Sauce.

Step 5. Sprinkle each squash with Parmesan cheese.

Step 6. Pour 1/2 cup boiling water into pan and add 2 tablespoons butter. Bake for 15 to 20 minutes.

Grecian Gourmet

PASTITSO I

Macaroni and Meat Sauce Casserole

Temperature: 350°
Pan Size: 9" x 13"
Yield: 24 servings

MEAT SAUCE:
1 onion (small or medium),
   chopped
1/4 stick butter
1-1/4 pounds ground round
1 tsp. salt
1/4 tsp. pepper
1/4-1/2 tsp. cinnamon
1/8 tsp. nutmeg
1 Tbsp. parsley
1 14-1/2 ounce can Italian
   pear tomatoes, mashed
4 Tbsp. tomato sauce
1/8 cup sherry

MACARONI MIXTURE:
1/2 pound long, spaghetti-
   like macaroni
2 Tbsp. vegetable oil
1/4 stick butter
2 ounces grated Romano
   cheese
2 eggs
1/2 cup milk
1 ounce grated Romano
   cheese to use in
   layering

CREAM SAUCE:
1/2 stick butter
3 Tbsp. flour
1/2 tsp. salt
1-1/2 cups cold milk
3 eggs
1 ounce grated Romano
   cheese

Step 1. Sauté onions in butter in dutch oven. Add ground meat and brown. Add seasonings, tomatoes, and tomato sauce. Add sherry. Cook over medium heat about 1/2 hour or until there is not much liquid left (almost dry). Stir occasionally. Do not cover.

Step 2. Add vegetable oil to boiling, salted water; add macaroni; cook for 10-12 minutes. Remove from heat, add 1 cup cold water, and strain. Return macaroni to pot. Melt butter and pour over macaroni; heat macaroni and butter for 5 minutes; stir occasionally to keep from sticking. Remove from heat. Sprinkle with cheese; mix well. Beat eggs with milk until thoroughly blended; combine with macaroni.

Step 3. Butter pan. Spread half of macaroni mixture into pan; add meat sauce in an even layer; sprinkle with cheese; add remaining macaroni; gently shake pan to settle contents; cover and set aside while preparing cream sauce.

Step 4. Melt butter in saucepan. Remove from heat, stir in flour, and blend until smooth; add salt; return to heat. Gradually add milk, stirring constantly with wooden spoon until thickened and to the boiling point. Remove from heat.

Step 5. In large bowl, beat eggs with electric mixer until lemon colored. Slowly add the milk mixture; blend well.

Continued...

Step 6. Gently loosen top layer of macaroni; carefully ladle sauce all over macaroni (this will form a creamy crust when baked); sprinkle with cheese. Bake at 350° for 35 minutes or until knife inserted into center comes out clean.

Notes: Don't overbake as this casserole is generally reheated. Cut into squares before reheating for neater looking pieces.

May be prepared up to 3 days in advance and refrigerated. To reheat, cover pan with aluminum foil and heat for 1 hour at 275°. Or bake, cool; cut into serving pieces; prepare foil-wrapped packages containing desired number of servings; freeze. To serve, bake unthawed, sealed packages at 350° for 30 minutes or until hot.

Mrs. Bruce Erskine (Helen)

DOMATES YEMISTES
Stuffed Tomatoes

GREEK

Temperature: 350°
Yield: 6 servings

12 medium tomatoes
Sugar
1 large onion, chopped
1/2 stick butter
1-1/2 pounds ground beef
Salt and pepper to taste
1 clove garlic, minced
1 cup tomato sauce
2 Tbsp. chopped parsley
  or mint
1/4 cup vegetable oil
1/4 cup toasted bread
  crumbs
1/2 cup mushrooms,
  chopped (optional)
1/2 cup uncooked rice
Flour
1 cup water

Step 1. Wash tomatoes and cut a thin slice from stem end to make a cap. Scoop out seeds and some of the pulp. Sprinkle inside with a little sugar and turn upside down to drain.

Step 2. Sauté onions in butter until transparent. Add mushrooms (if desired) and continue stirring for a few minutes.

Step 3. Add meat, salt, pepper, and garlic, stirring frequently until juices are absorbed. Add tomato sauce, mint or parsley, and rice.

Step 4. Fill tomatoes and cover with caps. Arrange in a shallow baking dish and pour oil over tomatoes. Srinkle with breadcrumbs or dust with flour. Add water and bake for 1 hour.

Note: Bell peppers, which have been blanched in boiling water for 5 minutes, may be used instead of or combined with tomatoes.

Grecian Gourmet

PASTITSO II

GREEK

Macaroni and Meat Sauce Casserole

Temperature: 350°
Pan Size: 11" x 14" x 2"
Yield: 40 pieces

2 sticks butter
2 pounds ground chuck
2 large onions, chopped
3 cloves garlic, chopped
1/4 cup parsley, chopped
1 8-ounce can tomato sauce
Salt, pepper and cinnamon
  to taste

2 Tbsp. salt
1 pound macaroni
1-1/2 sticks butter, melted
5 eggs, beaten
3 cups Romano cheese,
  grated

CREMA:
1-1/2 sticks butter
1 cup flour
2 quarts milk
9 eggs, beaten
Salt and pepper to taste

Step 1. Melt 1 stick butter and add ground chuck. Stir until browned.

Step 2. In another pan, melt the other stick butter; brown onions and garlic and add to ground chuck; add parsley, tomato sauce, salt, pepper, and cinnamon; cook for 1 hour.

Step 3. In a deep kettle, add salt to boiling water and cook macaroni until almost done; drain and put into large bowl; add melted butter; add beaten eggs.

Step 4. Grease pan with butter, sprinkle with part of grated cheese. Put 1/3 of macaroni mixture into pan, cover with 1/2 of the meat sauce, and sprinkle with part of grated cheese; repeat layers of macaroni mixture and meat sauce, sprinkle with part of grated cheese; finish with macaroni mixture and part of grated cheese.

Step 5. Prepare crema. Melt butter in heavy saucepan over medium heat; add flour and stir well; blend until smooth. Add milk slowly, stirring constantly. Cook until thick.

Step 6. In mixing bowl, beat eggs and pour in hot crema mixture, a little at a time, stirring constantly. Mix well and spread sauce on top of macaroni mixture. Sprinkle with rest of grated cheese and baked for 1 hour.

Mrs. John Touliatos (Voula)

PASTITSO III

GREEK

Macaroni and Meat Casserole

Temperature: 350°
Pan Size: 9" x 13"
Yield: 20 2"-squares

1 pound ground beef
2 Tbsp. butter
1 medium onion, chopped
1 clove garlic, minced
Salt and pepper to taste
1 Tbsp. tomato paste
1/2 cup water
2 Tbsp. chopped parsley
1/4 tsp. cinnamon
3/4 pound macaroni
1/2 stick butter, melted
1/4 pound grated Parmesan
  cheese

CREMA SAUCE:
6 Tbsp. butter
6 Tbsp. flour
3 cups milk
6 eggs, beaten
1/4 cup Parmesan cheese
1/4 tsp. ground nutmeg
Salt and pepper to taste

Step 1. Brown meat until juices are absorbed. Add onion, butter, garlic, salt, pepper, parsley, cinnamon, tomato paste, and water. Simmer until thickened, about 20 minutes.

Step 2. Cook macaroni in boiling salted water until almost done. Pour into a colander, rinse with hot water, and drain well. Mix macaroni with melted butter.

Step 3. Brush baking pan with melted butter. Line with half of macaroni. Sprinkle with half of cheese. Spread meat mixture on top of cheese, and then repeat macaroni and cheese layers.

Step 4. Crema: Melt butter. Add flour, stirring constantly. Remove from heat, and gradually stir in milk. Return to heat, stir constantly until thickened.

Step 5. Add eggs slowly. Blend in Parmesan cheese, salt, pepper, and nutmeg.

Step 6. Pour crema sauce over top of casserole and bake for 1 hour or until golden brown.

Grecian Gourmet

STEAK GREEK STYLE

GREEK

Pan Size: Frying Pan
Yield: 4 servings

4 Tbsp. butter
4 choice sirloin strip steaks
  (one inch thick)
1 lemon, juice of
Garlic (granulated)
Oregano
Cavender's prepared Greek
  seasoning

Step 1. Sprinkle steaks on both sides with lemon and a mixture of garlic, oregano, and seasoning.

Step 2. Melt butter in pan.

Step 3. Place steaks in melted butter and cook until rare or medium done. Can also be broiled or barbecued.

Mrs. Harry Yavis (Sophie)

SARMA
Cabbage Rolls

SERBIAN

Yield: 3 dozen rolls

3/4 pound ground pork
1/4 ground ground beef
1/4 cup raw rice
1/2 cup finely chopped onion
2 cloves garlic, minced
2 Tbsp. lard or other
shortening
Salt and pepper
1 medium size cabbage
Tomato juice or sauce

ROUX:
1/2 onion, finely chopped
1 Tbsp. lard
1 Tbsp. flour
2 tsp. paprika
Cabbage broth

Step 1. Remove core from cabbage. Separate leaves and blanch 3 or 4 at a time.

Step 2. Cool, pare heavy veins but not completely through the leaf.

Step 3. Sauté onion and garlic in shortening until tender. Add meat and rice. Cook mixture until meat is browned, stirring constantly.

Step 4. On each cabbage leaf, place a large spoonful of filling at the core end in the center of the leaf. Flip the right end of the leaf over the meat. Roll up and tuck in left side of the leaf into the sarma.

Step 5. Place leftover cabbage leaves in bottom of kettle. Place larger cabbage rolls on leaves at bottom; finish with smaller ones.

Step 6. Heat enough water to boiling to cover about 3/4 of the cabbage rolls. Bring to a boil. Add tomato juice or sauce until all cabbage rolls are immersed in liquid.

Step 7. Cook on medium heat for 1 to 1-1/2 hours.

Variation I: If roux is desired, sauté 1/2 onion in lard until tender. Stir in flour until lightly browned. Remove from heat. Add paprika and stir well. Stir cabbage broth into roux. When well blended, pour over cabbage rolls; add to sarma at least 1/2 hour before end of cooking time.

Variation II: For a sauerkraut flavor, place cabbage leaves in a large bowl or porcelain pot. Spread sauerkraut on some of the layers. Pour kraut juice over all. Cover with plastic wrap. Place a dish with a heavy object on it on the plastic wrap. Cover and keep in a cool place for several days or until ready to use.

Mrs. Rodney Arnokovich
Tucson, Arizona

YEMISTES MELIDZANES I   GREEK
Stuffed Eggplant

Temperature: 350°
Yield: 14 servings

1 large onion, chopped
1/2 stick butter
3 Tbsp. olive oil
7 medium eggplants
1/4 cup parsley
1-1/2 pounds ground beef
6 eggs, beaten
1/2 cup Parmesan cheese
1 tsp. cornstarch
Salt
Pepper
Sugar

Step 1. Cut eggplants in half lengthwise, dip into boiling water, and remove immediately. Allow to cool.

Step 2. Scoop out pulp of each half and sprinkle shells with a little salt, pepper, and sugar. Place hollow shells close together in a baking dish.

Step 3. Sauté onions in butter and oil until soft. Add meat and 3 tablespoons pulp to onions. When meat begins to brown, add parsley. Remove from heat and set aside to cool.

Step 4. Add grated cheese to the beaten eggs, and mix well. Reserve 3/4 cup of this mixture and add the rest to meat mixture, blending well.

Step 5. Fill each shell with meat mixture, and bake for 30 minutes. Remove from oven.

Step 6. Add cornstarch to remaining egg mixture and spoon over the top of each eggplant. Return to oven and bake until brown on top, about 15 minutes.

Grecian Gourmet

YEMISTES MELIDZANES II

GREEK

Stuffed Eggplant Deluxe

Temperature: 350°
Pan Size: 9" x 13" x 2"
Yield: 4-8 servings

2 medium eggplants
1/2 pound ground beef
4 Tbsp. cooking oil
4 ounces tomato sauce
1 large onion, chopped
3 cloves garlic, chopped
1/4 cup fresh parsley,
  chopped
1/8 tsp. dill, dried
1/8 tsp. mint, dried
1/8 tsp. oregano, dried
1/4 tsp. pepper
1 tsp. salt
1 cup water
3/4 cup long grain rice, or
  3/4 cup wild rice
1/4 cup bread or cracker
  crumbs
1/4 cup grated Parmesan
  cheese, or grated
  American cheese

Step 1. Wash eggplants and cut in half lengthwise. Remove pulp leaving a 1/4 inch shell, sprinkle salt inside hull and set aside. Cut pulp into medium size cubes.

Step 2. Sauté ground beef, chopped onion, and garlic in oil. Add chopped pulp and cook until tender. Stir in parsley, dill, mint, oregano, salt, and pepper. Add tomato sauce and 1 cup of water; simmer until well blended. Add rice; and stir thoroughly.

Step 3. Rinse eggplant shells and stuff with meat mixture; sprinkle eggplant with crumbs.

Step 4. Place eggplant halves in baking dish. Pour 1/2 cup water and remaining meat mixture, if any, into pan around eggplant halves. Cover with foil and bake at 350° for about 30 to 45 minutes or until rice is tender. Remove foil and top each half with grated Parmesan cheese. Bake an additional 5 minutes or until cheese has melted.

Note: Eggplant halves may be cut in two, yielding 8 servings when ready to serve.

George L. Koleas

SAUCES

ASPRI SALTSA
Bechamel Sauce

GREEK

Yield: 2 cups

2 cups milk, heated
3 Tbsp. flour
2 Tbsp. butter
2 Tbsp. grated Parmesan
  cheese
1/2 tsp. salt
1/4 tsp. ground nutmeg

Step 1. Melt butter in saucepan. Stir in flour. Add hot milk slowly, stirring constantly until mixture thickens and begins to boil.

Step 2. Remove from heat and add cheese, salt, and nutmeg.

Grecian Gourmet

BASIC AVGHOLEMONO SAUCE
Egg and Lemon Sauce

GREEK

Yield: 2 cups

3 eggs, well beaten
2 lemons, juice of
1 cup hot chicken broth

Step 1. Beat eggs until light and fluffy and add lemon juice slowly, beating well.

Step 2. Gradually add hot broth, beating constantly at low speed.

Grecian Gourmet

CREMA
Cream Sauce

GREEK

Yield: 4 cups

6 Tbsp. butter
6 Tbsp. flour
3 cups milk
6 eggs, beaten
1/4 cup Parmesan cheese,
  grated
1/4 tsp. nutmeg, ground
Salt and pepper to taste

Step 1. Melt butter and add flour, stirring constantly. Add milk gradually, stirring until thickened.

Step 2. Slowly add eggs, Parmesan cheese, salt, pepper, and nutmeg.

Note: This recipe covers a 9" x 13" pan.

Grecian Gourmet

EASY AVGHOLEMONO GREEK-AMERICAN
Easy Egg-Lemon Sauce

Yield: 1 cup

1 stick butter, melted
3 egg yolks
2-1/2 Tbsp. lemon juice
1/2 tsp. salt
1/2 cup boiling water

Step 1. Bring water to a boil.

Step 2. Melt butter.

Step 3. Combine butter, egg yolks, lemon juice, and salt in blender or processor. Blend until smooth (5 seconds). Gradually add boiling water and continue blending.

Step 4. Pour mixture in top of double boiler and cook over hot water (not boiling). Stir constantly until sauce thickens to consistency of soft custard. Remove from heat and serve.

Note: Sauce can be stored in refrigerator in covered container up to 2 weeks. Reheat as needed over hot water in double boiler.

Mrs. Michael C. Speros (Carolyn)

KEMA I GREEK
Meat Sauce

Yield: 6-8 servings

1 medium onion, chopped
1/2 stick butter
1 pound chopped lamb or beef
1 8-ounce can tomato sauce or 1 14-ounce can whole tomatoes, chopped
Salt and pepper to taste
1 clove garlic, minced
1/2 cup wine
3 Tbsp. chopped parsley
1 bay leaf (optional)
1/4 tsp. cinnamon

Step 1. Sauté onion in butter until golden brown. Add meat, stirring until well browned. Add tomato sauce or whole tomatoes.

Step 2. Add other ingredients, cover and simmer for about 30 minutes until sauce thickens.

Note: This sauce may be served over macaroni, spaghetti, noodles, or rice.

The Cookbook Committee

KEMA II

Meta Sauce

Yield: 8-10 servings

2 onions, chopped
2 cloves garlic, mashed
1/4 cup olive oil
1-1/2 pounds ground beef
2-1/2 cups tomato juice
1-1/2 cups tomato puree
1 6-ounce can tomato paste
1 tsp. salt
1/4 tsp. pepper
1 tsp. sugar

Step 1. Sauté onions and garlic in oil.

Step 2. Add meat and brown slowly.

Step 3. Heat tomato juice, puree, and paste in deep saucepan.

Step 4. Add meat mixture, salt, pepper, and sugar.

Step 5. Simmer 2-1/2 to 3 hours until thickened.

Grecian Gourmet

KEMA III

Meat Sauce   GREEK

1/2 pound ground chuck
1/2 pound mild sausage
1/4 cup water
2 Tbsp. minced dry onion
1/4 tsp. garlic powder (or
  1 whole clove garlic)
1/4 tsp. freshly ground
  black pepper
1 dash ground cinnamon
1 bay leaf
1 tsp. dry parsley leaves
1 pinch of rosemary leaves
  (optional)
1/2 cup red wine
1 12-ounce can tomato
  sauce
1/2 can very hot water
Salt

Step 1. Put meats and water into a heavy saucepan and break up meats; cook over high heat, stirring constantly until meat has separated into granules.

Step 2. Add all other ingredients except wine and tomato sauce and continue stirring until meat absorbs all liquids and begins to brown. Add wine, stirring constantly. When wine has evaporated, reduce heat to medium and add tomato sauce and water; stir to blend; cover and cook at least 30 minutes; stir occasionally to prevent sticking. Taste and correct seasonings; add salt if required. Serve over spaghetti, macaroni or use as pizza sauce.

James A. Lenis

YAOURTI
Yogurt

Yield: 8 cups

2 quarts milk
3 Tbsp. yogurt (culture)

Step 1. Heat milk and bring to a boil, stirring constantly. Remove from heat and allow to cool to lukewarm.

Step 2. Dilute culture with a little of cooled milk. Stir this mixture into remainder of milk slowly, blending well.

Step 3. Pour into large bowl or small individual bowls. Cover and keep in warm place for several hours or until set; then refrigerate.

Note: This process takes from 4 to 7 hours, depending on your room temperature. Plain commercial yogurt may be used for culture. For richer yogurt, add 1/2 cup heavy cream.

Grecian Gourmet

SKORTHALIA I
Garlic Sauce

GREEK

Yield: 2 cups

3 medium potatoes
Salt to taste
8 buttons garlic
4 slices bread
1/4 cup lemon juice
1/2 cup oil
1 Tbsp. vinegar
1 egg
1/4 cup boiling water

Step 1. Boil potatoes. Drain well and mash with electric beater. Add salt.

Step 2. With a garlic press, squeeze garlic into potatoes.

Step 3. Trim crusts from bread. Soak in water; squeeze water from bread and add to potatoes.

Step 4. Beat potatoes, garlic and bread well. Add lemon juice and oil alternately. Then add vinegar.

Step 5. Add egg and beat well. Add boiling water and beat until creamy. Allow to set before serving.

Note: May be used as a sauce for fish or as a dip for raw vegetables.

Mrs. Kosta N. Taras (Loretta)

SKORTHALIA II

GREEK

Garlic Sauce

Yield: 2 cups

4 or 5 cloves garlic, peeled
1/4 tsp. salt
18 slices white bread
  (day old), trimmed
3/4 cup Wesson oil
4 tsp. cider vinegar
1 tsp. lemon juice
1 or 2 Tbsp. cold water

Step 1. Crush garlic well and add salt. Garlic will "disappear" after being crushed. Set aside.

Step 2. Soak bread, one piece at a time, just long enough to wet. Squeeze out excess water until almost dry.

Step 3. In bowl of electric mixer, add 2 or 3 slices of bread at a time. Beat thoroughly. Scrape garlic mixture into bread and blend thoroughly.

Step 4. When mixture is smooth, add oil, 1 teaspoon at a time. Continue beating as you add lemon juice and vinegar; add cold water; blend well. Mixture should be the consistency of mayonnaise. If a thinner sauce is desired, add more water.

Note: Serve as sauce for fried frish, fried eggplant, squash, beets, cucumber, and as a salad dressing. Excellent for dips. Sauce will keep refrigerated for 2 weeks or longer and will freeze well.

Mrs. Ray Guidi (Sophia)

SKORTHALIA III

GREEK

Garlic Sauce, Blender Method

Yield: 1-3/4 cups

4 to 6 cloves garlic, minced
  or mashed
1/2 tsp. salt
1 Tbsp. lemon juice
2 Tbsp. white wine vinegar
2 egg yolks
1/2 cup olive oil
1/2 cup salad oil
1/2 cup finely ground,
  blanched almonds

Step 1. Put garlic, salt, lemon juice, vinegar, and egg yolks in blender. Blend a few seconds; gradually add oils.

Step 2. Remove mixture from blender container into bowl and stir in almonds. Chill before serving.

Note: Use as dip with a variety of fresh, raw vegetables, boiled or baked potatoes, fried squash, eggplant, fish, seafood, etc.

Mrs. Stephen S. Lenis (Mary)

VEGETABLES

ANGINARES AVGHOLEMONO

GREEK

Artichokes with Egg-Lemon Sauce

2 bunches green onions,
  chopped
1/3 cup olive or other
  cooking oil
2 cans artichoke hearts
Water
1 tsp. dill weed
Salt and pepper to taste

Step 1. Sauté green onions in oil until soft. Add artichokes, dill, and enough water to cover. Simmer for 20 minutes.

Step 2. Pour Avgholemono Sauce over artichokes and serve immediately. Refer to Basic Avgholemono Sauce, page 100.

Helen Ritsos Pappas

BAMYES ME DOMATES

GREEK

Okra and Tomatoes

Yield: 4-6 servings

1 pound okra
1/2 cup vinegar
1/2 cup olive oil
3 onions, chopped
1/2 cup canned tomatoes
1 Tbsp. chopped parsley
1/2 tsp. sugar (optional)
Salt and pepper to taste

Step 1. Wash okra and cut off stems. Allow to stand for 1 hour in vinegar and enough water to cover. Rinse thoroughly and drain well.

Step 2. Sauté onions in olive oil. Add okra and cook for 5 minutes. Add tomatoes, parsley, sugar, salt, pepper, and enough water to cover. Bring to a boil. Cover and reduce heat. Cook for 45 minutes.

Grecian Gourmet

DOLMATHES YIALANDJI

GREEK

Stuffed Grapevine Leaves, Lenten

Yield: 3 dozen

3 medium onions, finely
   chopped
1/4 cup pine nuts (optional)
1 tsp. salt
1/2 tsp. pepper
3/4 cup rice
3/4 cup olive oil, divided
1 Tbsp. fresh mint, chopped
1 Tbsp. fresh dill, chopped
   (or 1/2 tsp. dry)
1/2 cup fresh parsley,
   chopped (reserve stalks)
1 bunch scallions, finely
   chopped
Salt and pepper
1 lemon, juice of
1/4 cup water
1 12-ounce jar of grapevine
   leaves

Step 1. Remove leaves from jar and scald in hot water; drain.

Step 2. In a skillet, sauté onions in 1/4 cup oil until transparent; add rice, salt, pepper, mint, dill, parsley, and scallions; mix well. Add half of the lemon juice and 1/4 cup water; cover and steam for 10 minutes. Cool.

Step 3. Separate grape leaves carefully. Snip off thick stems. Cut large leaves in half. Put the dull side of leaf up. Place one rounded teaspoonful of rice mixture at base of leaf. Fold left side of leaf to center, then right side, and then roll.

Step 4. Spread parsley stalks over bottom of deep 3-4 quart saucepan. Arrange the dolmathes in layers over stalks. Add remaining lemon juice, salt, and pepper and drizzle remaining oil over dolmathes. Place heavy plate (inverted) on top of dolmathes to keep them from falling apart during cooking. Pour boiling water over them (enough to cover the top of the dolmathes). Bring to full simmer, lower heat and cook over low heat 45 minutes to an hour, until rice is cooked. (Check pan during cooking and add more boiling water if necessary.) Cool in pan. To serve: Arrange dolmathes on serving platter. Squeeze lemon juice over all; garnish with very thin slices of lemon.

Mrs. Bill K. Taras (Bessie)

FASOULAKIA YIAHNI

GREEK

Greek-Style Green Beans

Yield: 6 servings

2 pounds string beans
2 medium onions, chopped
3/4 cup olive oil
1 cup tomato sauce
1/4 cup chopped celery
2 carrots, quartered
2 Tbsp. chopped parsley
1-1/4 cup water
Salt and pepper to taste

Step 1. Sauté onions lightly in oil. Add tomato sauce, salt, and pepper and simmer for 15 minutes.

Step 2. Add string beans and remaining ingredients. Cover and simmer for 1 hour or until tender.

Grecian Gourmet

PATATES BRIANI
Greek-Style Potatoes

GREEK

Temperature: 375°
Pan Size: 9" x 13"
Yield: 6 servings

6-7 white baking potatoes, peeled and quartered lengthwise
1/2 green pepper, cut in large pieces
1 medium onion, cut in large pieces
1 large clove garlic, minced
1 to 1-1/2 sticks butter, cut into pieces
2 Tbsp. water
Salt and pepper to taste
1/2 tsp. paprika

Step 1. Arrange all the ingredients in 9" x 13" pan and sprinkle with salt, pepper, and paprika.

Step 2. Put in oven and stir vegetables as soon as butter melts.

Step 3. Stir and baste occasionally as potatoes bake.

Step 4. Bake 1 to 1-1/4 hours until potatoes are cooked through and golden brown.

Note: May add bouillon cube to water or use drippings from roast for basting.

Mrs. Bruce Erskine (Helen)

KOLOKITHAKIA
Squash in Tomatoes

GREEK

Yield: 4 servings

3 yellow squash
2 zucchini squash
1 large onion, chopped
1 cup water
1 Tbsp. chicken base
1/2 stick butter
1 tsp. salt
1/2 tsp. pepper
1/2 tsp. Accent
1/2 tsp. dill weed
1 8-ounce can tomato sauce
1 cup water

Step 1. Clean squash and cut into 1 inch slices. Set aside.

Step 2. Cook onion in water, chicken base, and butter until onion is soft. Add salt, pepper, Accent, and dill weed.

Step 3. Add tomato sauce and water. Cook for 10 minutes.

Step 4. Add squash and cook until squash is tender.

Mrs. Kosta N. Taras (Loretta)

KOLOKITHÓPETA
Squash and Feta Casserole

GREEK

Temperature: 350°
Yield: 6-8 servings

8 medium yellow squash
1 Tbsp. butter
1 onion, chopped
2 Tbsp. canned tomato sauce
3/4 cup Feta cheese,
  crumbled
3 Tbsp. cracker meal crumbs
2 well beaten eggs
Salt and pepper to taste
Butter

Step 1. Slice squash in 1-inch slices. Cook squash in boiling salted water until tender. Drain well.

Step 2. Put butter in saucepan and sauté onions until lightly browned.

Step 3. Add tomato sauce. Remove from heat; add squash, 1/2 cup crumbled Feta cheese, and 1 tablespoon cracker meal crumbs.

Step 4. Fold in eggs and season with salt and pepper.

Step 5. Put mixture in greased 8" casserole. Sprinkle top with remaining crumbled Feta cheese and cracker crumbs. Dot with butter.

Step 6. Place casserole dish in pan of hot water and bake in oven at 350° for approximately 30 minutes. Serve immediately.

Note: May be prepared ahead and frozen before baking.

Mrs. George A. Futris (Jane)

FRIED PEPPERS AND ONIONS

GREEK

3 large green peppers
1 large onion
1/3 cup olive oil
Salt and pepper to taste

Cut peppers and onions in slices and add to hot oil in frying pan. Sauté until vegetables are slightly limp. Add salt and pepper, reduce heat, cover, and cook until tender but firm. Serve as a side dish to meats, especially hamburgers and liver. This is also a good lenten dish.

Variation: Add potato slices. When vegetables have finished cooking, a pinch of thyme or oregano may be added.

Mrs. James Varnavas (Helen)

RIZI ME MANITARIA
Rice with Mushrooms

GREEK

Yield: 4 servings

2 medium onions, chopped
1/2 cup olive oil
1 8-ounce can sliced
  mushrooms
1/2 cup chopped celery
1/2 cup chopped parsley
2-1/2 cups broth or water
1/4 cup dry white wine
1 tsp. salt
1/4 tsp. pepper
1 cup rice

Step 1. Sauté onions in olive oil until soft.

Step 2. Drain mushrooms and add to onions. Cook for 2 minutes over medium heat.

Step 3. Add celery, parsley, broth, wine, salt and pepper; cover and simmer for 20 minutes.

Step 4. Add rice. Cover and continue to simmer until rice is tender and all liquids are absorbed.

Grecian Gourmet

SPANAKOPETA I
Spinach Peta

GREEK

Temperature: 450°
Pan Size: 11" x 15" x 2"
Yield: 40 squares

3 pounds fresh spinach
  or 5 boxes frozen spinach
3 bunches fresh green onions,
  chopped
2 Tbsp. dry dill weed
1 bunch chopped parsley
7-8 well beaten eggs
1 Tbsp. farina (or Cream
  of Wheat)
1/2 pound crumbled Feta
  cheese
1/4 cup grated Parmesan
  cheese
1/4 cup olive oil
Salt to taste
3 sticks butter, melted
1 pound filo

Step 1. Wash spinach and drain well. (If using frozen spinach, thaw overnight and press out *all* water.) Sprinkle with salt and cut. Combine with onions, dill, parsley, farina, cheeses, oil and eggs.

Step 2. Line pan with 8 filo leaves brushing with melted butter between each layer. Pour in spinach mixture. Cover with 8 more filo leaves brushing each with butter. Brush top with butter and sprinkle lightly with water.

Step 3. Bake in 450° over for 15 to 20 minutes, until filo begins to turn a light golden color and puffs in the center. Reduce oven to 350° and bake 30 minutes longer until golden brown.

Step 4. Let peta stand 15 to 20 minutes before cutting.

Mrs. Charles Vergos (Tasia)

SPANAKOPETA II
Spinach Pie—A Third Generation Way

GREEK

Temperature: 350°
Pan Size: 12" x 18"
Yield: 40-50 pieces

**4 10-ounce packages frozen
  chopped spinach
4-5 bunches green onions,
  chopped
2 pints sour cream
1-1/2 pints cottage cheese
1/2 cup crumbled Feta cheese
5 eggs, well-beaten (about
  2 minutes)
1 tsp. cream of wheat
4 Tbsp. dried dill weed
Salt and pepper to taste
1 pound melted butter
1 pound filo**

Step 1. Place spinach in colander and thaw overnight. Squeeze water completely out of spinach.

Step 2. Cook onions in very little water and drain thoroughly.

Step 3. Mix thawed spinach, onions, sour cream, cottage cheese, Feta cheese, dill weed, salt, pepper, eggs and cream of wheat in a large bowl.

Step 4. Generously butter sides and bottom of pan. Fold one sheet filo in half and place at short end of pan with folded side hanging over pan. Repeat at other end of pan and on long sides. Brush all folded sheets with butter. Place one full sheet on bottom of pan and sprinkle with butter. Repeat this process until you have 8 sheets on bottom.

Step 5. Spread spinach mixture in prepared pan.

Step 6. Fold the folded end in, over spinach mixture. Layer 8 more sheets on the top, following same procedure as with bottom sheets —layering sheets and butter. Filo sheets do not have to be smooth. Butter top layer completely.

Step 7. With a sharp knife, score top layers of filo in squares. Sprinkle with a few drops of water.

Step 8. Bake for 1 hour until golden brown.

Note: May be frozen before baking or partially bake, cool completely and freeze.

Mrs. Dimitri Taras (Mary Katherine)

SPANAKORIZO
Spinach with Rice

Yield: 4-6 servings

2 pounds fresh spinach
1 bunch green onions,
  chopped
1/2 cup olive oil
1 clove garlic, minced
2 Tbsp. dill weed
2 sprigs parsley, chopped
4 ounces tomato sauce
1 cup water
1 cup rice
1/2 cup Feta cheese (optional)
Salt and pepper to taste

Step 1. Wash spinach; drain.

Step 2. Sauté onions in oil until soft. Add all other ingredients except rice and cheese. Cook until spinach is wilted.

Step 3. Add rice, cover and simmer until rice is tender. Remove from heat and add Feta cheese, if desired. Do not stir.

Note: Two 10-ounce boxes of frozen leaf or chopped spinach may be used instead of fresh.

Variations: You may add shrimp, scallops or squid when you sauté the onions. This makes an excellent Lenten dish (omit cheese).

Grecian Gourmet

VEGETABLE CASSEROLE

Temperature: 350°
Pan Size: 9" X 13"
Yield: 6-13 servings

1 onion, slivered
3 stalks celery, sliced thinly
4 small yellow squash, sliced
1 cup cut green beans
1 small eggplant, cubed
1 to 2 carrots, sliced
4 small red potatoes, halved
1 can tomato wedges
1 can tomato sauce
1 bouillon cube (optional)
2 bell peppers, sliced
Salt and pepper to taste
1 sprig mint leaves, chopped
2 Tbsp. parsley, chopped
1/4 cup oil

Step 1. Arrange prepared vegetables in pan.

Step 2. Sprinkle salt, pepper, mint and parsley over them.

Step 3. Pour oil over vegetables.

Step 4. Cover with aluminum foil.

Step 5. Bake for 45 minutes. Uncover and bake 15 minutes more.

Note: Fresh tomatoes may be used instead of canned; substitute any of your favorite vegetables.

Mrs. Helen Valsamakis
Clarksdale, Mississippi

BREADS

GLYKO PSOMI
Holiday Sweet Bread

GREEK

Temperature: 350° reduce to 325°
Yield: 5 1-pound loaves

2 cups milk, scalded
2 sticks butter
2 sticks margarine
2-1/2 cups sugar
2 Tbsp. salt
5 packages yeast
1 cup lukewarm water
5 pounds flour, all-purpose
1-1/2 tsp. ground cloves
2 tsp. ground cinnamon
1 tsp. mastiha, crushed
  (optional)
1/2 cup orange juice
1 jigger cognac or whiskey
1 tsp. vanilla
5 eggs, beaten
1 egg, slightly beaten (for
  glazing)
Sesame seeds
Honey, for glazing
Powdered sugar

Step 1. Scald milk, remove from heat and add butter, margarine, sugar and salt. Stir to dissolve and set aside.

Step 2. Add yeast to water and allow to rise.

Step 3. Sift flour and spices into a large basin and make a well in flour; add milk mixture, yeast mixture, orange juice, cognac, vanilla and eggs. Stir to blend, incorporating flour until dough is formed. Turn out onto floured surface and knead until smooth and elastic. Place dough into a well oiled basin and set in a warm place to rise until doubled in bulk (approximately 1 hour).

Step 4. Punch down dough; turn out of bowl; knead slightly. Divide dough by cutting with a sharp knife into as many loaves as are desired. Retain a portion of dough for any applied decorations. Knead into desired shape. Place in oiled pans. Shape and apply the desired decorations (See page 30); cover and set in a warm place to rise. When dough has doubled in size and is ready for baking, brush top with beaten egg, being careful not to let egg run onto top edge of pan as it will cause bread to stick to pan. Sprinkle with sesame seeds. Bake at 350° for 20 minutes, then check for degree of browning. If loaves have browned lightly on tops of decorations and around sides, reduce heat to 325°. If not yet browned, check every 10 minutes before reducing heat. Bake small loaves (up to 1 pound) 45 to 55 minutes (total time). Bake loaves, 1 pound and larger, 50 to 60 minutes. Should loaves require more baking, check every 5 minutes to prevent overbaking. Test loaves for doneness by thumping in center for a hollow sound. Turn out of pans onto wire racks.

Step 5. Brush top and sides of hot loaves with honey and dust with powdered sugar. Allow to cool completely before storing.

Note: Unbleached flour makes this recipe especially delicious.

Mrs. James Varnavas (Helen)

PSOMI I

Greek Bread

Temperature: 350°
Yield: 6 loaves

2-1/2 cups milk
1 cup sugar
1-1/2 Tbsp. salt
1 stick butter
1 cup Crisco
4 packages granulated
  yeast
1 Tbsp. sugar
2 cups warm water
5 eggs, beaten
4 pounds flour
  (approximately 15 cups)
1 egg, beaten (for glaze)

Step 1. Scald milk; add sugar, salt, butter, Crisco; stir until sugar dissolves. Set aside to cool to lukewarm.

Step 2. Sprinkle yeast and 1 tablespoon sugar into 2 cups warm water. Allow yeast to dissolve (10 to 15 minutes).

Step 3. Pour lukewarm milk mixture into large mixing bowl. Add beaten eggs, yeast mixture, and begin adding flour. When dough starts forming ball, turn out onto floured surface and knead (adding flour as necessary) until dough is smooth and not sticky. Cover and let rise in warm place until doubled in bulk.

Step 4. Punch down dough. Turn out onto lightly floured surface. Divide into 6 equal parts. Shape dough as desired (round loaves, braided, twisted, etc.) and place in greased pans. Cover and let rise again to double in bulk.

Step 5. Before baking, brush tops with beaten egg for dark, glossy crust. If desired, sprinkle with sesame seeds.

Step 6. Bake at 350° for 30 to 45 minutes, depending on size of loaf. Test for doneness by thumping. It should have a hollow sound.

Note: If fewer loaves are desired, this recipe may be divided, equally.

Mrs. Kosta Taras (Loretta)

PSOMI II
Greek Bread

Temperature: 350°
Yield: 2 loaves

5 cups sifted plain flour
1/2 cup sugar
1 Tbsp. salt
2 eggs, beaten
2 sticks margarine, melted
2 yeast cakes or
   2 packages dry yeast
2-1/4 cups warm water
1 egg yolk, beaten
Sesame seeds

Step 1. Sift flour, sugar and salt in a large mixing bowl. Add beaten eggs and melted margarine to flour. To this mixture add 2 cups of warm water to make a soft dough.

Step 2. Dissolve yeast in 1/4 cup warm water, add to mixture and knead until mixture is smooth and elastic—15 to 20 minutes. Cover and let rise in warm place until double in size.

Step 3. Divide dough in half and shape to fit two greased loaf pans and allow to rise again. Brush top with beaten egg yolk, and sprinkle with sesame seeds. Bake for about 1 hour.

Grecian Gourmet

TSOUREKI
Sweet Bread

GREEK

Temperature: 325°
Yield: 4-5 loaves

3 yeast cakes or
   3 packages dry yeast
1/2 cup lukewarm water
1/2 cup shortening
1 cup milk
7 eggs, beaten
2-1/2 cups sugar
1-1/2 sticks butter, melted
4 tsp. baking powder
1/2 tsp. salt
3/4 tsp. mastiha, crushed
3-1/2 to 4 pounds flour
Milk or beaten egg yolk
Sesame seeds

Step 1. Dissolve yeast in lukewarm water and set aside. Add shortening to hot milk and allow to cool to lukewarm. Beat eggs with sugar until light. Add melted butter and beat well. Stir in lukewarm milk and shortening, dissolved yeast and remaining ingredients.

Step 2. Gradually add enough flour to make a soft dough. Knead until smooth. (All flour may not be used.) Place in greased bowl, cover, and let rise for a few hours or until doubled in bulk.

Step 3. Divide dough and shape into plain or braided loaves. Place in greased pans, cover, and let rise until double, about 1 hour. Brush top of bread with milk or beaten egg yolk. Sprinkle with sesame seeds. Bake for 40 minutes.

Grecian Gourmet

EASTER BREAD

Temperature: 400° for 10 minutes, 350° for 1 hour
Pan Size: 2 loaf pans, 9" x 5"
Yield: 2 loaves

2 cakes yeast
2 cups lukewarm milk
3 cups flour, sifted
5 egg yolks, beaten well
1 cup sugar
1/2 cup butter, melted
1 cup raisins
1 Tbsp. vanilla
6 cups sifted flour

Step 1. Dissolve yeast in lukewarm milk in a large bowl. Add 3 cups flour, and mix, then cover with a towel.

Step 2. After beating egg yolks, mix in sugar, butter, raisins, and vanilla. Add to yeast mixture with enough remaining flour to make a light dough. Let rise in a warm place until double in bulk, about 2 hours.

Step 3. Turn out onto a floured board and knead, using enough flour to make a medium firm dough. Divide into 2 loaves, knead until smooth and place in well-greased loaf pans. Let rise again until double in bulk, about 1-1/2 hours.

Step 4. Bake in a 400° oven for 10 minutes; reduce the heat to 350° and bake for 1 hour or until a deep golden brown. Remove from pans; cool.

Mrs. Steve Hlavka (Anne)
Linden, New Jersey

CYPRIOT CHEESE BREAD

Temperature: 375° - 400°
Pan Size: angel food pan

5 eggs
1 cup olive oil
1 jigger brandy
5 cups flour
3 tsp. baking powder
1 cup milk
2 cups grated Parmesan
  cheese
2 tsp. chopped mint
  (optional)

Step 1. Beat eggs; add olive oil and brandy. Set aside.

Step 2. Sift flour and baking powder. Add milk and stir.

Step 3. To the flour mixture, add the egg mixture, grated cheese, and mint.

Step 4. Pour into greased angel food pan. Bake about 45 minutes at 375° - 400°. Test with sharp knife or toothpick for doneness.

Mrs. George Demas (Victoria)

POVITICA

Walnut and Date Sweet Bread

Temperature: 350°
Pan Size: 10" tube pan
Yield: 12-16 servings

2 packages dry yeast
1/4 cup lukewarm water
1/2 tsp. sugar
2-1/2 cups flour
1/4 tsp. salt
2 Tbsp. sugar
3 beaten egg yolks
1 cup melted margarine
  (2 sticks)
1 cup milk

FILLING:
1 cup ground walnuts
2 tsp. cinnamon
1/2 cup milk
6 Tbsp. sugar
1 cup chopped dates
4 egg whites
1-1/3 cup sugar

Step 1. Mix 2 packages dry yeast and 1/4 cup lukewarm water with 1/2 teaspoon sugar and set aside to proof.

Step 2. Sift together 2-1/2 cups flour, 1/4 teaspoon salt and 2 tablespoons sugar.

Step 3. In large bowl mix melted margarine, milk and beaten eggs yolks. Add yeast mixture. Blend in flour mixture and beat well. When dough is sticky, but comes away from sides of bowl, transfer to large plastic container which seals tightly (size allows for dough rising and lid prevents spilling). Refrigerate overnight.

Step 4. Remove dough from refrigerator and let stand at room temperature during preparation of filling.

Step 5. Filling: Mix walnuts, cinnamon, milk, sugar and dates. Cook over medium heat, stirring constantly to prevent burning and until dates have become paste.

Step 6. On a floured cloth, roll out half of dough into a 20" by 20" square. As you roll out dough, sprinkle with flour to prevent dough from sticking to cloth.

Step 7. Beat 4 egg whites well, add 1-1/3 cups sugar gradually, beating until whites are stiff but not dry. Fold into walnut and date mixture until well blended.

Step 8. Place half of the filling on each square of rolled-out dough. Using cloth, roll up each square, as you would a jelly roll.

Continued...

Step 9. Place rolls one on top of the other in well-oiled tube pan and bake at 350° for 1 hour and 5 minutes.

Step 10. Remove from oven and cool in pan for 20 minutes. Gently flip out of pan onto a cooling rack.

Note: This bread freezes well..

Anne Pekovich

KOLACHKY
Nut Roll Bread

RUSSIAN

Temperature: 375°
Pan Size: cookie sheet
Yield: 6 long rolls

1/2 cup evaporated milk
1 cup water
1 package dry yeast
3 Tbsp. warm water
1/4 cup sugar
Dash salt
1/2 cup Wesson oil
2 egg yolks, beaten
2 egg whites, beaten
6-1/2 cups flour, sifted

NUT FILLING:
6 cups walnuts, ground fine
1 cup sugar
1 cup milk

Step 1. Mix milk and water. Heat until lukewarm. Mix yeast with 3 tablespoons warm water and add to milk. Add sugar, salt, oil, egg yolks, and then whites. Add flour a little at a time. Add enough flour, so dough no longer sticks to hands. Shape into 6 balls. Place on cookie sheet, cover, and let rise about 2 hours.

Step 2. Filling: Mix nuts and sugar together, adding milk a little at a time. Be careful not to make the filling too thin.

Step 3. Take each ball, roll out to 1/2 inch thickness on a floured board, to approximately 12" x 18". Spread with filling and roll up as for jelly-roll. Place on greased pan. Cover and let rise 15 minutes. Brush with milk, and bake for 25-30 minutes.

Note: Other fillings may be bought ready-made, such as Solo poppyseed or apricot preserves. This may be served as dessert or as a breakfast pastry. To serve, cut into 1/2" thick slices. Sprinkle with powdered sugar, if desired.

Mrs. Anna Ostrosky
Coaldale, Pennsylvania

PSOMI STA TESSARA

Nick's #4 Bread

Temperature: 325°
Pan Size: standard loaf pans
Yield: 6 loaves

4 tsp. sugar
**4 packages yeast, dissolved
  in 1 cup water**
4 cups milk
4 ounces honey
4 ounces butter
4 large eggs, beaten
4 tsp. salt
4 pounds flour, approximately

Step 1. In a large bowl, add sugar and yeast mix and set aside to activate.

Step 2. Heat milk in saucepan until scalded; do not boil. Remove from heat, add honey and butter, stir and set aside to cool to lukewarm.

Step 3. Into warm milk mixture; add eggs and salt and mix with whisk or beater.

Step 4. Add active yeast mixture to lukewarm milk mixture. Stir well, cover and set aside until yeast activates again.

Step 5. Into a large mixing bowl or basin, put about 2 pounds of flour, add yeast mixture while stirring with a wooden spoon until a very soft dough is formed. Turn out onto floured surface and knead lightly, adding flour until dough is soft and silky and does not stick to your hands. Place dough into a large greased bowl, cover and let rise until double in size. Punch down and knead lightly. (Optional: At this point, if a very finely textured bread is desired, dough may be allowed to rise again before proceeding with next step.) Turn onto a lightly floured surface, divide dough equally into greased pans, cover lightly and set in a warm place to rise until double in size.

Step 6. Preheat oven to 325°. Bake loaves 45 to 60 minutes. Check after 20 minutes to see if loaves are rising and browning evenly; rearrange if necessary. Reduce oven to 300° and continue baking. Bread will be done when nicely browned and has a hollow sound when thumped in center of top.

Note: This recipe is very flexible. To make less bread, simply change the amount of ingredients from 4's to 3's or 2's for smaller amounts or increase to 5's or 6's for larger amounts.

Nick J. Vergos

VASILOPITA
Matula's New Year's Cake

Temperature: 250°
Pan Size: 12" x 3" round cake pan

6 ounces butter
1-1/2 cups sugar
1-1/2 to 2 pounds flour
  (6-8 cups, sifted)
1-1/2 cups milk
1 Tbsp. cinnamon
3 medium eggs, beaten
2 tsp. baking powder
1 tsp. baking soda
1 orange, grated rind of
1 orange, juice of
Sesame seeds
Whole cloves
1 pound blanched whole
  almonds

TOPPING:
1 egg
1 tsp. milk

Step 1. In large bowl of electric mixer, beat butter until light. Add sugar gradually and continue beating until thoroughly creamed.

Step 2. Add 6 cups flour gradually and alternately with 1 cup of the milk. Add cinnamon and eggs; blend well; continue beating.

Step 3. Dissolve baking powder and baking soda in remaining 1/2 cup milk and add to batter; blend thoroughly.

Step 4. Add orange juice and rind.

Step 5. Beat in remaining flour only until batter resembles heavy pound cake type batter.

Step 6. Pour into cake pan.

Step 7. Decorate as follows: Make the date of the new year across the top of the cake with rows of whole cloves (push stems into batter). Cover surface generously with sesame seeds. Place blanched whole almonds between and around the numbers. Brush top of cake lightly with topping mixture.

Step 8. Bake in slow oven until done. Test for doneness with cake wire or a piece of raw spaghetti; if it comes out clean, cake is done.

Note: A "lucky" coin is placed into the batter during mixing. When cake is cut to celebrate New Year's Day, the slices are named as they are served, starting with "for the house," and then for each member of the family and guests. Whoever finds the coin in his slice is supposed to have extra good luck in the new year.

Mrs. Matula Constantikes
Gouverneur, New York (Sparta)

VASILOPITA
New Year's Sweet Bread

Temperature: 350°
Yield: 5 loaves

2 cups milk
4 packages dry yeast
2 tsp. salt
5 pounds flour
1-1/2 sticks butter
1 stick margarine
2 Tbsp. Crisco
2 cups sugar
12 eggs (room temperature)
1 tsp. vanilla (optional)
1 tsp. mastiha (crushed)
1 egg

Step 1. Scald milk. Cool to lukewarm. Pour milk into large bowl. Add yeast, salt and 4 cups of flour. Mix thoroughly. Cover with clean towel. Set aside to rise until bubbly.

Step 2. Beat butter, margarine, Crisco and sugar. Add beaten eggs and flavoring. Beat well. Add egg mixture to yeast mixture. Add remaining flour. Knead until dough is satiny and elastic.

Step 3. Place in greased bowl and allow to rise until double in size.

Step 4. Punch down dough. Divide into 5 portions and work each piece until smooth.

Step 5. Place into greased, round or square baking pans. Cover with tea towel and allow to rise for about 1 hour.

Step 6. Brush with beaten egg and bake in pre-heated oven at 350° for 20 minutes, reduce heat to 325°. Care must be taken in the baking process that bread does not get too brown. Place foil over loaves, if necessary.

Note: See instructions for inserting coins in recipe on page 121.

Mrs. George Karkatsugas (Agori)

DESSERTS/PRESERVES

CHRISTINA'S DELIGHT

GREEK

Temperature: 350°
Pan Size: 13" x 9" x 2"
Yield: 20 pieces

2 sticks butter
3 cups sugar
8 eggs
4 cups flour
4 tsp. baking powder
1/2 tsp. salt
1 cup milk
2 tsp. vanilla
1/2 pound medium ground
  walnuts (reserve about
  1 cup for the top)

SYRUP:
4 cups sugar
3 cups water
1 slice lemon

Step 1. Cream butter until fluffy. Add sugar, a little at a time, and beat until light and fluffy.

Step 2. Add eggs two at a time and beat well after each addition.

Step 3. Sift flour, baking powder and salt 3 times. Reserve about 1 cup to mix with nuts.

Step 4. Add flour mixture alternately with milk, a small amount at a time, blending well after each addition. Add vanilla.

Step 5. Mix nuts with flour and fold into mixture.

Step 6. Bake for 45 minutes. Cool cake completely.

Step 7. Syrup: Bring water, sugar and lemon slice to a boil. Reduce heat and simmer for 15 minutes or until syrup begins to thicken.

Step 8. Cut cake into squares and pour hot syrup over cake, slowly.

Step 9. Sprinkle with powdered sugar, cinnamon and nuts.

Mrs. John Zepatos (Alice)

124

KARITHOPETA I
Almond Cake

GREEK

Temperature: 375°
Pan Size: 11" x 16"
Yield: 35-40 pieces

10 large eggs, separated
1 cup sugar
1/2 tsp. salt
1 cup ground Zwieback or
  cracker meal
2 tsp. baking powder
1 to 1-1/2 cups ground
  almonds
1/2 stick butter, melted

SYRUP:
4 cups sugar
3 cups water
1/2 cup honey
1/2 lemon, juice of

Step 1. Mix Zwieback or cracker meal, salt, and baking powder together, add nuts and set aside.

Step 2. Beat egg yolks until light; add sugar very slowly and beat until light and fluffy.

Step 3. Add dry ingredients and mix well with a spoon.

Step 4. Beat egg whites until stiff but not dry. Fold into mixture.

Step 5. Pour melted butter into 11" x 16" pan. Tilt pan to coat entirely with butter.

Step 6. Pour batter into pan.

Step 7. Bake 30-35 minutes. Cool completely.

Step 8. Syrup: Combine sugar, water, and lemon juice. Bring to a boil. Reduce heat and simmer 10 minutes. Remove from heat and add honey.

Step 9. Pour warm syrup over cake very slowly with spoon.

Mrs. Gerry Touliatos (Olga)

ORECHNIK

Nut Cake

Temperature: 350°
Pan Size: 9" tube, spring form
Yield: 1 medium size cake

1-1/2 cups sifted flour
1 tsp. baking powder
1/2 tsp. salt
3 eggs
1 cup sugar
3/4 cup sour cream
1/2 tsp. baking soda
1/2 tsp. vanilla
1/2 cup chopped nuts
1/2 cup fine bread crumbs

Step 1. Sift together first 3 ingredients. Beat eggs until thick; then gradually add sugar. Stir in sour cream, soda, and vanilla, beating well. Blend in nuts.

Step 2. Fold in sifted dry ingredients and bread crumbs. Pour into greased spring form tube pan.

Step 3. Bake 35 to 40 minutes or until done. Remove from pan when cool. Cake may be glazed or eaten plain.

Mrs. George Ostrosky (Helen)

POUTINGA

Cake with Pudding Topping

Temperature: 375°
Pan Size: 10" x 14"

SYRUP:
2 cups sugar
1 cup water
2 jiggers cognac or whiskey

CAKE:
9 eggs, separated
1/2 cup plus 2 Tbsp. sugar
1/2 cup regular Cream
  of Wheat
1 cup ground almonds,
  divided
1 Tbsp. cocoa
1 tsp. vanilla
1 box (3-3/4 ounce) chocolate
  pudding, regular

Step 1. Prepare syrup. Dissolve sugar in water; bring to a boil; reduce heat and allow to simmer about 10 minutes to form a light syrup. Stir in flavoring; set aside to cool.

Step 2. Beat egg yolks with sugar until light and fluffy. Add Cream of Wheat, 2/3 cup almonds, cocoa and vanilla; stir until thoroughly blended.

Step 3. Beat egg whites until stiff but not dry. Fold into Cream of Wheat mixture. Pour into greased pan. Bake for 30 minutes. Remove cake from oven; pour cooled syrup over cake and return it to the oven to bake 5 minutes longer. Remove cake from oven and cool.

Step 4. Prepare pudding according to directions on box. Spread in a thin layer over cake. Sprinkle with 1/3 cup ground almonds.

Cookbook Committee

PANTESPANI PORTOKALI
Orange Sponge Cake

Temperature: Pre-heat 375°; lower to 350°
Pan Size: 8" x 10" or 7" x 11" pan
Yield: 10-12 servings

1 cup sugar
5 eggs, separated
1/2 pound butter, melted
1 orange, juice and grated
  rind
1 jigger cognac or
  orange liqueur
1 cup flour
3-1/2 tsp. baking powder

SYRUP:
2-1/2 cups water
1 cup sugar
1 stick cinnamon
2 jiggers orange liqueur
  or cognac

Step 1. Beat sugar and egg yolks well.

Step 2. Stir in melted butter, orange juice, cognac or liqueur, flour (which has been sifted with baking powder), and orange rind.

Step 3. Carefully fold into stiffly beaten egg whites.

Step 4. Pour into buttered pan.

Step 5. Bake 10 minutes at 375°–then lower to 350° and bake 30 minutes or until done. Cool completely in pan.

Step 6. Bring sugar, water and cinnamon to a boil. Simmer for 10 minutes. Remove from heat and add orange liqueur or cognac. Slowly pour hot syrup over cake.

Step 7. Cut into square or diamond shapes.

Mrs. Angelo D. Liollio (Tina)

KARITHOPETA II
Walnut Cake

Temperature: 350°
Pan Size: 10" x 4" tube pan

1 cup butter
1-1/2 cups sugar
6 eggs
2 cups walnuts, ground
1 tsp. cinnamon
1/2 cup milk
2 cups flour
4 tsp. baking powder

Step 1. Cream butter and sugar until light and fluffy; add eggs one at a time, blending thoroughly after each addition.

Step 2. Stir in walnuts, cinnamon, and milk, blend thoroughly. Add flour which has been sifted with baking powder; blend thoroughly.

Step 3. Pour batter into well buttered baking pan and bake 30 minutes or until cake tests done. Cool; dust with powdered sugar.

Mrs. Charles Vergos (Tasia)

RAVANI

Almond Cake

Temperature: 350°
Pan Size: 11" x 16"
Yield: 30 or more pieces

12 eggs, separated
1 pound sweet butter
(preferably 3/4 butter and
1/4 Crisco)
1 cup sugar
2-1/2 cups flour
2-1/2 cups farina or Cream of
Wheat
4 tsp. baking powder
1/2 cup milk
2 tsp. lemon extract
1/2 cup chopped almonds

SYRUP:
6 cups sugar
7 cups water

Step 1. Beat egg whites stiff, but not dry; set aside.

Step 2. Beat egg yolks until light; set aside.

Step 3. Cream butter and sugar together, then add beaten egg yolks; blend.

Step 4. Sift flour, farina and baking powder together and add to butter mixture; blend. Add milk and blend. Fold in stiffly beaten egg whites. Add lemon extract.

Step 5. Pour into greased pan and sprinkle almonds over batter.

Step 6. Bake 40 minutes, or until cake tests done.

Step 7. Syrup: Bring sugar and water to a boil, simmer about 15 minutes.

Step 8. When cake is removed from oven, pour hot syrup over it. Cover pan with aluminum foil and allow to set overnight.

Note: To serve, cut into squares or diamond shapes.

Mary G. Dentiste

WALNUT TORTE

UKRAINIAN

Temperature: 350°
Pan Size: 2 9" round
Yield: 12 - 15 servings

CAKE:
2 cups sifted flour
2-3/4 tsp. baking powder
1/4 tsp. salt
2/3 cup butter
1 cup sugar
2 tsp. vanilla or your choice
  of any fruit liqueur
Rind of 1 lemon, grated
3 eggs, separated
3/4 cup milk at room
  temperature
1-1/4 cups ground walnuts
1 lemon, juice of
1 Tbsp. cognac, or choice of
  liqueur
1 Tbsp. water

FILLING:
1 12-ounce jar orange
  marmalade
1/2 pint heavy cream
2 Tbsp. confectioners' sugar
1/4 cup ground walnuts

MOCHA BUTTERCREAM:
1/2 ounce unsweetened
  chocolate
3 Tbsp. milk
3 Tbsp. strong coffee
1 stick very soft butter
1 cup confectioners' sugar
1 tsp. liqueur of your choice

Step 1. Sift dry ingredients together, set aside.

Step 2. Beat butter, sugar, vanilla or liqueur, and lemon rind together. Add egg yolks and beat until fluffy, about 5 minutes.

Step 3. Alternately, add dry ingredients and milk and beat until smooth. Add ground walnuts.

Step 4. Beat egg whites and fold into mixture. Pour into well-buttered pans and bake 30 minutes or until cake tests done. Remove from oven and cool for 10 minutes in pans. Invert onto wire racks and cover with tea towels and allow to cool completely.

Step 5. When completely cool, split each layer horizontally so that there are 4 layers. Set aside.

Step 6. Combine lemon juice, cognac and water (enough to make 1/4 cup) and brush each layer with this mixture. Be generous but do not make cake too soggy. Set aside.

Step 7. Filling: Spread 2 of the layers with orange marmalade. Whip 1/2 pint heavy cream with confectioners' sugar and fold in ground walnuts. Spread 1 layer with this mixture. Assemble the layers on a cake plate and refrigerate while making buttercream.

Step 8. Mocha Buttercream: In a double boiler melt chocolate and milk; stir in coffee to make a smooth paste (the consistency of pudding). Cool. Beat in butter, remaining heavy cream, and liqueur. Whip until light and fluffy.

Step 9. Spread over entire cake and refrigerate overnight or at least 6 hours.

Larysa Matiash-Folk

YAOURTOPETA I

Yogurt Nut Cake with Lemon-Honey Syrup

Temperature: 350°
Pan Size: 13" x 9" x 2"
Yield: 20-24 pieces

LEMON-HONEY SYRUP:
1 small lemon
1/2 cup sugar
1-1/3 cups water
1 small cinnamon stick
(1-1/2")
2 whole cloves
1 Tbsp. rose water (optional)
or brandy
1/2 cup honey

YOGURT CAKE:
1/2 cup (1 stick butter or
margarine)
2 cups sugar
2 eggs
2-1/2 cups sifted
all-purpose flour
1/2 tsp. baking soda
Pinch salt
1 container (8 ounce)
plain yogurt
1 tsp. vanilla
1/4 cup toasted whole
blanched almonds

Step 1. Lemon-Honey Syrup: Remove rind (thin yellow, not white) from lemon; squeeze out 1-1/2 teaspoons lemon juice into a small cup; set aside.

Step 2. Place lemon rind, sugar, water, cinnamon stick and cloves in a heavy medium-size saucepan. Bring to a full boil, stirring constantly; lower heat; simmer at least 20-25 minutes, no stirring.

Step 3. Stir in honey; when completely dissolved, pour through strainer into a 2-cup measure. Stir in reserved lemon juice and rose water; or brandy. Cool to lukewarm.

Step 4. Yogurt Cake: Grease pan and dust with flour.

Step 5. Beat butter and sugar in large bowl with electric mixer until thoroughly blended. Add eggs, one at a time, beating well after each.

Step 6. Sift flour, baking soda and salt together.

Step 7. Stir flour mixture into creamed mixture alternately with yogurt, just until blended. Stir in vanilla. Pour into baking pan.

Step 8. Bake in a moderate oven at 350° for about 45 minutes, or until center springs back when lightly pressed with fingertip. Cool in pan on wire rack 5 minutes.

Continued...

Step 9. Pierce the surface all over with thin utility fork (a round toothpick would accomplish the same results). Spoon syrup evenly over the warm cake, reserving about 1/2 cup of syrup. Score cake into diamonds or squares, spoon remainder of syrup over cake. Place a toasted almond in the center of each. Cool to room temperature.

Note: Cake is best when prepared the day before or several hours before serving. If prepared the day before, do not refrigerate; however, reserve about 1/2 cup of prepared syrup, heat the next day and pour over cool scored cake; then place toasted almonds on top.

Evangeline "Scottie" Koleas

YAOURTOPITA II
Yogurt Nut Cake

GREEK

Temperature: 350°
Pan Size: 9" x 13"
Yield: 25-30 servings

1 cup soft butter
1-1/4 cup sugar
6 eggs, well beaten
2 cups flour
1 tsp. cinnamon
1 tsp. cloves
1 cup yogurt
2 tsp. baking soda
1 jigger whiskey
1 cup finely chopped
almonds

SYRUP:
2 cups sugar
3 cups water
1 stick cinnamon

Step 1. Beat butter and sugar together for 10 minutes. Add well beaten eggs; beat 5 minutes longer.

Step 2. Sift flour and spices together. Add to butter mixture gradually. Add yogurt and blend well.

Step 3. Dissolve baking soda in whiskey and add to mixture. Add almonds.

Step 4. Pour into greased pan and bake 45 minutes or until toothpick comes out clean.

Step 5. Combine syrup ingredients in saucepan; stir to dissolve sugar; bring to a boil; simmer (do not stir) for 10 minutes. When cake is completely cooled, cut into diamond or square shaped pieces and pour hot syrup over cake (while in pan) *very slowly*. Allow to set, undisturbed, at least 1 hour or until syrup is absorbed.

Mrs. Costa B. Taras (Nancy)

XANTHO MELACHRINO
GREEK

Yellow Cake with Spiced Meringue

Temperature: 375°
Pan Size: 11" x 15"
Yield: 35 pieces, approximately

2 sticks butter
1 cup sugar
4 eggs, separated
2 cups sifted flour
1 tsp. baking powder
1 cup chopped almonds
1 oz. cognac or whiskey
1 tsp. vanilla extract
1 tsp. grated lemon rind

8 eggs, separated
1 cup sugar
1 cup crushed Zwieback
1 tsp. baking powder
2 cups chopped pecans
1 tsp. cinnamon
1/2 tsp. ground cloves
1/2 tsp. nutmeg

SYRUP:
3 cups sugar
3 cups water
1 lemon, juice of

XANTHO:
Step 1. Cream butter and sugar and add egg yolks. Beat until light.

Step 2. Add flour which has been sifted with baking powder. Add almonds, cognac, vanilla and grated lemon rind.

Step 3. Fold in stiffly beaten egg whites. Pour into greased pan.

MELACHRINO:
Step 1. Beat eggs with sugar. Add Zwieback, to which baking powder has been added. Add pecans, cinnamon, cloves, and nutmeg and blend thoroughly.

Step 2. Fold in stiffly beaten egg whites. Pour on top of Xantho cake. Bake for 45 minutes. Cool cake completely. Pour warm syrup over cool cake.

Syrup: Bring sugar and water to a boil. Reduce heat and simmer for 10 minutes. Remove from heat and add lemon juice. Cool slightly before pouring over cake.

Note: Allow cake to absorb syrup completely before cutting.

Mrs. Sam Larigakis (Mary)
Clarksdale, Mississippi

FINIKIA
Honey Dipped Cookies

GREEK

Temperature: 350°
Yield: Makes 10 dozen cookies

1-1/2 cups sugar
1 cup butter
2 cups oil
3 eggs
1 cup orange juice
5 pounds flour or less
1 tsp. baking powder
Vanilla
1 tsp. cinnamon
1/4 tsp. cloves
1/8 tsp. nutmeg

FILLING:
1 pound dates, chopped
1 cup ground nuts
1/2 tsp. cinnamon
1/2 tsp. cloves
1 Tbsp. honey

SYRUP:
2 cups sugar
1-1/2 cups water
1-1/2 pounds honey

Extra Honey for Dipping

TOPPING MIXTURE:
Cinnamon
Grounded nuts
Powdered sugar

Step 1. Melt butter. Pour into bowl large enough to hold all ingredients and finished product. Add oil and sugar. Mix well and place in refrigerator to set. This step may be done a day in advance.

Step 2. Beat butter mixture until light in color. Add eggs and orange juice and beat well. Sift baking powder and flour. Add vanilla and flour to form a soft cookie dough.

Step 3. Chop dates coarsely; add chopped nuts. Combine with spices and honey. Mix well.

Step 4. Break off pieces of the dough about the size of a walnut and roll into a ball, flatten slightly and place about 1/2 teaspoon of filling in center. Fold dough around filling in the shape of an oval.

Step 5. Bake on cookie sheet until lightly brown, about 20 minutes.

Step 6. Remove cookies from oven and cool on racks.

Step 7. Prepare syrup by combining sugar and water in saucepan. Stir. Bring to a boil, reduce heat and simmer for about 10 minutes. Add honey; stir well.

Step 8. Dip each cookie quickly into hot syrup as it simmers.

Step 9. Drain on racks or in colander.

Step 10. Dip top of each cookie in honey.

Step 11. Sprinkle with ground nuts, cinnamon and powdered sugar mixture.

Mrs. George Karkatsugas (Agori)

HAMALIA
Almond Cookies
GREEK

Temperature: 300°
Yield: 3 dozen

3 cups blanched almonds, finely ground
1 cup sugar
1/4 cup warm water
3 oz. orange flower water or rose water
Confectioners' sugar

Step 1. Mix almonds, sugar and water. Blend well.

Step 2. Use amount of mixture necessary to make desired shape (ball, crescent, thumbprint, etc.) Place on well-greased pan.

Step 3. Bake 15 to 20 minutes or until edges of pastry are slightly golden.

Step 4. Cool and remove from pan. Sprinkle with orange flower water or with rose water and dust with confectioners' sugar until well covered.

Mrs. Helen Valsamakis
Clarksdale, Mississippi

KIFLE
Crescent Cookies
SERBIAN

Temperature: 375°
Yield: 10 dozen

4 cups flour
1 ounce compressed yeast
1-1/2 cups butter
1/2 cup sour cream
3 egg yolks beaten
1 lemon, grated rind of
Granulated sugar

FILLING:
3 egg whites
1 cup sugar
1/4 pound ground walnuts

Step 1. Combine flour, yeast and butter. Mix until ingredients look like pie crust. Mix in sour cream, beaten egg yolks and lemon rind.

Step 2. Knead and divide into 5 or 6 balls.

Step 3. Roll out dough on granulated sugared board into circles approximately 10" in diameter. Cut into 2" pie wedges.

Step 4. Mix filling: Beat egg whites until stiff and add sugar and ground walnuts. Put about 1/2 teaspoon of filling at wide edges of dough and roll it up. Place on cookie sheet.

Step 5. Bake 12 to 15 minutes.

Mrs. George Cavic (Mileva)
St. Louis, Missouri

KOLACHKY
Frozen Dough Cookies

Temperature: 350°
Yield: Approximately 12 dozen

1 pound Crisco
1 pound butter
9 cups sifted flour
3 small yeast cakes
Little warm water
8 eggs, separated
1 pint sour cream
Powdered sugar

NUT FILLING:
6 cups finely ground
  walnuts or pecans
1 cup granulated sugar
1/2 to 1 cup cold milk

Step 1. Mix Crisco, butter, and flour by hand. Crumble yeast into warm water; then add to flour and mix well. Add yolks to flour mixture, blending well. Next add sour cream and 4 beaten egg whites to mixture. Add enough flour at the end until the dough no longer sticks to hands.

Step 2. Place covered in refrigerator for several hours or overnight until it is very cold.

Step 3. Nut Filling: Mix ingredients with spoon, adding only enough milk to moisten, making it easy to spread on the dough.

Step 4. Roll out dough about 1/4" thick, a small portion at a time, on a board sprinkled with powdered sugar. Cut dough into small 2" squares or wedges. Spread filling on squares of dough; then pick up corner with small knife and roll to look like a crescent roll. Or you may pinch only 2 ends together, if desired.

Step 5. Bake at 350° until lightly browned. Remove from oven and sprinkle lightly with powdered sugar. These keep well in an air-tight container. You may also fill with fruit fillings such as apricot preserves, Solo brand prune filling or poppyseed filling.

This is a traditional Easter and Christmas cookie.

Mrs. Anna Ostrosky

KOULOURAKIA I

Easter Cookies

GREEK

Temperature: 350°
Yield: 11 dozen

1/2 cup Crisco
1/2 cup Wesson oil
2 sticks butter
2 cups sugar
1/2 cup milk or orange juice
2 Tbsp. baking powder
6-1/2 cups flour
2 eggs
1 tsp. vanilla
1 egg yolk, beaten with 1/2
  tsp. sugar for glaze
1 cup sesame seeds (optional)

Step 1. In mixer bowl, combine Crisco, Wesson oil, butter and sugar; beat well until creamy.

Step 2. Beat in milk or orange juice.

Step 3. Add eggs and vanilla.

Step 4. Sift baking powder and flour and add gradually to mixture, until consistency of cake batter.

Step 5. Remove from mixer and add remaining flour, kneading by hand.

Step 6. Test dough by rolling the dough in the palm of your hand; if it sticks, knead in more flour.

Step 7. Roll dough about 3" long and 1/2" thick; then shape into small doughnuts, pressing the ends together with your fingers to form a circle.

Step 8. Brush with egg yolk and dip in sesame seeds if desired.

Step 9. Place on a cookie sheet.

Step 10. Bake at 350° for 15-20 minutes until lightly browned.

Mrs. Jerre Duzane (Madeline)

KOULOURAKIA II

Traditional Easter Cookies

Temperature: 350°
Yield: Approximately 120-140 depending on size

1 dozen eggs
4 cups sugar
1 pound butter, melted
2 tsp. vanilla, or 2 packets
  imported vanilla
3 level Tbsp. baking powder
5 pounds all-purpose flour,
  approximately

Step 1. Using electric mixer, beat eggs with the sugar until light and fluffy.

Step 2. Add cooled melted butter to egg mixture; continue beating until light in color and creamy; add vanilla.

Step 3. Sift baking powder with 2 cups of flour. Add to egg mixture and continue beating.

Step 4. Gradually add remaining flour. When mixture becomes too thick for beaters, turn dough into larger mixing basin and continue kneading the flour in until the dough is soft but not sticky. Set aside and allow dough to rest approximately 1 hour.

Step 5. Pinch off a small piece of dough and work until elastic. Shape into desired form. Place on cookie sheet and bake for approximately 20 minutes or until light golden brown around edges. Cool thoroughly before storing.

Note: Dough can be refrigerated for later use, but allow to come to room temperature before shaping.

Mrs. John C. Vergos (Fannie)

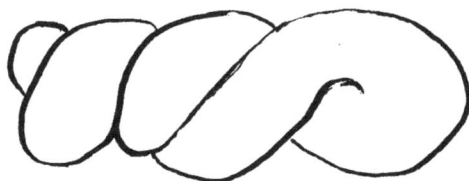

The circle and the twist are the two most traditional shapes. The circle represents eternity and the twist represents the dual nature of Christ, God and man.

KOURABIEDES I

GREEK

Sugar-Coated Butter Cookies

Temperature: 350°
Yield: 90 cookies

1 pound sweet butter
3 Tbsp. powdered sugar
1/4 jigger bourbon
1 whole egg, beaten
2 pounds sifted cake flour
(approximately)
1/2 tsp. vanilla
3/4 cup toasted and ground
almonds
2 boxes powdered sugar

Step 1. Melt butter and allow to cool completely.

Step 2. Beat until light and fluffy. (This will take about 15 minutes.)

Step 3. Add bourbon and powdered sugar and beat well. Add beaten egg and mix well. Add almonds and vanilla.

Step 4. Add flour, a little at a time, beating well until it forms a soft dough.

Step 5. Using 1 tablespoon per cookie, form dough into desired shape–round or crescent.

Step 6. Bake on a buttered baking sheet for 15 to 20 minutes at 350°.

Step 7. On waxed paper, sift enough powdered sugar to cover paper. Place hot cookies on sugar. Immediately sift powdered sugar over cookies, covering completely. Allow to absorb sugar about 1 hour.

Step 8. With spatula, place in paper baking cups.

Mrs. John G. Touliatos (Voula)

KOURABIEDES II

Sugar-Coated Butter Cookies

Temperature: 350°
Yield: Approximately 5 dozen

1 pound butter, clarified
3 Tbsp. powdered sugar
1 cup almonds, toasted and
  finely chopped
1 large egg
1 jigger whiskey
Whole cloves (optional)
6-8 cups flour (1-1/2 to
  2 pounds)
2 boxes confectioners'
  sugar

Step 1. Prepare surface for cookies by laying waxed paper on a countertop. Sift generously with powdered sugar.

Step 2. Beat butter and sugar until light and fluffy.

Step 3. Beat in egg and add whiskey.

Step 4. Add nuts and sifted flour alternately. Continue adding flour, kneading until dough is soft but not sticky.

Step 5. Take a small amount of dough and shape into a ball; place on cookie sheet, depress center slightly and press a whole clove into the center (stem down).

Step 6. Bake about 20 minutes or until bottoms are very lightly browned.

Step 7. Remove from oven and place carefully on prepared surface. While cookies are still hot, generously sift additional powdered sugar over top and sides. Cool thoroughly before storing.

Mrs. John C. Vergos (Fannie)

MELOMAKARONA I

GREEK

Honey Dipped Cookies

Temperature: 350°
Yield: 180 pieces

2 cups Wesson oil
2 sticks butter
1 cup sugar
2 eggs
1/2 cup orange juice
1-1/2 tsp. vanilla
1 tsp. baking powder
2 to 2-1/2 pounds flour, sifted
1-1/2 cups walnuts, ground

FILLING:
1 pound dates,chopped
1-1/2 cups nuts, chopped
1 tsp. cinnamon

SYRUP:
2 cups sugar
2 cups water
1/2 lemon, juice of

TOPPING:
Honey
2 cups walnuts or pecans,
   ground
Cinnamon
Powdered sugar or walnut or
   pecan halves

Step 1. Sift flour with baking powder and set aside.

Step 2. Heat oil until very hot. Set aside to cool slightly; then add butter.

Step 3. When thoroughly cool, add sugar, gradually, and beat well. Add eggs, one at a time.

Step 4. Add orange juice, vanilla, and 1 cup of nuts.

Step 5. Add as much of the flour as mixer will allow; then knead in remaining flour with hands. Work dough with hands until soft and glossy, but not sticky.

Step 6. Break off pieces the size of a walnut and roll into ball, flatten slightly and place about 1/2 teaspoon of filling (if desired) in center, forming dough around in the shape of an oval.

Step 7. Bake on cookie sheet until lightly brown, about 20 minutes.

Step 8. Remove cookies from oven and cool on racks.

Step 9. Syrup: Bring sugar, water and lemon juice to a boil. Reduce heat and simmer 15-20 minutes, until thickened.

Step 10. Dip each cookie quickly into hot syrup as it simmers. Drain on racks or in colander.

Step 11. Dip tops of each cookie in honey.

Step 12. Sprinkle with ground nuts; then sprinkle a little cinnamon and powdered sugar, or, instead, place half of pecan or walnut on each cookie.

Mrs. Gerry Touliatos (Olga)

Note: These cookies may be filled with stuffing or not. Melomakarona keep well in tightly covered tins and may also be frozen.

140

MELOMAKARONA II   GREEK
Honey Cookies

Temperature: 375°
Yield: 10 dozen

**2 sticks butter, at room
  temperature**
1-1/4 cups sugar
2 cups Wesson oil
1 egg
1-1/2 cups orange juice
1 tsp. baking soda
1 tsp. vanilla flavoring
1 tsp. baking powder
Dash cinnamon
Dash cloves
**2-1/2 pounds Gold Medal
  flour (approximately)**

FILLING:
2 cups pecans, chopped
**1 8-ounce package pitted
  dates, chopped**
1/2 tsp. cinnamon
**Honey, enough to hold nuts
  together**

SYRUP:
4 cups sugar
4 cups water
1 cinnamon stick
1/2 cup honey
**2 cups pecans, chopped,
  for topping**

Step 1. Beat softened butter with mixer for 15 minutes. Add sugar and beat well. Add oil slowly and beat 10-15 minutes. Add whole egg. In separate bowl, mix orange juice and baking soda; let foam and add quickly to butter mixture and beat in thoroughly; add vanilla. Mix 2 cups flour, baking powder, cinnamon, and cloves together and add, gradually, to first mixture; add enough of the remaining flour to form a very soft, but not sticky, dough.

Step 2. Combine pecans, dates, cinnamon, and honey to make cookie filling.

Step 3. Using 1 tablespoon dough to each cookie, roll into oval shape; press out and add 1/2 teaspoon filling and shape back into an oval cookie. Place crease side down on baking sheet. Bake about 20 minutes.

Step 4. Syrup: Combine sugar and water; stir to dissolve sugar; bring to a boil, add cinnamon, reduce heat; simmer 10-15 minutes to thicken. Remove from heat and stir in honey. Cool.

Step 5. Dip cookies into cooled syrup. Let drain. Dip top of each cookie into honey. Sprinkle with ground nuts.

Mrs. John Touliatos (Voula)

PASTA FLORA
Fruit Squares

Temperature: 350°
Pan Size: 11" x 7" x 1" pan
Yield: 16 pieces

1 can apricot halves
3/4 cup peach jam or
preserves
1/2 orange, juice of
1/2 lemon, juice of
2 Tbsp. dry sherry
5 tsp. cornstarch
1/4 tsp. cinnamon

PASTRY DOUGH:
1/3 cup soft butter
1/2 cup sugar
1 egg, beaten
1/2 tsp. grated orange rind
1 Tbsp. brandy
1 tsp. vanilla
2 cups flour
1 tsp. baking powder
1/2 tsp. salt
1/4 cup ground, toasted
almonds

Step 1. To prepare filling, drain apricots and reserve 1/4 cup juice. Set apricots on paper towel to drain.

Step 2. Combine peach jam, orange juice, lemon juice and sherry in saucepan.

Step 3. Slowly mix apricot juice in cornstarch and add to fruit mixture.

Step 4. Cook over low heat, stirring frequently until thickened. Set aside to cool.

Step 5. To prepare pastry dough, cream butter and sugar, add beaten egg and mix until creamy. Add orange rind, brandy, and vanilla.

Step 6. Sift flour with baking powder and add to mixture, blend thoroughly. Knead until smooth.

Step 7. Grease pan. Press half of dough into pan.

Step 8. Carefully lay apricots in rows, cut side down and spoon on filling, covering fruit entirely.

Step 9. Roll remaining dough into 1/2" rope strips and lay over filling, making lattice design.

Step 10. Bake for 40 minutes in 350° oven. Cool completely before cutting.

Mrs. Angelo Liollio (Tina)

SKALTSOUNAKIA

Nut Filled Cookies

GREEK

Temperature: 375°
Yield: 4-5 dozen cookies

4 cups sifted flour
1 tsp. baking powder
3 Tbsp. sugar
Dash of cinnamon
2 sticks butter, softened
2 egg yolks, beaten
1 jigger brandy (apricot preferred)

FILLING:
1 cup orange marmalade or apricot preserves
1 cup white raisins
1 cup chopped nuts
1/2 cup candied fruit, finely chopped
Rose water
Powdered sugar

Step 1. Sift flour, baking powder, sugar and cinnamon together. Add butter and rub into dry ingredients with palms of hands, until well blended.

Step 2. Add egg yolks and brandy, kneading slightly.

Step 3. Roll out dough until thin and cut into 4" or 5" circles.

Step 4. Filling: In a separate bowl, mix marmalade, raisins, nuts and fruits.

Step 5. Place 1 teaspoon of filling in the middle of dough. Wet edges with water and fold over to form a half-moon. Press the edges with a fork to seal.

Step 6. Bake on greased cookie sheets for 20 minutes.

Step 7. Remove from oven, sprinkle with rose water and roll hot cookies in powdered sugar.

Grecian Gourmet

MAZURKI

Fruit Cookies

Temperature: 300°
Pan Size: 10" x 14", 1/2" deep
Yield: Approximately 3 dozen

1 cup seedless raisins, chopped
1 cup dried apricots, chopped
1 cup currants
1 cup walnuts, chopped
1 cup blanched almonds, chopped
1 cup raspberry jam (or strawberry)
2 eggs, beaten
1 lemon rind, grated
2 cups sifted all-purpose flour

Step 1. Combine all ingredients except flour. Sprinkle with flour and mix thoroughly.

Step 2. Spread dough in greased shallow baking pan. Bake in 300° oven for about 35 minutes. Remove from oven. Cut into diamond shapes while still in the warm pan. Return pan to oven for 5 additional minutes to dry out the cookies.

Mrs. George Ostrosky (Helen)

PAXIMATHIA I

GREEK

Tea Cookies

Temperature: 375°
Yield: 8 dozen

1 pound softened butter
1-2/3 cups sugar
4 eggs
1 tsp. vanilla
1 tsp. baking powder
1 tsp. baking soda
5-1/2 to 6 cups flour
1 cup chopped nuts
Sesame seeds (optional)

Step 1. Cream butter with sugar. Add 4 eggs and beat well. Add vanilla.

Step 2. Sift flour with baking powder and soda. Mix flour with nuts. Blend into butter mixture with a spoon. (You may have to knead flour in with hands.)

Step 3. When soft dough is formed, shape into a long narrow flat loaf, about 2 to 2-1/2" wide and 1/2" thick.

Step 4. Place on cookie sheet for baking. With knife, mark flattened loaf with slight indentation, indicating width of cookies.

Step 5. Brush top of loaf with slightly beaten egg. Sprinkle with sesame seed if desired.

Continued...

Step 6. Bake at 375° for 20 minutes or until lightly brown. Remove from oven and slice through indentations to form cookies.

Step 7. Return to oven and toast lightly on both sides until lightly brown.

Mrs. Nicholas L. Vieron (Bess)

AHLADAKIA
Cookie Pears

GREEK

Temperature: 350°
Yield: 50 cookies

1 cup vegetable oil
1-1/2 cups sugar
2 eggs
1 orange, juice and rind of
2 tsp. baking powder
1/2 tsp. baking soda
4 cups sifted flour
** (approximately)**
Whole cloves

SYRUP:
2 cups water
1 cup sugar
1 lemon, juice of

Step 1. Cream oil and sugar together; add eggs, 1 at a time, beating constantly.

Step 2. Dissolve baking soda in orange juice and add to creamed mixture.

Step 3. Add baking powder and enough flour to make a soft dough. Pinch off a small piece of dough, about the size of a walnut and shape into small ball. Pinch one side to resemble a pear, and press a clove into wider end of cookie.

Step 4. Place on greased baking sheet and bake for 20-25 minutes in 350° oven. Remove from baking sheet and cool.

Step 5. Combine water and sugar and bring to a boil; add lemon juice; reduce heat and keep warm.

Step 6. Dip cookies quickly one by one in warm syrup. Sprinkle immediately with mixture of granulated sugar and cinnamon.

Note: Syrup should coat rather than penetrate cookie; otherwise, it becomes soggy.

Mrs. George Futris (Jane)

PAXIMATHIA II

Greek Tea Cookies

Temperature: 350°
Pan Size: Approximately 18" cookie sheet
Yield: Approximately 170 cookies

2 cups granulated sugar
3 sticks sweet butter
1 stick margarine
7 eggs
1 jigger bourbon or brandy
(optional)
Approximately 3 pounds (12
cups) all-purpose flour
(Gold Medal)
1 tsp. baking powder
1/2 tsp. baking soda
1 cup pecans, chopped
Sesame seeds (optional)

Step 1. Preheat oven to 350°. In large mixing bowl cream sugar, butter and margarine until smooth (electric beater at medium speed).

Step 2. Add 6 eggs to butter mixture, 1 at a time, and beat until smooth. Add jigger of whiskey.

Step 3. Sift flour, baking powder, and baking soda together. Gradually add 2 cups of dry ingredients to creamed mixture (with electric mixer on medium speed) until mixture is too stiff for electric mixer. Continue blending dry ingredients by hand until thoroughly mixed; add pecans. Dough should be buttery and should not stick to hands.

Step 4. Take enough of mixture (about 7 ounces) and shape a loaf about 16" long and approximately 3" wide and about 3/4" high. Two loaves this size will fit on 1 baking sheet.

Step 5. Beat remaining egg with about 1 teaspoon water. Brush loaves lightly. If desired, sprinkle lightly with sesame seeds.

Step 6. Bake loaves for 30 minutes and remove from oven. With a sharp knife slice loaves (as if slicing loaves of bread) into strips about 3/4" wide. Turn pieces flat, scatter around baking sheet and return to oven for about 10-12 minutes, until golden brown and crisp. Set aside to cool.

Mrs. Gus Vantis (Agnes Koleas)
Miami Beach, Florida

CREMA GLEEKI
Sweet Custard

GREEK

Yield: 6 servings

1/2 cup sugar
3 cups milk
2 egg yolks
3 Tbsp. cornstarch
1 Tbsp. flour
1/4 tsp. salt
1-1/2 tsp. vanilla
1 Tbsp. butter

Step 1. Combine sugar, milk, yolks, cornstarch, flour and salt in saucepan. Beat well with hand beater to mix ingredients.

Step 2. Cook over low heat until thick, stirring constantly.

Step 3. When thickened, remove from heat and add butter and vanilla. Pour into individual custard cups and refrigerate when cooled.

Grecian Gourmet

CREMA KARAMELA I
Caramel Custard

GREEK

Temperature: 350°
Pan Size: 2-quart mold or individual ramekin cups
Yield: 12 servings

1-3/4 cups sugar
5 eggs, slightly beaten
1 quart warm milk
1 tsp. vanilla or
 zest of 1 lemon (optional)
Brandy, few drops (optional)

Step 1. Melt 1 cup of the sugar over low heat, stirring constantly until of caramel consistency. Brandy may be sprinkled over melted sugar if desired. Pour into mold and distribute evenly over bottom of pan and tilt pan to coat sides.

Step 2. Heat milk until slightly warm; add lemon zest.

Step 3. Beat eggs with 3/4 cup sugar and vanilla. Gradually add warm milk (remove lemon zest before combining ingredients).

Step 4. Pour into mold or cups. Place into pan of hot water and bake 45 minutes or until custard is firm and until knife comes out clean when inserted in center.

Step 5. Cool thoroughly and place in refrigerator. When ready to serve, run a knife around edge of custard to loosen from pan. Turn upside down on serving plate.

Grecian Gourmet

CREMA KARAMELA II

GREEK

Caramel Custard

Temperature: 350°
Pan Size: 2-quart mold or individual ramekin cups
Yield: 12 servings

1/4 cup water
2 cups sugar, divided
**6-8 medium eggs, slightly
  beaten**
1 quart half and half, warm
1-1/2 tsp. vanilla
Brandy (optional)

Step 1. To caramelize, mix 1/4 cup water with 1 cup sugar. Cook over over low heat; stir until bubbling and light brown. Carefully sprinkle with a few drops of brandy. Pour into mold quickly. Tilt to distribute evenly over bottom.

Step 2. Whisk the other cup of sugar into eggs and gradually add half and half.

Step 3. Pour into prepared mold and place into a pan of hot water. Bake 45 minutes or until knife comes out clean when inserted in center. Cool completely and refrigerate.

The Cookbook Committee

CREMA KARAMELA III

GREEK

Caramel Custard

Temperature: 350°
Pan Size: 1-1/2 quart mold or 12 5-ounce custard cups
Yield: 12 servings

1-3/4 cups sugar
1 quart milk
1 tsp. vanilla
8 eggs

Step 1. Caramelize 1 cup of sugar over medium heat and pour into bottom of mold or custard cups.

Step 2. Heat milk with remaining 3/4 cup sugar. Add vanilla.

Step 3. Beat eggs lightly. Avoid overbeating of eggs. Mix milk with eggs and strain.

Step 4. Pour mixture over caramelized sugar. Place mold into pan of hot water. Bake for 1 hour or until firm when tested with knife.

Step 5. Cool and place in refrigerator at least 6 hours or overnight. When ready to serve, unmold on serving plate.

MOUSTALEVRIA
Grape Pudding

GREEK

Yield: 8 servings (1/2 cup)

**2 bottles white grape juice or
   1 bottle white and
   1 bottle red
1/2 cup sugar
3 Tbsp. arrowroot or
   cornstarch
1/2 cup water
Finely ground nuts, any kind**

Step 1. Bring grape juice and sugar to a boil. Reduce heat to medium.

Step 2. Mix arrowroot or cornstarch and water together. Stir into grape juice. Cook stirring until thickened. About 5 minutes.

Step 3. Pour into individual dishes. Garnish with ground nuts.

Ms. Lynda Liollio

RIZOGALO I
Rice Pudding

GREEK

Yield: 8 servings

**1 quart milk
1/2 cup rice
1/2 stick butter
2 eggs
1 cup sugar
1 tsp. vanilla
Cinnamon**

Step 1. In a large, deep saucepan, bring milk, rice and butter to a boil. Reduce heat after 10 minutes and cook 20 minutes longer at medium heat until rice is tender. Remove from heat.

Step 2. Beat eggs with sugar until light. Add vanilla.

Step 3. Stir egg mixture slowly into milk and cook over medium heat, stirring until thickened.

Step 4. Pour into individual serving dishes and sprinkle with cinnamon. Allow to cool completely before refrigerating.

Mrs. Harry Cotros (Margaret)

HALVA I

Spiced Wheat Pudding

GREEK

Pan Size: 9" x 9" or 1 quart mold
Yield: 12 pieces

SYRUP:
2 cups water
2 cups milk
1 cup sugar

1 stick butter
1 cup Cream of Wheat
1/2 cup chopped nuts
Cinnamon

Step 1. In saucepan, combine water, milk and sugar; bring to a boil, reduce heat and cook for 5 minutes.

Step 2. In a deep saucepan, melt butter and stir in Cream of Wheat over medium heat. Cook until golden brown, stirring constantly. Remove from heat.

Step 3. Pour liquids into Cream of Wheat, using a wooden spoon, and stir until Halva begins to thicken. Add nuts. Cover and let stand 8-10 minutes.

Step 4. Press into mold or pan; then turn out onto platter. Sprinkle with cinnamon.

Grecian Gourmet

HALVA II

Halva Provincial

GREEK

Yield: 50 servings

1 cup sugar
1 cup water
1 cup oil
3 cups flour, more if
   needed
Ground cinnamon

Step 1. Melt sugar in cold water.

Step 2. In a large frying pan, heat the oil over high heat. (Oil will be hot enough when a pinch of flour sprinkled into the hot oil appears to foam or boil.) Begin adding flour, stirring continuously until all flour is used. The flour must be thoroughly cooked; it is necessary to keep stirring so that it will not burn; cook until golden brown; lower heat to keep from burning.

Step 3. Add the sugar-water mixture in a steady stream while stirring flour mixture very quickly to avoid creating lumps. (Caution: Be sure to use a long handled spoon for stirring as the cold liquid will "explode" when it hits the hot flour mixture.) Continue stirring until all liquid is absorbed and mixture forms a mass. Remove from heat.

Continued...

Step 4. With a tablespoon (use a teaspoon for petite servings) take a rounded spoonful of halva, and using cupped palm of hand, press gently to form smooth, rounded shape. Turn out of spoon onto a serving dish. When all halva mixture has been shaped, dust with powdered sugar and then sprinkle with cinnamon.

Mrs. James Varnavas (Helen)

LITSA'S HALVA
Spiced Wheat-Almond Pudding

GREEK

Pan Size: 1 to 1-1/2 quart mold

SYRUP:
3 cups sugar
4 cups water

Step 1. SYRUP: Stir sugar into water stirring until sugar dissolves. Bring to a boil, reduce heat and cook over medium heat for 5 minutes.

PUDDING:
1 cup oil
2 cups Cream of Wheat
1 cup almonds, ground
1 tsp. cinnamon, ground
1/2 tsp. cloves, ground

Step 2. Heat oil in heavy skillet until hot. With wooden spoon stir in Cream of Wheat. Stir constantly until Cream of Wheat turns golden brown. Add almonds and spices. Blend well and slowly add syrup. Continue stirring vigorously to prevent lumps from forming. Cook until mixture thickens and all liquid is absorbed.

Step 3. Pour into buttered mold.

Step 4. Set aside to cool for at least 1 hour before serving.

Note: Halva can be refrigerated and served the following day, but it should come to room temperature before serving.

Mrs. Evangelia Karvouni (Litsa)
Natpaktos, Greece

RIZOGALO II
Rice Pudding

GREEK

Yield: 12 4-ounce servings

1 quart milk
2 cups hot water
1/2 cup rice, white plump
  grain, regular
1 cup sugar
1 tsp. vanilla
2 eggs, large
Ground cinnamon

Step 1. Combine milk and water in deep 4-quart saucepan; bring to a boil. Add rice and stir with a wooden spoon until mixture returns to boiling point. Reduce heat to medium and stir for about two minutes; cover; reduce heat to low. Cook undisturbed for 20 minutes; remove cover and stir thoroughly. Replace cover and cook for 10 minutes or until rice is very, very tender. Turn heat very low and allow to continue cooking, uncovered; stir occasionally.

Step 2. In a large bowl, combine sugar, vanilla and eggs and beat together with rotary beater or whisk until "soupy." Add hot rice mixture to egg mixture in small amounts, stirring egg mixture constantly with wooden spoon until sugar has dissolved.

Step 3. Pour egg mixture into rice mixture (which is still cooking), stirring constantly. Increase heat to medium and continue stirring until pudding is thickened, approximately 15-20 minutes, and pudding thinly glazes wooden spoon and rice is fully suspended in pudding.

Step 4. Remove from heat and pour into serving cups or into a flat 2-quart bowl, and dust generously with ground cinnamon. Serve chilled. Recipe may be doubled.

Mrs. Stephen Lenis (Mary)

AMIGTHALOTA FLOGERES
Almond Flutes

Temperature: 350°
Yield: 4 dozen

3 eggs
1/2 cup sugar
1/2 tsp. almond extract
1 cup ground almonds
1 Tbsp. brandy
3 Tbsp. light cream
12 sheets filo
1/2 pound butter, melted
1/2 tsp. cinnamon

SYRUP:
2 cups sugar
1-1/2 cups water
1 stick cinnamon
1/4 lemon, juice and rind of
1 Tbsp. brandy

Step 1. Beat eggs until very thick.

Step 2. Combine sugar, cinnamon and almonds.

Step 3. Fold into eggs.

Step 4. Add cream.

Step 5. Using 1/2 sheet of filo, brush with butter; fold in half, brush top with butter.

Step 6. Place 1 tablespoon of filling on filo and fold sides in, brushing with butter.

Step 7. Roll up in jelly roll fashion.

Step 8. Brush seam with butter and place on cookie sheet, seam side down.

Step 9. Note: Flutes may be frozen at this point before baking and used at a later date.

Step 10. Bake at 350° for 20 minutes until golden brown.

Step 11. Prepare syrup: Bring all ingredients to a boil. Reduce heat and simmer 10 minutes. Remove from heat. Cool slightly. Add brandy.

Step 12. When flutes have cooled, arrange in a single layer in deep pan.

Step 13. Pour warm syrup over flutes. Allow to stand at least 1 hour in syrup before serving.

Step 14. Store with syrup, but not in refrigerator.

Step 15. When serving, arrange on platter or tray and sprinkle with powdered sugar and cinnamon.

Mrs. Angelo D. Liollio (Tina)

BAKLAVA I

Honey Nut Pastry

GREEK

Temperature: 300° for 1-1/2 hours, then 350° for 15 minutes
Pan Size: 11" x 14" x 2"
Yield: Approximately 40 pieces

2 pounds butter
2 pounds filo pastry
Whole cloves

FILLING:
9 cups ground nuts
  2 cups almonds
  4 cups walnuts
  3 cups pecans
1/2 cup sugar
2 tsp. cinnamon
2 tsp. nutmeg
1/2 tsp. cloves

SYRUP:
4 cups sugar
3 cups water
2 cinnamon sticks
10 whole cloves
1/2 orange, sliced
1 whole lemon, sliced
1-1/2 cups honey

Step 1. Clarify the butter by melting it in a large pot. Bring to a boil and boil until the foam rises to the top and turns a golden or honey color (approximately 15 minutes). Skim off any foam on surface. Carefully pour off honey colored oil, discarding sediment in bottom of pan. This should yield approximately 3 cups of clarified butter. Refrigerate until needed.

Step 2. Coarsely grind all nuts. It is recommended that you grind whole nutmeats, rather than use packaged pieces.

Step 3. Mix ground nuts with 1/2 cup sugar and spices. Cover and set aside.

Step 4. Prepare the syrup by combining all the ingredients except honey and bring to a boil. Boil until it thickens (at least 15 minutes) to 225° on candy thermometer. Add honey. Set aside to cool.

Step 5. Assembling the baklava: Melt clarified butter and grease bottom and sides of pan with pastry brush. Line bottom and sides of pan with filo, brush well with melted butter, and repeat until 8 layers cover bottom, brushing each with melted butter. Sprinkle 3/4 cup nut mixture on top of 8th sheet of buttered filo. Cover with another sheet of filo, butter and sprinkle another 3/4 cup of nuts. Continue this procedure until all nuts are used. Finish with 9-10 fila on top, brushing each with melted butter. Do not butter top filo.

Step 6. Cut pastry lengthwise in 1-1/2" strips. Cut each strip at 1-1/2" intervals diagonally to form diamond shape. (See Basic Techniques section.) Place whole clove in center of each diamond.

Continued...

Step 7. Heat remaining (approximately 1 cup) clarified butter until it turns dark. Allow to cool and pour over top of baklava. Brush to cover all of the filo. Sprinkle cool water with fingertips over top of baklava. Bake in 300° oven 1-1/2 hours. Increase oven to 350° and bake 15 minutes.

Step 8. Cool baklava completely in pan. Pour warm syrup slowly over it and allow syrup to penetrate pastry at least 24 hours before serving.

Mrs. James G. Sousoulas (Sophie)

GALATOBOUREKO
GREEK
Margaret's Custard Dessert

Temperature: 350°
Pan Size: 11" x 14"
Yield: 20-25 pieces

6 cups milk
6 eggs
1 cup Cream of Wheat, regular
1 cup sugar
1 stick butter
1 Tbsp. vanilla extract
1/2 pound filo
3 sticks butter, melted

SYRUP:
1 cup sugar
1-1/2 cups water
1/2 lemon, juice of and
  reserve rind

Step 1. In deep saucepan, add milk, eggs, Cream of Wheat, and sugar. Cook over medium heat, stirring constantly, until thickened; add butter and vanilla, stir until butter is absorbed and set aside to cool.

Step 2. Using melted butter, generously grease pan and lay filo to cover, buttering each layer, for 5 layers. Pour custard mixture into pan and turn all filo ends inward over filling. Top with remaning 5 layers of filo, brushing each layer with butter.

Step 3. Cut through top layers of filo to make 4 lengthwise rows. Bake in preheated oven, 350°, for 45 minutes to 1 hour. Remove from oven, cool.

Step 4. Syrup: Stir sugar, water, lemon juice and rind until sugar dissolves; bring to boil; cook 7-10 minutes until it thickens. Ladle hot syrup over entire surface (use all of syrup); cut dessert into squares or diamond-shaped pieces.

Mrs. Harry Cotros (Margaret)

BAKLAVA II
Honey Nut Pastry

Temperature: 350°
Pan Size: 9" x 13"
Yield: 42 small diamond-shaped pieces

1 pound filo
4-5 sticks butter (clarified)

FILLING:
2 cups walnuts, finely ground
1/4 cup sugar
1 tsp. cinnamon
Dash nutmeg
1/2 orange, grated rind of

SYRUP:
2 cups sugar
2 cups water
1 Tbsp. honey
1/2 Tbsp. lemon juice

Step 1. Cut filo sheets with sharp knife to fit 9" x 13" pan. Keep filo covered with damp dish towel when not in use—dries very fast. Save scraps for layering.

Step 2. Set aside 10 sheets of filo for finishing layers.

Step 3. Combine filling ingredients.

Step 4. Butter pan, using clarified butter. Place 5 sheets of filo in pan, buttering each sheet well. Add 1 more sheet (not buttered).

Step 5. Distribute about 1/3 cup nut mixture evenly over filo.

Step 6. Add 2 more sheets (whole or scraps) buttering each well. Add a third sheet (no butter on this); spread 1/3 cup nut mixture. Repeat layering of filo and nuts until nut mixture is used up.

Step 7. Finish with the 10 whole sheets of filo previously set aside. Butter each of these top sheets generously, especially the final top sheet.

Step 8. Refrigerate at least 10 minutes for easier cutting. With sharp, smooth-edged knife, cut in 6 rows (7 diamond-shaped pieces in each row). Cutting through to bottom before baking allows pastry to bake through, syrup to soak through, and pieces to look more attractive.

Step 9. Prepare syrup by combining sugar and water in a 2 quart saucepan. Bring to a boil, then reduce heat and cook for 18 minutes. Add honey and lemon juice and simmer a few minutes longer. Cool.

Continued…

Step 10. Bake pastry at 350° for 20 minutes; then at 300° for 40-45 minutes. Remove from oven. Cool for 20 minutes. Pour lukewarm syrup slowly and evenly over top. (Best to use 1/4 cup less of syrup.) Do not cover. Pastry will soak up the syrup and be ready to serve by the next day. Place each piece in paper muffin cups to serve.

Mrs. Bruce Erskine (Helen)

DIANA'S GALATOBOURIKO   GREEK
Custard Pastry

Temperature: 350°
Pan Size: 12" x 18"
Yield: 45 servings

1/2 gallon milk
1-1/2 cups Cream of Wheat, regular
1 pound butter, divided
1/2 tsp. vanilla
1-1/2 cups sugar, divided
10 eggs
1/2 Tbsp. orange extract
1 pound filo

SYRUP:
2 cups sugar
2-1/2 cups water
1/2 lemon
1/2 stick cinnamon

Step 1. Combine milk, Cream of Wheat, 1 stick butter, vanilla, and 3/4 cup sugar. Cook over medium heat, stirring constantly, until it thickens. Set aside to cool.

Step 2. Combine eggs, remaining 3/4 cup sugar, and orange extract in mixer bowl and beat well. Stir into Cream of Wheat mixture.

Step 3. Butter 12" x 18" pan, place half of filo sheets (8) on bottom brushing each sheet with butter. Carefully pour in mixture. Top with remaining filo sheets, brushing each sheet layer with butter.

Step 4. Slit *top* filo sheet lengthwise into 5-6 strips. Pour remaining butter over top. lightly sprinkle with water, and bake at 350°, 45 minutes to 1 hour, until golden brown.

Step 5. Remove from oven and let stand 10 minutes.

Step 6. Syrup: Bring to a boil the sugar, water, lemon, and cinnamon. Reduce heat, simmer until syrup thickens (approximately 15 minutes). Let cool. Pour cooled syrup over hot pastry. Let cool about 1 hour and cut into squares.

Mrs. Diana C. Mazas

KADAIFE

GREEK

Shredded Pastry with Nuts

Temperature: 350°
Pan Size: 9" x 13"
Yield: 3 dozen pieces

**1 pound kadaife dough,
   divided in half
1 pound (4 cups shelled)
   walnuts, ground
1/2 pound (1-1/2 cups
   shelled) almonds, ground
1 Tbsp. cinnamon
3 Tbsp. water
1/2 cup sugar
1-1/2 cups unsalted butter,
   melted**

**HONEY SYRUP:
1 cup sugar
1/2 cup honey
2 tsp. grated lemon peel
1 Tbsp. lemon juice
1 cup water**

Step 1. Butter pan and place half of the kadaife dough into it and pat evenly.

Step 2. Mix together walnuts, almonds, cinnamon, sugar and water and spoon over dough.

Step 3. Brush 1/2 the melted butter over the nut mixture, and pat remaining kadaife dough over the top. Brush the top with remaining butter.

Step 4. Bake in 350° oven for 35 minutes or until golden brown.

Step 5. In saucepan combine water, sugar, honey, lemon peel and lemon juice. Bring to boil and simmer for 5 minutes. Cool.

Step 6. Remove pastry from oven and place pan on rack. Pour cool honey syrup evenly over hot pastry. Then cover with a piece of cheesecloth to keep moist. Let stand until cool, then cut into rectangular or diamond-shaped pieces.

Mrs. Charles Vergos (Tasia)

Kadaifi is a shredded dough, prepared pastry, and is available at specialty shops.

TRIGONA
Nut Filled Triangles

GREEK

Temperature: 375°
Yield: 4-5 dozen

2 pounds chopped pecans
  or ground almonds
9 Zwieback slices
1 pound sugar
1 tsp. cinnamon
4 eggs
1 pound butter
1 pound filo

SYRUP:
3 cups sugar
3 cups water
1/2 lemon, juice of
3 cups honey

Step 1. Grind nuts and Zwieback slices together.

Step 2. Mix nuts with sugar, cinnamon and 1 stick melted butter.

Step 3. Beat eggs until light and add to nut mixture. Set this aside.

Step 4. Cut filo in 2" strips. Melt remaining butter.

Step 5. Brush 1 strip with melted butter; place another strip on top and brush with melted butter. Place 1 teaspoon of mixture on one end and fold diagonally to form a triangular shape. (See diagram in Basic Techniques section.) Brush each triangle with melted butter.

Step 6. Place on cookie sheet and bake for 20-30 minutes or until golden brown. Remove from oven and cool.

Step 7. Syrup: Bring sugar, water and lemon to a boil. Reduce heat and simmer 15-20 minutes until it begins to thicken. Remove from heat, add honey, and let syrup stand 5 minutes.

Step 8. Puncture each triangle with a fork and dip into syrup. Allow triangles to absorb syrup 2 or 3 minutes. Remove with slotted spoon and drain on racks.

Note: These may be frozen before baking. They keep well.

Mrs. Gerre Touliatos (Olga)

KOLOKITHOPETA GLIKI

Sweet Pumpkin Peta

GREEK

Temperature: 350° 25 minutes; 300° 25 minutes
Pan Size: 9" x 13" glass
Yield: 25-30 pieces

5 cups pumpkin, raw
1/4 tsp. salt
6 eggs, beaten
3/4 cup sugar
1-1/2 tsp. cinnamon
1/4 tsp. cloves
1-1/2 tsp. farina
1/8 tsp. nutmeg
10 fila
1/2 pound butter
1 cup chopped pecans
   or walnuts

SYRUP:
1-1/2 cups sugar
1 cup water
1 cinnamon stick
1/8 orange
1/8 lemon
1/4 cup honey

Step 1. Peel pumpkin and cut in small pieces. Chop it in food processor or grate it. Sprinkle salt over pumpkin, set aside.

Step 2. Combine sugar, cinnamon, cloves, nutmeg and farina.

Step 3. See basic techniques for preparing baking pan. For this size pan place 3 whole fila, allowing them to extend over sides; then fold 2 fila in half and lay them on over these.

Step 4. Squeeze out excess water from pumpkin; add combined spices and beaten eggs. Mix well. Pour into prepared pan, sprinkle a little melted butter over filling and finish with remaining fila; score; sprinkle with water and bake.

Step 5. Pour lukewarm syrup over warm peta.

Step 6. Syrup: Combine all ingredients except honey and lemon. Boil until it thickens, about 15 minutes. Add honey. Squeeze lemon into syrup and also add the lemon wedge. Set aside to cool.

Mrs. Bill K. Taras (Bessie)

LOUKOUMATHES

GREEK

Sweet Fritters

Yield: 12-15 puffs

8 ounces yogurt, plain
1/4 tsp. baking soda
1 ounce whiskey
2 eggs
1 cup flour, all-purpose
Oil for frying
Honey
Powdered sugar (optional)
Cinnamon
Chopped nuts

Step 1. Add baking soda and whiskey to yogurt; stir to blend. Beat eggs and add to yogurt mixture. Gradually blend in flour.

Step 2. Heat oil in a deep saucepan until very hot (360°). Drop tablespoonsful of batter into oil and cook until puffs are golden brown, turn as necessary to brown evenly. Remove puffs from oil; drain on paper towels. Dip puffs into heated honey and sprinkle with powdered sugar, cinnamon, and nuts. Serve warm.

Grecian Gourmet

ZVINGES

GREEK

Sweet Fritters

Yield: 8 servings

1 cup water
1/2 cup milk
1 Tbsp. butter
2 Tbsp. sugar
1/2 tsp. salt
1/2 tsp. grated orange rind
1 cup flour
4 eggs
Wesson or Mazola oil for
   frying
Honey
Cinnamon

Step 1. In a medium saucepan, bring water, milk, butter, sugar, salt and orange rind to a boil. Remove from heat.

Step 2. Add flour all at once and stir very quickly with a wooden spoon.

Step 3. Return to low heat and stir until dough comes away from sides of saucepan. Remove from heat and cool completely.

Step 4. Add eggs, 1 at a time, beating well after each addition.

Step 5. Heat oil until hot. Drop teaspoonfuls of dough into oil and fry until puffed and golden.

Step 6. Drain on paper toweling. Pile on serving plate; drizzle generously with honey and sprinkle with cinnamon. Serve hot. Fritters may be kept in warm oven until ready to serve.

Mrs. Alex Carayiannis (Voula)

DIPLES

Rolled Honey Pastries

Yield: 3 dozen

1/8 cake of yeast or 1/4 tsp. dry yeast
1-1/2 Tbsp. warm orange juice
1 jigger whiskey
Pinch of salt
3 beaten eggs
2-3 cups flour

SYRUP:
3 cups water
2 cups sugar
1 cup honey

2 tsp. cinnamon
1/4 cup finely ground nuts

Oil for frying

Step 1. Dissolve yeast in orange juice, whiskey and salt. Add this to beaten eggs.

Step 2. Add flour, gradually, to make a soft dough.

Step 3. Divide in 1" balls and set in lightly greased pan. Place a dry towel over dough and a damp towel over the dry towel. Allow to sit for 1 hour.

Step 4. Flour board lightly. Roll out 1 ball at a time into paper thinness. With a pastry wheel, cut dough into strips 2" x 6".

Step 5. Drop strip into hot oil. Using 2 forks, turn dough over immediately and roll loosely in jelly roll fashion.

Step 6. Fry until golden. Drain in a colander and cool.

Step 7. Syrup: Bring sugar and water to a boil. Reduce heat and simmer 15 minutes. Add honey and bring to a boil again and remove from heat.

Step 8. Quickly immerse diples into syrup or drizzle lavishly with syrup. Place on racks to drain.

Step 9. Sprinkle with cinnamon and nuts.

Traditional Recipe

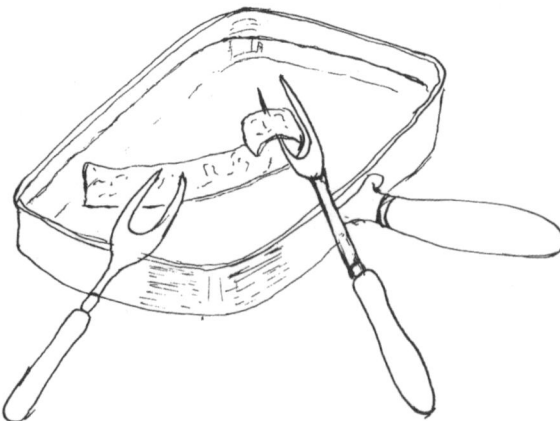

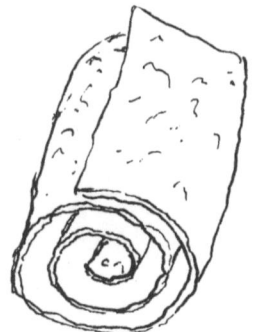

FRAOLES GLYKO

GREEK

Strawberry Preserves

Yield: 2 pints

4 cups strawberries
4 cups sugar
1 lemon, juice of

Step 1. Wash and hull strawberries, place in deep saucepan, add sugar and juice of lemon. Heat slowly to a boil; boil 10-12 minutes at high speed. Spread in baking pan until cool.

Step 2. Stir and heat again; pack into sterilized jars; cover with paraffin or store in freezer.

Mrs. Harry Yavis (Sophie)

PORTOKALI GLYKO

GREEK

Orange Preserves

3 navel oranges,
thick-skinned
3 cups sugar
3 cups water
1 lemon, juice of

Step 1. Grate all color from whole oranges. Cover with water and cook until skins are fork-tender.

Step 2. Drain; cut each orange into 8 or more sections. Do not remove pulp. Trim heavy membranes. Roll each section tightly and hold together with a toothpick.

Step 3. Boil sugar, water and lemon juice together for about 5 minutes. Add oranges and boil gently until syrup thickens.

Mrs. Harry Yavis (Sophie)

STAFILI GLYKO

GREEK

Grape Preserves

Yield: 1 pint

1-1/2 cups sugar
1-1/2 cups water
1/2 lemon, juice of
1 cinnamon stick
3 cups white seedless grapes,
washed and stemmed

Combine sugar, water, cinnamon and lemon juice; bring to a boil. Cook for 10 minutes; add grapes and cook until syrup thickens and color turns pinkish. Pour into sterilized jar; seal; allow to cool; refrigerate.

Mrs. Charles J. Vergos (Tasia)

FRAPA GLYKO
Grapefruit Preserves
GREEK

Yield: 1 quart

**8 whole white or pink
grapefruits**

SYRUP:
4 cups sugar
2 cups water
1 stick cinnamon
1/2 lemon
1/2 orange

Step 1. Grate grapefruit skins. Half, then quarter the grapefruits. Remove pulp. Roll each piece and secure with toothpick, or thread each roll on long thread.

Step 2. Place in deep pot and cover with water. Bring to a boil and boil for 1 minute. Drain. Repeat this process 6-8 times. This removes bitterness from grapefruits.

Step 3. Syrup: Bring sugar and water to a boil. Reduce heat; add cinnamon, lemon and orange. Simmer 10-15 minutes to form a light syrup.

Step 4. Add syrup to drained grapefruits and bring to a boil. Simmer together for 20 minutes or until thickened. Discard cinnamon, lemon and orange. Allow to cool completely before canning.

Mrs. James Liollio (Helen)

FRAPA GLYKO
Grapefruit Preserves
GREEK

3 thick-skinned grapefruits
3 cups sugar
3 cups water
1 lemon, juice of

Step 1. Grate all color from grapefruits; cut in half and remove pulp; pull out all membranes. Cover rinds with water and soak overnight. Rinse; cover with cold water and boil 15 minutes. Rinse. Repeat 2 more times.

Step 2. Cut rinds in half again. Starting from outer edge, slice into pieces 3/4" wide. Roll up each piece and skewer with a toothpick. Set aside.

Step 3. Cook sugar, water, and lemon juice until syrup is medium thick. Add rinds and cook gently until rinds are translucent and syrup is quite thick.

Mrs. Harry Yavis (Sophie)

WINES & CHEESES/ BEVERAGES

WINES AND CHEESES

If you are going to be "cooking Greek," you may as well go all the way and serve a Greek wine to complement your new-found culinary talents. While Greek wines do not compare with the best that France, Germany and the United States have to offer, there are, nevertheless, several choices available in this country that offer a pleasant accompaniment to a Greek meal. Especially encouraging is the fact that when compared with wines from other countries, Greek wines are still very reasonably priced. You should be able to find at least one of the wines listed below in any store that has a varied selection of wines. The list is by no means intended to be exhaustive.

Generally speaking, three companies account for most of the wine imported from Greece into the United States: Achaia Claus, Cambas and Nicolaus. Sometimes, all three companies will produce a wine with the same name. No attempt will be made to identify which company's wine provided the basis for the description below. All wines with a particular name will have similar characteristics. If you like, for example, the Achaia Claus brand of "Mavrodaphne," you might consider purchasing the Cambas or Nicolaus version in order to make a comparison.

Finally, it should be emphasized that these brief comments are the opinion of only one person and your impressions, perceptions and preferences may vary from mine. In the final analysis what really counts in wine tasting is discovering what you like, not what someone else says you should like.

WHITE

Demestica – One of the most popular wines in Greece and one of the more easily obtainable in the United States. It has the typical characteristics of many Greek white wines, i.e., light and dry. If you are just beginning to drink Greek wines, this wine would be a good one with which to start.

Retsina – Very popular in Greece, not so in the United States. The ultimate in dryness, this wine is flavored with resin that will startle your tastebuds on the first sip. I would not recommend that you begin with this wine for your initial sampling of Greek wines. You may have to acquire a taste for it. In fact, it is not a bad idea to have a large group of people on hand to consume a bottle. It is a Greek classic that you will love or hate; there is no in between.

Saint Helena – Very similar to Demestica, a beautiful amber color and gentle fragrance. Often found on restaurant and hotel lists.

Saint Laoura – A cousin to Saint Helena, that is also popular in Greece. It comes from the Peloponnese region which is the most important viticultural area of Greece. Recommended with chicken or fish dishes.

Hymettus – Perhaps the lightest of the white wines listed here, this wine goes well with seafood. It is simple with a smooth finish; a nice bargain.

Mantinia – Unlike many whites, this wine has staying power and may improve for several years after other whites begin to decline. Full-bodied and dry; it is well balanced. It comes from the central part of the Peloponnese.

Mont Ambelos – A bit more expensive than some of the other whites listed, but still a good bargain. It has a nicely balanced flavor and can be drunk with or without food.

REDS

Demestica – Like its white counterpart, this wine is readily available, and most people will find it palatable. More light-bodied than many reds, it will go well with lamb or pork dishes.

Hymettus – A light-bodied, pleasant wine that is a best buy selection, if price is a consideration (and it usually is). Almost akin to a rosé in some respects, this wine will go with almost any meal.

Castel Danielis – More full-bodied than many of the other wines listed here, this wine is very dry. It lacks the complexity and bouquet of a great red and needs considerable aging to develop. This wine is worth a try if you can find it.

Pendeli – This robust wine will go well with a highly seasoned souflakia or kapama dish. You might even try it with spaghetti as an alternative to an Italian red. As wine enthusiasts are apt to say, "It's got good legs".

Mont Ambelos – This medium-bodied dry red will go well with moussaka, pastisio or pilafi. Some people think it has a pronounced resin taste to it, and you may notice this.

Chateau Claus – This wine lacks body and bouquet in my opinion and is a bit more expensive than the other wines listed here. It comes in vintage years and may vary in quality from year to year. A deep red color distinguishes it.

Mavrodaphne – This wine is a Grecian classic. High in sugar and alcoholic content, it has a luscious texture and memorable aroma. A delicious dessert wine, it is meant to be sipped and savored. One bottle will go a long way.

OTHER NOTABLE LIBATIONS

Roditis – The best of the Greek rosés, this wine compares well with the rosés of other countries and can easily be consumed in considerable quantities, if you like this type of wine.

Kokkinelli – A very dark rosé, that is flavored heavily with resin (see Retsina above). Emanating from Cyprus, this is a popular resinated wine, and if you like that sort of thing, it may be worth a try. Reasonably priced.

Metaxa – This well known Greek distilled spirit comes in three, five and seven star varieties. The medium priced five star offers formidable competition to any similarly priced brandy or cognac. Readily available in most areas.

Ouzo – "The Greek liqueur," it's sipped nightly in tavernas all over Greece. Its licorice aroma and taste have been likened to everything from pernod to paragoric. When served on the rocks or with water, its clear color becomes a cloudy white. At some point in time, you must try some; but be forewarned, it is very potent.

Wine has been a part of Greek culture since before the time of Homer. Dionysus, the god of wine, was one of the most popular of the Greek gods. Hopefully after partaking of some of these wines of Greece, you will share the Greek affection for this fitting accompaniment to any meal. With a raised glass, I toast you, "Ees Eeyian"!

CHEESES

And while we're on the subject of wine, it brings to mind the natural accompaniment – cheeses. Cheese is the mainstay of life in Greece. Cheeses are served at breakfast, lunch, dinner or with wine and fruit as a late night snack. Among the most accessible and popular Greek cheeses imported in America are Feta, kefalotiri, kasseri and mizithra. Enjoying Greek cheeses is an acquired taste.

FETA: The most popular of all Greek cheeses. Feta is a salty cheese packed in brine. It is used often in Greek cooking, as it is soft and crumbles easily. Feta is very often served with fruit. Refrigerated, it will stay fresh for months.

KASSERI: A firm, golden, buttery tasting cheese, available in most specialty shops. It is often used in Greek cooking; the most popular Greek dish being "Saganaki" (fried cheese flambé).

KEFALOTIRI: A hard cheese most often grated. Kefalotiri gets its name from its shape which is like a head.

MIZITHRA: A hard mild cheese used as a table cheese or grated over pasta. This cheese resembles hard ricotta.

TRADITIONAL NOG   GREEK

Yield: 1-2 cups

1 egg yolk
2 to 3 tsp. sugar
1 to 2 cups hot beverage*

Step 1. In a cup, beat the egg yolk and sugar with a spoon until the sugar dissolves and the mixture is thick, creamy and light in color.

Step 2. Gradually add a small amount of hot beverage to egg mixture, stirring constantly. For 2 servings divide the egg mixture equally. Add hot liquid until cup is full.

*Note: Traditionally, the hot beverages most often used are hot chocolate and Greek coffee. This drink may be laced with brandy, cognac or whiskey.

Mrs. James Varnavas (Helen)

καὶ τὰ λοιπά

ET CETERA...

GALATOBOUREKO

This recipe was given to me by Carol Arnokovich Yarnes.

Temperature: 350°
Pan Size: 9" x 13"
Yield: 16 servings

7 egg yolks
1 cup sugar
3/4 cup cornstarch
1-1/2 quarts milk, heated
1 pound filo
3 sticks butter
1 tsp. vanilla extract
1/2 tsp. orange extract

SYRUP:
1-1/2 cups sugar
3/4 cup water
1 Tbsp. lemon juice
1 slice lemon
1/4 tsp. cinnamon

Step 1. In large pan, mix egg yolks, sugar, and cornstarch until smooth.

Step 2. Warm milk over medium heat. Pour slowly into first mixture. Put on low heat and stir constantly until mixture thickens. Add vanilla and orange extracts and blend. Cool. (May cover with waxed paper and refrigerate overnight.)

Step 3. Butter 9" x 13" pan. Place 12 filo sheets, buttering each, in bottom of pan and up the sides.

Step 4. Pour in custard mixture. Place 12 buttered filo sheets on top. To retain mixture, fold over overlapping filo to seal edges.

Step 5. Score top into diamond-shaped pieces. (See Basic Techniques section.)

Step 6. Bake at 350° for 1 hour.

Step 7. Syrup: Combine sugar, water, cinnamon, and slice of lemon. Bring to simmering point and simmer for 20 minutes.

Step 8. Add lemon juice and simmer 5 more minutes. Cool.

Step 9. Pour cooled syrup over hot galatoboureko.

Mrs. Harry T. Karris (Georgia Scondras)

TOURTA CHOCOLATA

GREEK

(Chocolate Torte)

The basic recipe was given to me 20 years ago by my sister-in-law, Mrs. Mike (Eleni) Kourtessis who was then living in Lagos, Nigeria, and in Athens, Greece.

Pan Size: 10" springform pan
Yield: serves 12-16

2 dozen ladyfingers, fresh-bakery type
1/2 pound butter, lightly salted
1-1/2 cups powdered sugar
8 eggs (extra large), separated
8 ounces semi-sweet chocolate, melted and cooled
Brandy or amaretto liqueur
1-1/2 cups whipping cream
3 Tbsp. sugar
1/2 tsp. vanilla
1/3 cup sliced almonds, lightly toasted
1 Hershey bar for chocolate curls
Chopped glacé fruits, (candied cherries, pineapple, orange peel) for decoration

Step 1. Whip butter with powdered sugar until light and fluffy. Wash beaters.

Step 2. Melt chocolate in heavy skillet on very low heat. Stir well and remove from heat to cool.

Step 3. Separate eggs. Beat yolks in small mixer bowl until light. Wash beaters.

Step 4. Add beaten yolks to butter mixture, using spatula to fold in completely. Add cooled chocolate to this mixture, folding in thoroughly with wire whisk.

Step 5. Whip egg whites in large mixer bowl until stiff but not dry. Fold into the butter mixture in thirds, using wire whisk. Refrigerate this mixture while preparing ladyfingers.

Step 6. Split ladyfingers in half, brush or sprinkle with brandy or amaretto. Place on bottom of springform pan. Put half of chocolate mixture on top of ladyfingers. Cover this with another layer of ladyfingers brushed with liqueur. Pour remaining chocolate mixture on top. Refrigerate at least 6 hours.

Step 7. Whip whipping cream with sugar and vanilla. Remove tourta from refrigerator and remove sides of springform pan. Place tourta on large platter. Cover with whipped cream.

Step 8. Decorate with almonds, glacé fruits, and chocolate curls. Refrigerate until serving.

Mrs. Harry T. Karris (Georgia Scondras)

SPICE PAXIMATHIA

GREEK

Temperature: 375°
Yield: 10 dozen

1/2 cup Mazola oil
1/2 pound butter (preferably unsalted)
2 cups sugar
6 eggs, well beaten
1 tsp. vanilla
7 cups flour (approximately), sifted
3 tsp. baking powder
1/2 tsp. baking soda
3 tsp. cinnamon*
1 tsp. allspice
1/2 tsp. cloves

*I prefer to use 5-6 teaspoons cinnamon instead of the 3 recommended.

Step 1. Cream oil, butter, and sugar together for 15 minutes.

Step 2. Gradually add eggs to creamed sugar mixture and blend thoroughly. Add vanilla.

Step 3. Sift flour, baking powder, baking soda, and spices together.

Step 4. Slowly add dry ingredients to sugar and egg mixture to make a medium dough that leaves the sides of the bowl.

Step 5. Knead dough slightly. Divide into 5 parts. Shape into long, narrow, flat loaves, about 2-1/2" wide and 1" thick. Place on greased cookie sheets, 2" apart to allow for baking. Score each loaf in 1/2" slices.

Step 6. Bake until lightly browned (about 20 minutes). Remove from oven. While still warm, slice where previously scored.

Step 7. Toast slices on both sides in moderate oven until lightly browned. Allow to cool before storing in covered container.

Mrs. George Demas (Victoria)

YIAOURTOPETA
Yogurt Cake

GREEK

Temperature: 350°
Pan Size: 9" x 13"

2 sticks soft butter
1-1/2 cups sugar
6 eggs, separated
2 tsp. baking soda
2 ounces cognac or
  bourbon
1 cup yogurt (plain)
1 cup walnuts/pecans,
  chopped
1 tsp. cinnamon
1 tsp. cloves
2 cups flour

SYRUP:
3 cups water
2 cups sugar
1/2 tsp. lemon juice
2 thin slices of lemon rind

Step 1. Cream butter and sugar. Add egg yolks.

Step 2. Dissolve soda in bourbon and add to butter mixture. Beat well.

Step 3. Add yogurt and remaining ingredients. Fold in beaten egg whites.

Step 4. Pour into greased pan. Bake 45 minutes.

Step 5. SYRUP: Combine all syrup ingredients in saucepan; bring to a boil; simmer for 10 minutes.

Step 6. After cake has cooled, spoon hot syrup evenly over cake. Cut into diamond-shaped pieces. Allow to set in pan until syrup is absorbed.

Mrs. Manuel P. Scarmoutsos (Georgia A.)

SAVAYIAR
Mocha Torte

GREEK

Yield: 12 servings

8 ounces whipped sweet
  butter
1 stick sweet butter
5 eggs
1 pound box confectioners'
  sugar
1-1/2 cups roasted ground
  almonds
1 1-ounce square of
  unsweetened chocolate,
  melted
2 Tbsp. boiling water
2 tsp. instand coffee
1-1/2 cups milk
1-1/2 Tbsp. whiskey
4 3-ounce boxes
  ladyfingers

Step 1. Combine both types of butter and sugar. Beat at high speed until fluffy. Add eggs, 1 at a time, and beat well. Add half of the almonds and the melted chocolate.

Step 2. Combine boiling water and instant coffee and add to mixture; beat well. Set aside.

Step 3. In a small bowl, combine milk and whiskey. Separate ladyfingers and brush them on both sides with the milk-whiskey mixture.

Step 4. Place 1 layer of ladyfingers on the bottom of a 12" platter. Spread a thin layer of mocha mixture over the ladyfingers. Repeat this procedure for a total of 4 layers; finish with mocha mixture.

Step 5. Sprinkle remaining almonds on top and sides. Keep refrigerated until ready to serve. (May be decorated with maraschino cherries.)

Mrs. Anna Eramo Denton

OLYMPIAN CAKE

Temperature: 350°
Pan Size: Two 8-inch cake pans

1/2 cup Crisco
1 cup sugar
3 eggs
2 cups Honey Graham
  Crackers, ground fine
1/2 cup milk
2 tsp. baking powder
Pinch of salt
1 tsp. vanilla

FILLING:
1/2 cup powdered sugar,
  divided
1 cup fig preserves (any
  fruit preserve may be
  substituted)

Step 1. Cream together the Crisco and sugar. Add the eggs one at a time, beating well after each.

Step 2. Blend in the graham cracker crumbs. Add milk and blend well.

Step 3. Add the baking powder, salt, and vanilla. Blend well.

Step 4. Lightly grease 2 cake pans. Divide batter evenly between them.

Step 5. Place on middle rack of oven that has been preheated to 350°. Bake until brown on top and a tester comes out clean, about 30 minutes.

Step 6. Sift 1/2 powdered sugar on cake plate. Place one layer on plate and spread preserves evenly over layer. Place remaining layer on top and sprinkle it with remaining powder sugar.

Erasmia D. Touliatos

RUSSIAN TEA   RUSSIAN

Yield: 6 servings

1/3 cup granulated sugar
1 tsp. grated lemon rind
1 tsp. grated orange rind
1/2 cup water
1/2" stick cinnamon
1/8 tsp. powdered cloves
1/4 cup orange juice
2 Tbsp. lemon juice
1/4 cup canned pineapple
  juice
3 cups boiling water
1/4 cup tea leaves

Step 1. Combine first 6 ingredients and boil 10 minutes; then remove cinnamon stick.

Step 2. Add fruit juices. Place over low heat. Pour boiling water over tea leaves; let steep 10 minutes. Strain into fruit juices, and serve hot. Tea may be served with lemon or orange slices. Nice served in punch cups.

Mrs. George Ostrosky (Helen)

ROAST LEMON LAMB GREEK

This recipe was contributed by Sophie Yavis who received it from her sister, Olga Touliatos.

Temperature: 350°
Yield: 15 servings

8 to 10 pounds leg of lamb
4 cloves garlic
2 lemons, juice of
Oregano
Pepper
1 package onion soup mix
1/2 stick butter, chopped
in bits

Step 1. Wipe lamb with damp cloth. Trim excess fat.

Step 2. Insert garlic in 4 slits 1/2" deep in meat. Rub with lemon, oregano, and pepper.

Step 3. Place lamb in foil and cover with onion soup mix. Place butter over top. Seal sides of foil, leaving a small opening on top.

Step 4. Bake about 4 hours. Juices should stay in foil. Pierce with fork, at intervals, to test if done; fork should turn easily.

Step 5. Uncover top for only the last 30 or 40 minutes to brown. Lamb may be cooked all night at 300°, then uncovered in the morning to brown.
Serve juices separately in gravy bowl.

Mrs. Gerry Touliatos (Olga)

SHRIMP AND FETA CHEESE A LA GRECQUE GREEK

This is usually served at waterfront taverns on the Greek island of Hydra.

Yield: 4 servings

3/4 pound medium shrimp,
cooked, shelled, and
deveined
1 pound Feta cheese,
crumbled
6 green onions, finely
chopped
1-1/2 tsp. dried oregano (or 4
tsp. fresh, minced)
4 tomatoes, peeled, cored,
seeded, and coarsely
chopped
Ground pepper and salt to
taste
1 pound pasta, freshly
cooked and drained

Step 1. Combine shrimp, Feta, onions, oregano, tomatoes, salt, and pepper in large bowl. Let mixture stand at room temperature at least 1 hour.

Step 2. Add pasta to sauce. Toss to coat well. Serve immediately.

Note: Feta is salty, so be careful when adding salt.

Mrs. A. D. Alissandratos (Urania)

PASTITSO

GREEK

Temperature: 350°
Pan Size: 9" x 13" x 2"
Yield: 12-16 servings

1 chopped onion
2 cloves garlic
1/2 pound ground lamb
1/2 pound ground beef
2 Tbsp. olive oil
Salt and pepper
1 8-ounce can tomato sauce
2 Tbsp. fresh parsley,
chopped
1/2 cup Port wine
1 tsp. cinnamon
1/2 pound elbow macaroni
(cooked)
1/4 cup butter, melted
1 cup cheeses, grated
(Romano and Parmesan)*
3 eggs

BECHAMEL SAUCE:
4 Tbsp. butter
4 Tbsp. flour
1 cup half and half
2 cups milk
6 eggs
1/2 cup cheeses*
Salt and pepper
1/4 cup cheeses*
Cinnamon and nutmeg to
taste

Step 1. Sauté onion and garlic in olive oil. Add meat and brown. Drain off grease. Salt and pepper to taste.

Step 2. Stir in tomato sauce, parsley, Port, and cinnamon. Simmer for 1 hour. (This can be done ahead of time.)

Step 3. Combine cooked macaroni, butter, 1 cup cheeses, and 3 eggs. Spread in greased pan. Spoon meat sauce over macaroni.

Step 4. Bechamel Sauce: Melt butter, stir in flour, and cook slowly until mixture is a golden brown.

Step 5. Slowly stir in milk and half and half; stir until thickened. Remove from heat; cool slightly.

Step 6. Add 6 eggs; blend in 1/2 cup cheeses, salt and pepper to taste. Pour over meat sauce.

Step 7. Pierce with fork all over. Sprinkle with remaining 1/4 cup cheeses, cinnamon, and nutmeg.

Step 8. Cook 1 hour at 350°. Let cool about 20 minutes for ease in serving.

Mrs. Alexandra (Si) Capadalis Dupre

CABBAGE SLAW

One head cabbage
1 onion
3/4 cup sugar

DRESSING:
3/4 cup vegetable oil
1/4 cup sugar
1 cup apple cider vinegar
1 tsp. dry mustard
1 tsp. celery seed
1 Tbsp. salt

Step 1. Cut up or shred cabbage, and chop onion. Place in large bowl.

Step 2. Pour sugar over slaw, cover, and set aside.

DRESSING:
Step 1. Combine all ingredients, heat to a boil. Pour over cabbage. Cover.

Step 2. Refrigerate for one day.

Mrs. Constantine Konstans (Sondra)

PSOMI TOU SPITIOU
Bread for the Home

GREEK

In a Greek home, good bread is as important with each meal as the courses served.

Temperature: 400° for 5 minutes
350° for 30 minutes
Pan Size: Loaf Pans
Yield: 2 loaves

1/2 cup water (should be warmer than lukewarm)
3 pkgs. rapid rise yeast
1 tsp. sugar (heaping)
2 cups warm water (warmer than lukewarm)
2 eggs (room temperature)
1/3 cup corn oil
1 tsp. salt
1 Tbsp. sugar
6-1/2 to 7-1/2 cups bread flour (Pillsbury preferred)

Step 1. *Proof yeast:* Add first 3 ingredients in large cup or small bowl. Cover with plastic wrap. Allow to activate at least 5 minutes.

Step 2. Place 2 cups warm water in mixer bowl. Add 2 eggs and beat well at high speed. Frothy mixture will rise to top of bowl. Add oil, salt and sugar and continue beating. Add yeast mixture. Add 3 cups bread flour and beat at medium speed about 2 minutes. Remove beaters from mixer and gradually add 3-1/2 to 4-1/2 cups bread flour while kneading by hand. (Flour amounts vary because different brands absorb liquid at different rates.) Test: When dough pulls away from bowl, do not add additional flour. At this point, hands may be lightly oiled to facilitate removal of dough from bowl and shaping it into a ball.

Step 3. Lightly grease bowl with white solid shortening and place dough in bowl. (Ceramic or hard plastic bowl preferred — not metal.) Lightly grease top of dough and place plastic wrap directly on top of dough; then cover entire bowl with clean dish towel. Place in warm oven to rise until double in size. (Turn oven to WARM for 2 minutes, then turn heat off. If oven is too hot, yeast will be destroyed and bread will not rise.)

Step 4. When dough is double in size, remove from oven and remove plastic. Punch dough down and allow to rest (covered with towel for 10 minutes).

Step 5. Divide into 2 parts. Shape each and place in greased loaf pans. Place again in oven and allow to double in size. Remove from oven. Brush tops with cold water.

Step 6. Bake in preheated 400° oven for 5 minutes. Lower temperature to 350° and bake 30 additional minutes. Remove from pans immediately and allow to cool on wire rack.

Mrs. James G. Sousoulas (Sophie)

SPINACH CHEESE CASSEROLE GREEK
(Lazy Day Version of Spanakopeta)

Temperature: 350°
Pan Size: 9" x 13" casserole
Yield: 15-20 servings

3 10-ounce packages frozen chopped spinach
2 bunches green onions, sliced
3 cups small curd cottage cheese
3/4 cup Feta cheese, crumbled
6 Tbsp. Parmesan cheese, grated
6 eggs, well beaten
1 tsp. short grain rice, uncooked
3 dashes nutmeg
3 tsp. seasoned salt
1 tsp. seasoned pepper
3/4 stick butter, thinly sliced

TOPPING:
1 stick butter
6 slices white bread, cubed

Step 1. Cook and drain spinach, thoroughly press out *all* water.

Step 2. Combine spinach, onions, cottage cheese, Feta cheese, Parmesan cheese, eggs, rice, nutmeg, salt, and pepper.

Step 3. Spread mixture in buttered 9" x 13" casserole. Dot with butter slices.

TOPPING:
Step 1. Melt butter in saucepan. Drop bread cubes in butter, coating thoroughly.

Step 2. Spread buttered cubes over top of casserole. Bake 20-25 minutes until golden brown and bubbly.

Note: For simpler and less caloric version, omit bread cube topping completely. In this case, do not mix the 6 tablespoons Parmesan cheese *into* the spinach mixture, but sprinkle it on *top* of the casserole before baking.

Mrs. Harry S. Zepatos (Polly)

CICVARA SERBIAN
(Cornmeal Dish)

Served with baked chicken as traditional Serbian Christmas breakfast.

Pan Size: Medium saucepan
Yield: 12 servings

1 pound creamed cottage cheese
1/2 pound unsalted butter
3 cups water
1 tsp. salt
1-1/2 cups yellow cornmeal
1 egg

Step 1. Combine water, butter, and cottage cheese in medium saucepan. Bring to a boil.

Step 2. Add cornmeal and salt and let it cook 45 minutes on low heat.

Step 3. Add whole egg and stir rapidly. Keep on mixing with a wooden spoon until entire mixture starts floating in butter.

Mrs. George B. Cavic (Mileva)

CEPHALONIAN MEAT PIE   GREEK
Kreatopeta

Temperature: 375°
Pan Size: 9" x 13"
Yield: 8-10 servings

**3 pounds leg of lamb or
   veal, boned
1 large onion, finely
   chopped
1/2 cup parsley, chopped
2 cloves garlic, minced
2 beaten eggs
1/2 cup Uncle Ben's rice
2 cups warm water
1 tsp. salt
1/4 tsp. pepper
1 tsp. oregano**

**DOUGH:
2-1/2 cups flour, sifted
2 Tbsp. vegetable oil or 3
   Tbsp. shortening
1/2 tsp. salt
1 egg yolk
2/3 cup water or milk**

Step 1. Cut meat in 1/2" pieces.

Step 2. Combine meat with remaining ingredients in a large bowl. Mix well. Set aside while preparing dough.

Step 3. Dough: Combine all ingredients to make smooth dough. Knead until well blended.

Step 4. Divide dough in half. Roll out to 1/4" thickness. Dust with flour or cornstarch to avoid sticking.

Step 5. Grease baking pan *well*. Arrange dough in prepared pan. (Dough should overlap over sides of pan.)

Step 6. Slowly pour in meat mixture.

Step 7. Roll out remaining dough; place over filling to fit pan. Turn in overlapping dough to seal edge. Brush top with oil and sprinkle with a few drops of water.

Step 8. Bake in 375° oven for 1-1/2 hours. Remove from oven. Let stand 10 minutes to absorb moisture.

Step 9. Place large platter or cutting board over pan. Turn over quickly.

Mrs. A. D. Alissandratos (Urania)

KOLOKITHAKIA
(Squash Casserole)

GREEK

Temperature: 350°
Pan Size: 9" x 13" casserole dish

2 pounds yellow squash
1 medium onion, chopped
1/2 stick butter
3 eggs
8 ounces cottage cheese
1 cup milk
2 Tbsp. Cream of Wheat
1 cup Parmesan cheese
Salt and pepper to taste
3-4 Tbsp. cracker crumbs
1/2 stick butter, melted

Step 1. Boil squash with onion in salted water until tender. Drain and mash with 1/2 stick of butter.

Step 2. Add eggs, cottage cheese, milk, Cream of Wheat, 1/2 cup Parmesan cheese, salt, and pepper. Pour into greased casserole dish.

Step 3. Sprinkle cracker crumbs on top with melted butter and 1/2 cup Parmesan cheese. Bake for approximately 30 minutes.

Mrs. Andrew Avgeris (Sophia)

MOUSAKA PATATA

GREEK

Temperature: 350°
Pan Size: 1-1/2 quart casserole
Yield: 6-8 servings

1-1/2 pounds lean ground
   chuck
1/4 stick butter
1 large onion, chopped
4 green onions, chopped
1 clove garlic, minced
2 Tbsp. parsley
1/2 tsp. oregano
1/2 cup Ragu sauce with
   mushrooms
2 cups water
Salt and pepper to taste
6 to 8 potatoes

Step 1. Sauté ground chuck, butter, onions, garlic, parsley, and oregano until lightly brown.

Step 2. Add Ragu sauce, water, salt, and pepper. Cook slowly until all is absorbed.

Step 3. Slice potatoes crosswise into medium thin slices.

Step 4. Layer meat and potatoes alternately until all is used with potatoes last. Add enough water to cover. Bake until potatoes are brown, about 1 hour.

Mrs. Harry Yavis (Sophie)

PATATOSALATA
(Greek Potato Salad)

GREEK

Yield: 6-8 servings

6 medium potatoes (do not peel)
1 large onion, chopped or sliced thinly
1/3 cup olive oil
1 lemon, juice of
Salt and pepper to taste
Oregano
1/2 cup Calamata olives
2 scallions

Step 1. Boil potatoes until tender. Remove from water, peel, cut into quarters, and then slice. Toss with onion.

Step 2. Beat olive oil, lemon juice, salt and pepper. Pour this dressing over potatoes; sprinkle with oregano, olives, and scallions. Serve warm.

Mrs. Alex Carayiannis (Voula)

SHRIMP WITH SPINACH

This recipe was one of many old country recipes my father brought from Glossa, Skopelos, in 1926 and later used in his restaurant, The Crystal Grill, in Greenwood, Mississippi. This was a popular lenten season dish.

Yield: 4 servings

2 ribs celery, chopped
2 cloves garlic, crushed
1 bay leaf
1 medium yellow onion, chopped
2 Tbsp. olive oil
2 Tbsp. butter
1/2 cup red wine
1 pound raw, cleaned large-size shrimp
2 pounds cleaned fresh spinach
2 Tbsp. tomato paste
Salt
Pepper

Step 1. In a 3 or 4-quart saucepan, sauté celery, garlic, bay leaf, and onion with olive oil and butter over medium heat until vegetables are tender.

Step 2. Add wine and shrimp to vegetables, cooking for 1 minute.

Step 3. Add spinach and cook for additional 5 minutes before adding tomato paste to thicken juices rendered from spinach. Salt and pepper to taste at this point.

Step 4. Turn heat to low, cover pan and cook until shrimp is tender, about 15 minutes longer.

Serve with crusty French bread and Feta cheese.

Ms. Lynda Liollio

YIANNIOTIKI PATSIARIÁ

Temperature: 375°
Pan Size: 11" x 16" baking pan

1 cup oil (1/2 olive; 1/2 corn)
3-1/2 cups cornmeal
2 pounds frozen chopped
  spinach, thawed and
  squeezed out
1/2 pound cheddar cheese,
  grated (reserve 3/4 cup
  for topping)
1 pound cottage cheese
2 eggs, beaten
1/2 cup flour
3 cups boiled milk
1 bunch scallions, chopped
1/2 bunch parsley, chopped
1/2 bunch dill, chopped (or 2
  tsp. dry)
Salt and pepper to taste

TOPPING:
1 small can evaporated milk
1 tsp. sugar
Reserved grated cheese

Step 1. Put about 1/4 of the oil in a large roasting pan. Spread a thin layer of cornmeal on bottom (thickness of a dime).

Step 2. In a large bowl mix spinach, cheddar cheese, cottage cheese, eggs, flour, boiled milk, scallions, parsley, dill, 1/2 of the oil, salt, and pepper. Pour mixture into pan. Drizzle the evaporated milk over the mixture.

Step 3. Spread remaining cornmeal and sugar over the top, then drizzle remaining oil and sprinkle with cheese.

Step 4. Bake 1 hour at 375°. Cut into squares.

May be used as a side dish or an appetizer, and squash may be substituted for the spinach.

Mrs. James Skefos (Alethea)

ARTICHOKE QUICHE

Temperature: 350°
Pan Size: 7" x 11" or 9" x 9"

2 6-ounce jars marinated
  artichoke crowns or hearts
1 small onion or 3 Tbsp.
  dehydrated onions
8 ounces sharp cheddar
  cheese, shredded
1/4 tsp. salt
1 clove garlic, minced
4 eggs
1/4 cup breadcrumbs
1/8 tsp. pepper
1/8 tsp. oregano
1/8 tsp. Tabasco sauce
2 Tbsp. dried parsley

Step 1. Drain juice from artichokes into small saucepan; add onions and sauté in juice about 8 minutes.

Step 2. Chop artichokes fine and place in mixing bowl. Add other ingredients and beat with a fork. Add ingredients from saucepan. Pour into greased baking dish or pan and bake 30 minutes at 350°. Cut into squares to serve, or cut smaller for hors d'oeuvres.

Note: This dish may be prepared a day ahead and refrigerated or frozen after it is baked. Heat to serve.

Mrs. Nick Futris (Kristine)

OLIVE BREAD

This recipe is from the island of Cyprus.

Temperature: 400° for 10 minutes; then 375° until done
Pan Size: Cookie sheet
Yield: 3 loaves

5 cups self-rising Pillsbury flour
1 cup olive oil
1 cup yogurt
1 cup fresh orange juice

FILLING:
2 cups olives, pitted and chopped (preferably black Mediterranean type)
1/2 cup grated onions
1 Tbsp. fresh chopped mint (dry mint may be used)

Step 1. Rub oil into the flour with fingers until all is well mixed. Add yogurt and fresh orange juice, mixing well with spoon.

Step 2. Divide dough into 3 parts and let rest for about 45 minutes before turning out.

Step 3. Prepare filling and set aside until dough is ready to be used.

Step 4. After dough's rest period, roll out each piece of dough with rolling pin into oblong shape, about 1/2" thick. Sprinkle filling over each piece of dough and then roll as you would a jelly roll.

Step 5. Place seam part down on greased cookie sheet and bake at 400° for 10 minutes; then at 375° for about 20 minutes or until done. When cool, slice about 1" thick.

Mrs. George Demas (Victoria)

TZATZIKI
(Yogurt and Cucumber Appetizer)

Yield: 1 cup

2 cucumbers
3 cloves garlic, minced
3 Tbsp. olive oil
1 Tbsp. lemon juice
1 cup plain yogurt (do not use low fat yogurt)

Step 1. Peel cucumbers. Cut lengthwise in four sections. Remove seeds. Place on plate, sprinkle generously with salt, and allow to stand 30 minutes.

Step 2. Pour off water, pat dry, and then pulverize in blender or Cuisinart. Discard liquid.

Step 3. Add cucumber, oil, garlic, and lemon juice to yogurt. Pour into cheese cloth lined strainer and allow to drain several hours or overnight. (Place strainer above liquid that is collecting.)

Serve with Melba toast. Excellent served with fish.

Mrs. James G. Sousoulas (Sophie)

YEMISER SELATTA
Lentil Salad

Yield: 6-8 servings

2 cups dried lentils
4 to 5 cups water
1 small green pepper
1 small red pepper
1/2 cup red or white onion, finely chopped
2 fresh hot chilies, finely chopped
2 Tbsp. vinegar or lemon juice
3 Tbsp. olive or vegetable oil
1-1/2 tsp. salt
1 Tbsp. garlic, finely chopped
1 Tbsp. mustard

Step 1. Wash lentils in cold water and drain.

Step 2. Combine lentils with water and boil until very tender, about 30 minutes. Drain in a sieve and set aside.

Step 3. Cut peppers into strips 1/2" wide and 1" long. Set aside.

Step 4. Combine vinegar (lemon juice), oil, salt, garlic, and mustard. Beat for about 2 minutes.

Step 5. Combine all ingredients and blend well. (It does not matter if lentils are mashed.) Serve cool with bread or alone.

In Ethiopia, lentil salad is eaten mainly during Lent.

Amsale Gebremeskel Gebreziabher

EGGPLANT PARMESAN

Temperature: 350°
Pan Size: 9" x 13"
Yield: 8 servings

3 medium eggplants
Vegetable oil
1 stick margarine
1/2 cup olive oil
2 medium-size onions, chopped
3 cloves garlic
1 Tbsp. chopped parsley
1/2 tsp. oregano
1 small can tomato sauce
2 Tbsp. tomato paste
1 cup water
Salt and pepper to taste
1/2 cup Parmesan cheese, grated
1 cup mozzarella cheese, grated

Step 1. Wash eggplants, slice lengthwise or crosswise in 1/2" wide thick slices. Soak in salt water for 15 minutes. Remove from water and dry on paper toweling. Put eggplant slices in broiler and brush with vegetable oil. Broil until light brown.

Step 2. In margarine and olive oil sauté onions, garlic, parsley, oregano, tomato sauce and tomato paste. Add 1 cup water and simmer for 15 minutes. Salt and pepper to taste.

Step 3. Put eggplant in casserole; sprinkle with half the Parmesan cheese; pour sauce over eggplant. Sprinkle remainder of cheese over the top.

Step 4. Bake in 350° oven for 30 minutes. Remove from oven, cover with grated mozzarella and return to oven for 15 more minutes.

Mrs. Charles J. Vergos (Tasia)

SALMON QUICHE

Temperature: 325°
Pan Size: pie pan

1 15-oz. can salmon
3 eggs, beaten
1 cup sour cream
1/4 cup mayonnaise
1/2 cup cheddar cheese,
   shredded
1 Tbsp. onion, grated
1/4 tsp. dill weed
3 drops Tabasco sauce
1 pie crust

TOPPING:
2 Tbsp. margarine, melted
1/3 cup whole wheat flour
1/3 cup cheddar cheese,
   shredded
1/8 cup almonds, chopped
1/4 tsp. salt
Paprika to taste

Step 1. Drain salmon and reserve liquid. Add water to reserved liquid to make 1/2 cup liquid.

Step 2. Flake salmon (removing bones and skin). Set aside.

Step 3. In a bowl, blend together eggs, sour cream, mayonnaise, and reserved salmon liquid. Stir in salmon, 1/2 cup cheese, onion, dill weed, and Tabasco sauce.

Step 4. Spoon filling into crust.

Step 5. Combine all topping ingredients and mix. Sprinkle topping over filling.

Step 6. Bake for 45 minutes or until firm in the center.

Mrs. Constantine Konstans (Sondra)

MUHALLEBI   ARMENIAN
(Armenian Custard)

Yield: 4 servings

2 cups milk
1/4 cup cornstarch
Pinch of salt
1/2 cup sugar
Cinnamon

Step 1. Put milk in a saucepan and bring to a boil. Mix cornstarch with 1/4 cup water and stir slowly into milk. Cook on low fire, stirring constantly for 15-20 minutes or until bubbles start forming on the top.

Step 2. Pour into individual dishes and chill. Sprinkle with cinnamon when served.

Mrs. Arthur Bedeian (Vikki)

GOMEN SEGÁ

ETHIOPIAN

Beef and Collard Greens

Yield: 6 servings

4 pounds fresh collard
  greens
2-1/2 pounds boneless beef
  (preferably chuck)
1 large onion
2 medium sized green
  peppers
2 tsp. salt
6 Tbsp. Niter Kebbeh*
  (6 Tbsp. butter may be
  substituted)
8 medium scallions
4 fresh hot chilies (optional)
  (see note below)
1/4 cup water

Note: When working with
  chilies wear rubber gloves
  and do not touch your face.
  Rinse in cold water. Cut or
  break off the stems, leaving
  the seeds.

*See recipe below

Step 1. Thoroughly wash the greens, strip away any very coarse stems, and chop green leaves coarsely. In a 10-quart pot place greens and water, cover tightly and cook over medium heat about 10 minutes or until wilted. Drain and set aside.

Step 2. Slice the meat 1/2" thick, 2" long and 1/2" wide.

Step 3. Wash and seed the green peppers. Cut one pepper into strips about 2" long and 1/2" wide, set aside.

Step 4. In a heavy ungreased 3- to 4-quart stewing pot combine beef, onion, green pepper strips and salt. Cook over high heat for 5 to 6 minutes, until the beef is lightly browned and the vegetables are tender. Stir frequently to prevent sticking. If necessary, lower heat. A little water may be added if necessary.

Step 5. Stirring constantly, add the reserved collard greens, Niter Kebbeh (or butter), scallions, chopped green pepper and whole chilies (optional). Continue cooking, partially covered, 25 to 30 minutes or until the meat is tender.

Yeweinishet (Wee) Dessalegn Begna

NITER KEBBEH

ETHIOPIAN

Spiced Butter

Yield: 1 cup

1 pound unsalted butter
1/2 small onion, chopped
2 tsp. ginger root, finely
  chopped
3/4 tsp. tumeric
Pinch of cardamom
1 piece of stick cinnamon,
  1/2" long
Pinch of nutmeg

Step 1. Melt butter until white foam appears. Stir in the remaining ingredients. Reduce heat and simmer uncovered for 30 minutes.

Step 2. Pour liquid through a very fine sieve into a jar. If any solids are left, strain again to prevent butter from becoming rancid. Cover tightly and store in the refrigerator.

Yeweinishet (Wee) Dessalegn Begna

YABESH DABO

Ethiopian Bread

Temperature: 375°
Pan Size: 15" x 11" x 4-1/2" Lasagne Pan

2 packages yeast
1 cup warm water
1 tsp. sugar
1 tsp. salt
2 Tbsp. bread flour

5 pounds bread flour
1 Tbsp. salt
4 Tbsp. sugar
1/4 tsp. ground cinnamon
1/4 tsp. ground cloves
1/2 tsp. coriander or ground cardamom
2-1/2 cups lukewarm water
1 cup vegetable oil

Step 1. Dissolve yeast in one cup warm water. Add 1 teaspoon sugar, 1 teaspoon salt and 2 tablespoons flour. Leave it to rise for about 15 minutes.

Step 2. Combine bread flour, 1 tablespoon salt, 4 tablespoons sugar, ground cinnamon, ground cloves, and coriander in a large mixing bowl. Add the raised yeast mixture and mix well. Gradually add the lukewarm water. Add the oil the same way mixing until the dough is smooth.

Step 3. When the dough is thoroughly mixed, knead until smooth and shape it like a ball. Cover and let stand in a warm place until doubled in bulk. Let it stand to rise for a second time. Punch down and knead lightly.

Step 4. Line the pan with foil and grease the foil. Turn the dough into the baking pan and lightly spread it to fill the space. Let it stand until it starts to rise again to almost double.

Step 5. Bake in preheated oven for 1 hour. Do not open the oven door before an hour.

Belaynesh (Mimi) Keskessa

DORO WOT
Chicken Sauce

ETHIOPIAN

Yield: 7 servings

**3-4 pound hen, cut into
serving pieces**
1 lemon, juice of
2 pounds red onion
**1 Tbsp. Ethiopian red
pepper**
2 cups tomato sauce
**4 Tbsp. spiced butter (refer
to page 186)**
**1 Tbsp. minced garlic and
ginger, combined**
**1/2 Tbsp. cardamom or
mixed spices**
4 Tbsp. red cooking wine
1/2 Tbsp. salt
1/2 tsp. black pepper
7 brown eggs

Step 1. Remove and discard the skin of the chicken. Thoroughly wash the chicken with cold water. Soak in fresh lemon juice and water for 10 minutes.

Step 2. Chop the onion in a food processor. Place 1 tablespoon spiced butter in a large heavy saucepan and sauté the onion. Add drops of water as needed to prevent the onion from sticking to the pan. When onion is lightly brown, add the Ethiopian red pepper and tomato sauce, the remaining 3 tablespoons spiced butter, minced garlic and ginger, cardamom and wine. Cook for 20 minutes, stirring occasionally.

Step 3. Remove chicken from the lemon juice mix. Rinse well and add to the sauce. Add salt and black pepper. Bring the sauce to a boil, cover, reduce heat and simmer until the chicken is tender.

Step 4. Place eggs in cold water, bring to a boil and cook for 15 minutes. Cover with cool water for a few minutes and peel. Add the hard boiled eggs to the chicken sauce. Simmer for 5 minutes.

Note: Traditionally, this sauce is served with Ethiopian bread (enjera) or pita bread and homemade cottage cheese. It also will go well with rice.

Woubayehu (Woube) Kassas

SATZIKI
Cucumber Dip

GREEK

Yield: 3 cups

3-1/2 cups plain yogurt
1 tsp. salt
1 cup cucumber, finely
  chopped
Salt
1 clove garlic, crushed
1 Tbsp. olive oil
1 Tbsp. fresh dill or mint
1 Tbsp. lemon juice or
  vinegar

Step 1. To thicken yogurt, place 3-1/2 cups yogurt mixed with 1 teaspoon salt in a dish towel. Hang over bowl until dripping stops, about 2 hours. Measure 2 cups yogurt and set aside.

Step 2. Sprinkle salt over cucumber and let stand for 15 minutes. Press dry.

Step 3. Combine 2 cups thickened yogurt, cucumber, garlic, olive oil, dill and lemon juice. Chill.

Alexandra Peters
Clarksdale, Mississippi

KOUSHARIE
Lentils With Rice

EGYPTIAN

Yield: 4-6 pieces

1 cup brown lentils
2 medium onions, chopped
1/2 Tbsp. butter of
  vegetable oil
3 cups boiling water
1/2 tsp. salt
1 cup rice
2 medium onions, thinly
  sliced
1/2 Tbsp. butter or
  vegetable oil

Step 1. Boil lentils in water in covered pan until slightly done, about 15 minutes. Drain.

Step 2. Brown chopped onions in butter until slightly brown. Add 3 cups boiling water and salt. Stir in drained lentils and boil until almost done. While still boiling, add rice. Stir and cover.

Step 3. Reduce heat to low. Cook for approximately 20 minutes or until rice is done.

Step 4. While lentils and rice are cooking, brown sliced onions in butter.

Step 5. Transfer lentil and rice mixture to serving dish and garnish the top with browned onions. Serve with yogurt, pita bread and mixed green salad.

Suzan Hanna

AMYGTHALOTA (ERGOLAVI)   GREEK
Almond Cookies

Temperature: 350° for 20 minutes
Yield: 20 pieces

1 cup almonds, blanched
1-1/2 cup sugar
3-4 egg whites
1 tsp. vanilla
10 almonds, blanched, cut in
    half

Step 1. Put the almonds through a fine mill or grind them in a blender or food processor. Add sugar, egg whites and vanilla and keep grinding until it becomes a soft mixture.

Step 2. Butter a shallow pan or line with parchment paper. Place spoonfuls of the mixture about 1-2 inches apart (to allow for spreading). Smooth out the top with a spatula and place a half almond in the center.

Step 3. Bake for 20 minutes or until they become golden brown. Let them stand for 5 minutes. Carefully remove to a wire rack to cool. Store in a cookie tin to avoid drying out.

Mrs. Jim Karas (Despina)

MAYERITSA III   GREEK
Easter Soup

Yield: Approximately 6 servings

2 pounds lamb, cubed*
1 stalk celery, cut up
1/2 onion
1/4 cup (1/2 stick) butter
1 large onion, finely chopped
1/2 cup white wine
3 bunches scallions, finely
    chopped
Salt to taste
Freshly ground pepper to
    taste
1/2 cup fresh dill, chopped
1/2 cup parsley, finely
    chopped
1/4 cup rice (optional)
4-5 cups water

*Lamb shoulder, shanks and
    chops may be used.

Step 1. Place bones from shanks and chops in a kettle. Add water to cover. Add celery and 1/2 onion. Bring to a boil and remove foam as it forms. Simmer for 30 minutes. Strain, reserving the broth. Chop meat into pieces no larger than 1/2".

Step 2. Sauté chopped onion in butter until transparent. Add cubed lamb and sauté until lightly browned. Add wine and broth. Bring to a boil. Add scallions, dill, parsley, salt and pepper. If rice is to be used, add rice plus 2 cups boiling water.

Step 3. Prepare avgholemono sauce (see "Sauce" section). Fold into soup just before serving.

Mrs. Bill K. Taras (Bessie)

GALATOBOUREKO
Custard Pastry

GREEK

Temperature: 350° for 1 hour and 10 minutes
Pan Size: 9" x 13"
Yield: 12-15 pieces

SYRUP:
1 cup sugar
1 cup water
Fresh lemon juice

CUSTARD:
2 quarts milk
1/4 cup (1/2 stick) butter
1/2 tsp. salt
1/2 cup Cream of Wheat
2 cups sugar
3 Tbsp. cornstarch (level)
1/2 cup milk
6 eggs
1 tsp. vanilla

CRUST:
1/2 pound filo
1/2 pound butter

Step 1. To make syrup, place sugar and water in saucepan. Boil until mixture thickens to syrup consistency. Add a few drops of lemon juice and set aside to cool.

Step 2. For custard, place 2 quarts milk in a large saucepan with butter and salt. Heat to boiling and gradually add the Cream of Wheat. Cook for 10 minutes, stirring constantly. Mixture will be thick but not stiff. Remove from heat and set aside.

Step 3. Mix together sugar and cornstarch. Add 1/2 cup milk, stir and set aside.

Step 4. Beat the eggs in a large bowl. Pour hot milk mixture slowly into beaten eggs, stirring constantly. Place the mixture into saucepan and add the sugar-cornstarch mixture. Stir well. Add vanilla.

Step 5. Cook mixture over low heat stirring constantly until it begins to boil. Simmer for about 5 minutes. Remove from heat.

Step 6. Line the bottom of the baking dish with 1/2 of the filo, brushing with butter between each layer. Pour the milk mixture over the filo crust and layer with the other half of filo on top, brushing with butter between each layer.

Step 7. Bake for 1 hour and 10 minutes. Remove from oven and pour the cooled syrup over the pastry. The galatoboureko cuts better when cool. Pastry must be refrigerated.

Note: Can be served cold or may be reheated in oven (not microwave) before serving.

Mrs. George Demas (Victoria)

COPENHI

Custard Pastry With Crust and Filo

Temperature: 375° for 60-75 minutes
Pan Size: 12" x 18"
Yield: Approximately 50 pieces

BOTTOM CRUST:
2 eggs
1-1/2 cups butter, softened
Flour (about 1-1/2 pounds)

FILLING:
2-1/4 pounds shelled walnuts
1-1/2 boxes Nabisco
  Zwieback
22 eggs (separated)
6 cups sugar
1 Tbsp. ground cinnamon
1 tsp. ground cloves
3 tsp. baking powder
1 fresh orange, zest of
Remainder of orange,
  ground in food grinder

TOPPING:
1/2 pound filo (8 pieces)
1/2 cup (1 stick) melted
  butter

SYRUP:
5 cups sugar
4 cups water
1 cup (8 ounces) honey
1 lemon, juice of

Step 1. To make bottom crust, add eggs to softened butter and mix well. Add enough sifted flour to form a very soft dough. With the palm of the hand spread dough over the bottom of pan to the edges. Dough will be sticky. Wet hands with water to keep dough from sticking. Set aside.

Step 2. For filling, chop walnuts and Zwieback together. Add 3 cups sugar, cinnamon, cloves, baking powder, orange zest and mix well with hands. Set aside.

Step 3. Beat egg yolks well with electric mixer until fluffy. Gradually add remaining 3 cups sugar and beat thoroughly (the longer the better).

Step 4. Add ground orange to dry mixture and mix just enough so that all ingredients are completely moistened.

Step 5. Beat egg whites until very stiff. Add egg yolk mixture to walnut mixture. Fold in egg whites and pour into pan.

Step 6. Place filo loosely over filling, one sheet at a time, brushing each sheet well with melted butter. Bake 1 hour to 1 hour and 15 minutes or until top is well browned. Test with toothpick until it comes out clean. When done, set aside to cool thoroughly, preferably overnight.

Step 7. When cooled, cut into diamond shaped pieces using a very sharp knife. Be careful not to press too hard with knife so as not to crush topping.

Continued...

Step 8. For syrup, boil sugar and water until mixture froths. Add lemon juice and honey and cook slowly until slightly thickened but not syrupy. Syrup should be thin enough to pour easily over the top. Gradually pour hot syrup over top working over entire area. Allow syrup to absorb before removing any pieces.

Note: This recipe is excellent for large gatherings. Recipe may be halved and baked in 9" x 13" pan for 50-60 minutes or until toothpick comes out clean.

Mrs. George Demas (Victoria)

FALAFIEL OR TAAMIYAH   EGYPTIAN
Fried Bean Patties

Yield: 10-12 servings

1-1/2 pounds dry fava or lima beans
1-1/2 pounds dry chickpeas
4 medium onoins, finely chopped
4 cups (1 bunch) fresh parsley, finely chopped
3 cups fresh cilantro (coriander), finely chopped
4 cloves garlic, crushed
1 tsp. ground coriander
1/4 tsp. cayenne pepper (optional)
1 tsp. salt or to taste
1/2 tsp. flour (optional)
1/2 tsp. baking soda
1 Tbsp. water
Vegetable oil for frying

Step 1. Soak fava or lima beans in water for 18 hours or overnight. Soak chickpeas in water for 18 hours or overnight. (If canned beans are used, soaking is not necessary.) Drain well and grind with electric grinder or food processor.

Step 2. Add onion, parsley, cilantro, garlic, coriander, cayenne pepper and salt. Mix and knead well. Let stand for 2-1/2 hours. If mixture appears soggy, add optional 1/2 teaspoon flour and mix to eliminate some of the moisture.

Step 3. Heat oil in pan on high until very hot.

Step 4. Mix baking soda with 1 tablespoon of water and thoroughly incorporate into the falafiel mixture. Shape into small circles, pat with the palm of hand, and then fry in oil for 3 minutes until brown. Drain.

Step 5. Serve with pita bread, chopped parsley, pickles, tahini and chopped tomatoes.

Note: It can be served as a side dish or appetizer.

Suzan Hanna

JIMMY'S ARNI PSITO
Roast Lamb

Temperature: 350°
Yield: 16-20 servings

8-10 pound boneless leg of
lamb, tied (use Domestic
only)
2-3 garlic heads, separated
into cloves and peeled
(do not use minced or
flavored garlic cloves)
2 cups fresh lemon juice or
bottled 100% lemon juice
(not imitation)
2 cups sherry wine (not
cooking sherry)
2 cups extra virgin olive oil
Salt
Pepper
Basil
Dill
Thyme
Rosemary
Marjoram
Oregano
Fennel seed

POTATOES (Optional)
Lamb drippings
6-8 red potatoes
1/2 cup olive oil
1/2 cup lemon juice
1/2 cup sherry
Salt
Pepper

Step 1. Lamb should be lean and boneless, if possible. Rinse lamb well and place in pan. With a paring knife, make about 25-30 incisions in meat and insert garlic cloves. Incisions should be made all over the lamb leg – top, bottom and sides.

Step 2. Using 1 cup each, generously rub lamb with lemon juice, then sherry and then olive oil. Make sure to do it in this order to capture the flavor of the seasonings within the meat. There will be a generous amount of lemon juice, sherry, and oil in bottom of the pan. Turn lamb over so that it is upside down in the pan and the top of the lamb is in the marinade.

Step 3. To season, start with the bottom and sides of the lamb. Sparingly use salt and pepper. Then use generous amounts of the following to make a crust – basil, dill, thyme, rosemary, marjoram, oregano and fennel seed. It is important to season in this order. The object is to end with a crust of oregano and then fennel seed. When the bottom and sides are covered with seasoning, turn meat over and repeat the seasoning, turn meat over and repeat the seasoning process on the top of the lamb, making sure to begin with salt and pepper and end with the fennel seed. All of the meat should be covered with seasoning.

Note: For best results, season a day ahead and allow marinate.

Step 4. Place a meat thermometer into the lamb leg. Place meat in a 400° preheated oven for 30 minutes; then lower the temperature to 350° for 2-3 hours. (Cooking time will vary with size of lamb and type of oven.) Lamb internal temperature should reach 175°. Baste every hour using remaining mixture of lemon juice, sherry, and oil. Add water to the bottom of the pan as needed to extend the liquid and prevent it from drying out.

Step 5. Upon removal of lamb from oven, cover with foil to keep it moist. When ready to serve, remove string before slicing.

Continued…

Step 6. (Optional) Roasted potatoes can be cooked after the lamb is done by using the drippings from the pan. Place peeled and quartered red potatoes in pan with drippings. Then use olive oil, lemon juice, sherry, salt, and pepper to season potatoes. Cook at 350° for approximately 45 minutes, basting and adding water as needed. Cook until potatoes are tender.

Jimmy Skefos

PHANOUROPITA
Saint Phanourios Cake

GREEK

Saint Phanourios is the patron saint of the "lost and found." According to tradition, whenever a treasured possession is lost, the owner pledges to bake a fruit cake for Saint Phanourios in the hope of finding it. When the article is found the owner honors his vow and presents the cake to his neighborhood church for blessing. Afterward, it is distributed to the parishioners present at the church service and to the poor.

Temperature: 325° for 1 to 1-1/2 hours
Pan Size: 7" fluted tube pan or 8" loaf pan
Yield: 12-16 servings

1 cup orange juice
1/2 cup brandy
2 Tbsp. unsalted butter
2 cups golden raisins
3/4 cup sugar
1/2 cup honey
1/2 tsp. salt
1 Tbsp. ground cinnamon
1/4 tsp. ground cloves
2 cups all-purpose flour
2 tsp. double-acting baking powder
1/2 tsp. baking soda
2 Tbsp. grated orange zest
1/2 cup sesame seeds (optional)
1/4 cup brandy

Step 1. Preheat oven to 325°.

Step 2. Combine orange juice, 1/2 cup brandy, butter, raisins, sugar, honey, salt, cinnamon and cloves in a large heavy-bottomed saucepan. Bring to a boil, reduce heat, and simmer for 10 minutes, or until thick and syrupy. Set pot in cold water to cool mixture completely.

Step 3. Sift flour, baking powder and baking soda into cooled syrup. Beat vigorously for 8 to 10 minutes, or until batter is smooth and bubbly. Stir in grated orange zest.

Step 4. Turn into a well-buttered 7" fluted tube pan or 8" loaf pan. Sprinkle with sesame seeds. Bake for 1 to 1-1/2 hours, or until a knife inserted in the center comes out clean. Sprinkle with brandy and cool cake in pan.

Submitted by Katherine Futris
as given to her by her cousin
Julie Fotiades of New Orleans

SPINACH PETA WITH CORNMEAL CRUST

GREEK

Temperature: 375° for 45 minutes
Pan Size: 2 baking dishes, 8" x 12"
Yield: 12-15 pieces per dish

FILLING:
4 to 5 bunches fresh spinach
6 bunches green onions, chopped
6 eggs
3/4 cup olive oil
1-1/2 to 2 pounds Feta cheese
Salt to taste
1/4 cup Cream of Wheat

CRUST:
4 cups yellow cornmeal
2 cups all-purpose flour
2 tsp. baking powder
1/3 cup olive oil or more
1-1/2 cups milk
Salt to taste
1/4 cup olive oil

Step 1. To prepare filling, thoroughly wash spinach and onions and drain. Chop into 1/2" pieces. Place in large bowl.

Step 2. Beat eggs well and add to spinach, along with onion, olive oil, Feta cheese and salt. Add Cream of Wheat to mixture. This will cut down on the liquid discharged from the spinach and will not alter the taste. Set filling aside.

Step 3. To make crust, mix dry ingredients. Add 1/3 cup oil (or more for added crispness) and rub into mixture with fingers until all oil is absorbed. Add milk and mix well. Batter will be a little thicker than cake batter.

Step 4. Divide dough into 2/3 and 1/3 portions and set smaller portion aside for later use. Grease pan with oil. Take 2/3 portion of batter and spread onto bottom and up sides of pan with hands. Moisten hands with water to keep dough from sticking to fingers.

Step 5. Pour spinach mixture over the batter. Dilute the 1/3 portion of batter with milk and 1/4 cup of olive oil to make a runny mixture.

Step 6. Pour this mixture over entire pita. Drizzle with additional olive oil before baking (optional). Bake until golden brown.

Mrs. George Demas (Victoria)

INDEX

A

A Carpatho-Russian Christmas Eve 18
Aegean Cocktail Buffet 22
Ahladakia *(Cookie Pears)* 145
Amigthalota Flogeres *(Almond Flutes)* 153
Amygthalota (Ergolavi) *(Almond Cookies)* 190
Angie's Easter Eggs 32
Anginares Avgholemono *(Artichokes with*
   Egg-Lemon Sauce) 106
APPETIZERS
   Baba Ga-Nooj *(Eggplant Appetizer)* 34
   Dolmathakia *(Stuffed Grapevine Leaves)* 34
   Keftethakia *(Cocktail Meatballs)* 35
   Kreatopetakia *(Meat Triangles)* 35
   Melidzana Caviar *(Eggplant Canape)* 36
   Saganaki *(Fried Cheese)* 36
   Satziki *(Cucumber Dip)* 189
   Spanakopetakia *(Spinach Puffs)* 37
   Tarama Keftethes *(Caviar Cakes)* 64
   Taramosalata *(Caviar Dip)* 37
   Tiropitakia *(Cheese Triangles)* 38
   Toursi *(Pickled Vegetables)* 38
   Tzatziki *(Yogurt and Cucumber Appetizer)* 183
ARMENIAN RECIPES
   Muhallebi *(Armenian Custard)* 185
Arni Fricassee *(Lamb in Egg-Lemon Sauce)* 74
Arni Me Spanaki *(Lamb with Spinach)* 74
Arni Psito *(Roast Lamb)* 75
Arni Tis Souflas *(Whole Lamb Barbecued on a Spit)* . . 76
Artichoke Quiche 182
ARTICHOKES
   Anginares Avgholemono *(Artichokes with*
     Egg-Lemon Sauce) 106
   Artichoke Quiche 182
   Kota Anginares Ke Manitaria *(Chicken with*
     Artichokes and Mushrooms) 69
Artos for Artoklasia 10
Artos I *(For Artoklasia)* 12
Artos II *(For Artoklasia)* 13
Aspri Saltsa *(Bechamel Sauce)* 100
Avgholemono Soupa *(Egg-Lemon Soup)* 40

B

Baba Ga-Nooj *(Eggplant Appetizer)* 34
Baked Kibbie 78
Baked Orzo 88
Baklava I *(Honey Nut Pastry)* 154
Baklava II *(Honey Nut Pastry)* 156
Bamyes Me Domates *(Okra and Tomatoes)* 106
Basic Avgholemono Sauce *(Egg and Lemon*
   Sauce) 100
BASIC TECHNIQUES
   Angie's Easter Eggs 32
   Basic Techniques 26
   Bread: Braided Method 30
   Byzantine Cross 30
   Decorations 30
   Easter Eggs 32
   Filled Braid 31
   Kouloura 30
   Kouloura with Eggs 30
   Pysanky *(Ukrainian Easter Eggs)* 32
   Red Easter Egg Tradition 32
   Working with Filo 26

BEANS

Faki *(Lentil Soup)* 42
Falafiel or Taamiyah *(Fried Bean Patties)* 193
Fasoulatha *(Bean Soup)* 40
Kousharie *(Lentils with Rice)* 189
Mavromatika Fasolia Salata
   (Blackeyed Pea Salad) 46
Yemiser Selatta *(Lentil Salad)* 184
BEEF
Beef Stroganoff 77
Cevapcici *(Serbian Sausage)* 77
Dolmathakia Me Avgholemono *(Stuffed*
   Grapevine Leaves with Egg-Lemon Sauce) 87
Dolmathes *(Stuffed Cabbage Leaves)* 86
Domates Yemistes *(Stuffed Tomatoes)* 93
Gomen Segá *(Beef and Collard Greens)* 186
Keftethes *(Meatballs)* 75
Kema I *(Meat Sauce–Lamb or Beef)* 101
Kema II *(Meat Sauce–Beef)* 102
Kema III *(Meat Sauce–Chuck and Sausage)* 102
Kolbasa *(Sausage)* 80
Kotlety *(Baked Meat Cutlets)* 79
Meat Dressing 88
Mousaka I *(Eggplant Casserole)* 89
Mousaka II *(Eggplant-Meat Casserole)* 90
Mousaka Patata 180
Papoutsakia Zucchini *(Stuffed Zucchini)* 91
Pastitso 176
Pastitso I *(Macaroni and Meat Sauce Casserole)* . . 92
Pastitso II *(Macaroni and Meat Sauce Casserole)* . 94
Pastitso III *(Macaroni and Meat Casserole)* 95
Psito Kreas *(Roasted Meat)* 84
Sarma *(Cabbage Rolls)* 96
Sikotaki *(Grecian Style Calf's Liver)* 82
Soutsoukakia *(Meatballs in Tomato Sauce)* 82
Souvlakia I *(Shish-Ka-Bob)* 83
Souvlakia II *(Shish-Ka-Bob)* 83
Steak Greek Style 95
Stefatho *(Stew)* 85
Yemistes Melidzanes I *(Stuffed Eggplant)* 97
Yemistes Melidzanes II *(Stuffed Eggplant Deluxe)* . 98
Youvarelakia *(Meatballs in Egg-Lemon Sauce)* . . . 85
Beef Stroganoff 77
BEVERAGES (See Also Wines)
Russian Tea 174
Traditional Nog 168
Wines, Commentary 166
Bread: Braided Method 30
BREADS
Artos I *(For Artoklasia)* 12
Artos II *(For Artoklasia)* 13
Byzantine Cross 30
Cypriot Cheese Bread 117
Easter Bread *(Ukrainian)* 117
Filled Braid 31
Glyko Psomi *(Holiday Sweet Bread)* 114
Kolachky *(Nut Roll Bread)* 119
Koliva *(Memorial Wheat Offering)* 10, 13, 14
Kouloura 30
Kouloura with Eggs 30
Lagana *(Feta Cheese Bread Roll)* 51
Olive Bread 183
Povitica *(Walnut and Date Sweet Bread)* 118
Proscuri *(Individual Church Altar Breads)* 11
Prosphora *(Antidoron)* 10

Psomi I (Greek Bread)...................115
Psomi II (Greek Bread)..................116
Psomi Sta Tessara (Nick's #4 Bread).......120
Psomi Tou Spitiou (Bread for the Home).....177
Tiropsomo (Cheese Bread)...............54
Tsoureki (Sweet Bread)................116
Vasilopita (Matula's New Year's Cake).......121
Vasilopita (New Year's Sweet Bread).........122
Yabesh Dabo (Ethiopian Bread)...........187
Breezoles Tis Skaras (Charcoal Broiled Lamb Chops).. 77

C

CABBAGE
Cabbage Slaw.........................176
Dolmathes (Stuffed Cabbage Leaves)........86
Sarma (Cabbage Rolls).................96
Cabbage Slaw........................176
CAKES
Christina's Delight (Nut Cake)............124
Karithopeta I (Almond Cake)............125
Karithopeta II (Walnut Cake)...........127
Olympian Cake......................174
Orechnik (Nut Cake)...................126
Pantespani Portokali (Orange Sponge Cake)...127
Phanouropita (Saint Phanourios Cake)....19, 195
Poutinga (Cake with Pudding Topping)........126
Ravani (Almond Cake)...................128
Vasilopita (Matula's New Year's Cake).......121
Walnut Torte........................129
Xantho Melachrino (Yellow Cake with
    Spiced Meringue).................132
Yaourtopeta I (Yogurt Nut Cake with
    Lemon-Honey Syrup)..............130
Yaourtopita II (Yogurt Nut Cake)...........131
Yiaourtopeta (Yogurt Cake)..............173
CAVIAR
Melidzana Caviar (Eggplant Canape)........36
Tarama Keftethes (Caviar Cakes).........64
Taramosalata (Caviar Dip)..............37
Cephalonian Meat Pie (Kreatopeta).........179
Cevapcici (Serbian Sausage).............77
CHEESE DISHES
Cheeses, Commentary...............168
Cicvara (Cornmeal Dish)...............178
Cypriot Cheese Bread.................117
Easy Tiropeta......................54
Gibanica I (Strudel and Cheese Cake Combination).. 50
Gibanica II (Cheese Peta)..............52
Lagana (Feta Cheese Bread Roll)...........51
Makaronopeta I (Macaroni and Cheese Peta)....52
Makaronopeta II (Macaroni and Cheese Peta)...53
Pascha (Traditional Easter Dessert).........55
Piroshki (Stuffed Dumplings).............56
Saganaki (Fried Cheese)................36
Tiropeta (Cheese Peta).................53
Tiropitakia (Cheese Triangles)............38
Tiropsomo (Cheese Bread)..............54
Yianniotiki Patsiariá..................182
CHICKEN
Doro Wot (Chicken Sauce)...............188
Kota Anginares Ke Manitaria (Chicken with
    Artichokes and Mushrooms)...........69
Kota Kapama I (Chicken in Tomato Sauce with
    Spaghetti).....................68
Kota Kapama II (Chicken in Tomato Sauce)....69
Kota Me Bamyes (Chicken with Okra).......67
Kota Melanaise (Chicken with Melanaise Sauce).. 70
Kota Pilaf (Chicken Pilaf)................71

Kota Riganato (Chicken with Oregano)........71
Kotopetakia Avgholemono (Chicken Rolls
    with Egg-Lemon Sauce)..............66
Pan Broiled Chicken..................72
Sikotakia (Fried Chicken Livers)...........72
Christina's Delight (Nut Cake)............124
Christmas Customs and Christmas Eve.....16, 18
Cicvara (Cornmeal Dish)...............178
COD
Psari Plaki II (Baked Fish with Vegetables)......63
COOKIES
Ahladakia (Cookie Pears)...............145
Amygthalota (Ergolavi) (Almond Cookies).....190
Finikia (Honey Dipped Cookies)...........133
Hamalia (Almond Cookies)..............134
Kifle (Crescent Cookies)...............134
Kolachky (Frozen Dough Cookies)..........135
Koulourakia I (Easter Cookies)...........136
Koulourakia II (Traditional Easter Cookies).....137
Kourabiedes I (Sugar Coated Butter Cookies)...138
Kourabiedes II (Sugar Coated Butter Cookies).. 139
Mazurki (Fruit Cookies)................144
Melomakarona I (Honey Dipped Cookies).....140
Melomakarona II (Honey Cookies)..........141
Pasta Flora (Fruit Squares).............142
Paximathia I (Tea Cookies).............144
Paximathia II (Greek Tea Cookies).........146
Skaltsounakia (Nut Filled Cookies).........143
Spice Paximathia....................172
Copenhi (Custard Pastry with Crust and Filo)....192
Crema (Cream Sauce).................100
Crema Gleeki (Sweet Custard)...........147
Crema Karamela I (Caramel Custard).......147
Crema Karamela II (Caramel Custard).......148
Crema Karamela III (Caramel Custard).......148
CUSTARDS
Copenhi (Custard Pastry with Crust and Filo)...192
Crema Gleeki (Sweet Custard)...........147
Crema Karamela I (Caramel Custard).......147
Crema Karamela II (Caramel Custard).......148
Crema Karamela III (Caramel Custard).......148
Diana's Galatobouriko (Custard Pastry).......157
Galatoboureko (Custard Pastry)...........170
Galatoboureko (Custard Pastry)...........191
Galatoboureko (Margaret's Custard Dessert)...155
Muhallebi (Armenian Custard)............185
Cypriot Cheese Bread.................117

D

Decorations..........................30
DESSERTS
Ahladakia (Cookie Pears)..............145
Amigthalota Flogeres (Almond Flutes).....153
Baklava I (Honey Nut Pastry)...........154
Baklava II (Honey Nut Pastry)..........156
Christina's Delight (Nut Cake)............124
Copenhi (Custard Pastry with Crust and Filo)...192
Crema Gleeki (Sweet Custard)...........147
Crema Karamela I (Caramel Custard).......147
Crema Karamela II (Caramel Custard).......148
Crema Karamela III (Caramel Custard).......148
Diana's Galatobouriko (Custard Pastry)......157
Diples (Rolled Honey Pastries)...........162
Finikia (Honey Dipped Cookies)...........133
Galatoboureko (Custard Pastry)...........170
Galatoboureko (Custard Pastry)...........191
Galatoboureko (Margaret's Custard Dessert)...155
Gibanica I (Strudel and Cheese Cake Combination).. 50
Halva I (Spiced Wheat Pudding)...........150

198

Halva II *(Halva Provincial)* 150
Hamalia *(Almond Cookies)*. 134
Kadaife *(Shredded Pastry with Nuts)* 158
Karithopeta I *(Almond Cake)* 125
Karithopeta II *(Walnut Cake)* 127
Kifle *(Crescent Cookies)*. 134
Kolachky *(Frozen Dough Cookies)*. 135
Kolokithopeta Gliki *(Sweet Pumpkin Peta)* 160
Koulourakia I *(Easter Cookies)*. 136
Koulourakia II *(Traditional Easter Cookies)*. 137
Kourabiedes I *(Sugar Coated Butter Cookies)*. . . 138
Kourabiedes II *(Sugar Coated Butter Cookies)* . . 139
Litsa's Halva *(Spiced Wheat-Almond Pudding)* . . 151
Loukoumathes *(Sweet Fritters)* 161
Mazurki *(Fruit Cookies)*. 144
Melomakarona I *(Honey Dipped Cookies)* 140
Melomakarona II *(Honey Cookies)* 141
Moustalevria *(Grape Pudding)* 149
Olympian Cake. 174
Orechnik *(Nut Cake)*. 126
Pantespani Portokali *(Orange Sponge Cake)*. . . 127
Pascha *(Traditional Easter Dessert)*. 55
Pasta Flora *(Fruit Squares)* 142
Paximathia I *(Tea Cookies)* 144
Paximathia II *(Greek Tea Cookies)* 146
Phanouropita *(Saint Phanourios Cake)* 19, 195
Poutinga *(Cake with Pudding Topping)*. 126
Povitica *(Walnut and Date Sweet Bread)* 118
Ravani *(Almond Cake)*. 128
Rizogalo I *(Rice Pudding)*. 149
Rizogalo II *(Rice Pudding)* 152
Savayiar *(Mocha Torte)*. 173
Skaltsounakia *(Nut Filled Cookies)*. 143
Spice Paximathia 172
Tourta Chocolata *(Chocolate Torte)* 171
Trigona *(Nut Filled Triangles)* 159
Vasilopita *(Matula's New Year's Cake)* 121
Vasilopita *(New Year's Sweet Bread)* 122
Walnut Torte. 129
Xantho Melachrino *(Yellow Cake with Spiced
    Meringue)*. 132
Yaourtopeta I *(Yogurt Nut Cake with Lemon-Honey
    Syrup)* 130
Yaourtopeta II *(Yogurt Nut Cake)* 131
Yiaourtopeta *(Yogurt Cake)* 173
Zvinges *(Sweet Fritters)* 161
Diana's Galatobouriko *(Custard Pastry)* 157
Diples *(Rolled Honey Pastries)*. 162
Dolmathakia *(Stuffed Grapevine Leaves)* 34
Dolmathakia Me Avgholemono *(Stuffed
    Grapevine Leaves with Egg-Lemon Sauce)* 87
Dolmathes *(Stuffed Cabbage Leaves)* 86
Dolmathes Yialandji *(Stuffed Grapevine
    Leaves, Lenten)* 107
Domates Yemistes *(Stuffed Tomatoes)* 93
Domatosalata *(Tomato Salad)* 46
Doro Wot *(Chicken Sauce)* 188

E

Easter 21
Easter Bread. 117
Easter Eggs 32
Easy Avgholemono *(Easy Egg-Lemon Sauce)*. . . . 101
Easy Tiropeta 54
EGGPLANT
    Baba Ga-Nooj *(Eggplant Appetizer)* 34
    Eggplant Parmesan 184
    Melidzana Caviar *(Eggplant Canape)* 36

Mousaka I *(Eggplant Casserole)*. 89
Mousaka II *(Eggplant-Meat Casserole)* 90
Vegetable Casserole. 112
Yemistes Melidzanes I *(Stuffed Eggplant)* 97
Yemistes Melidzanes II *(Stuffed Eggplant Deluxe)*. .98
Eggplant Parmesan. 184
EGGS
Angie's Easter Eggs 32
Avgholemono Soupa *(Egg-Lemon Soup)* 40
Basic Avgholemono Sauce
    (Egg and Lemon Sauce) 100
Crema *(Cream Sauce)*. 100
Easter Eggs 32
Easy Avgholemono *(Easy Egg-Lemon Sauce)* . . 101
Pysanky *(Carpatho-Russian/Ukrainian)* 32
The Red Easter Egg *(Greek)*. 32
EGYPTIAN RECIPES
Falafiel or Taamiyah *(Fried Bean Patties)* 193
Kousharie *(Lentils with Rice)* 189
ET CETERA
Amygthalota (Ergolavi) *(Almond Cookies)*. 190
Artichoke Quiche 182
Cabbage Slaw 176
Cephalonian Meat Pie *(Kreatopeta)*. 179
Cicvara *(Cornmeal Dish)* 178
Copenhi *(Custard Pastry with Crust and Filo)* . . . 192
Doro Wot *(Chicken Sauce)* 188
Eggplant Parmesan 184
Falafiel or Taamiyah *(Fried Bean Patties)* 193
Galatoboureko *(Custard Pastry)*. 170
Galatoboureko *(Custard Pastry)* 191
Gomen Segá *(Beef and Collard Greens)*. 186
Jimmy's Arni Psito *(Roast Lamb)*. 194
Kolokithakia *(Squash Casserole)* 180
Kousharie *(Lentils with Rice)* 189
Mayeritsa III *(Easter Soup)* 190
Mousaka Patata 180
Muhallebi *(Armenian Custard)* 185
Niter Kebbeh *(Spiced Butter)*. 186
Olive Bread 183
Olympian Cake. 174
Pastitso 176
Patatosalata *(Greek Potato Salad)* 181
Phanouropita *(Saint Phanourios Cake)* 19, 195
Psomi Tou Spitiou *(Bread for the Home)*. 177
Roast Lemon Lamb 175
Russian Tea 174
Salmon Quiche. 185
Satziki *(Cucumber Dip)* 189
Savayiar *(Mocha Torte)*. 173
Shrimp and Feta Cheese à la Grecque 175
Shrimp with Spinach 181
Spice Paximathia 172
Spinach Cheese Casserole *(Lazy Day
    Version of Spanakopeta)*. 178
Spinach Peta with Cornmeal Crust 196
Tourta Chocolata *(Chocolate Torte)* 171
Tzatziki *(Yogurt and Cucumber Appetizer)* 183
Yabesh Dabo *(Ethiopian Bread)* 187
Yemiser Selatta *(Lentil Salad)* 184
Yianniotiki Patsiariá 182
Yiaourtopeta *(Yogurt Cake)* 173
ETHIOPIAN RECIPES
Doro Wot *(Chicken Sauce)* 188
Gomen Segá *(Beef and Collard Greens)*. 186
Niter Kebbeh *(Spiced Butter)* 186
Yabesh Dabo *(Ethiopian Bread)* 187
Yemiser Selatta *(Lentil Salad)* 184

F

Faki (Lentil Soup) 42
Falafiel or Taamiyah (Fried Bean Patties) 193
Fasoulakia Yiahni (Greek-Style Green Beans). . . . 107
Fasoulatha (Bean Soup) 40
Filled Braid 31
Finikia (Honey Dipped Cookies). 133
FISH
 Marithes (Fried Smelts). 60
 Plaki IV (Baked Fish). 64
 Psari Marinato (Marinated Fish). 61
 Psari Mayoneza I (Chilled Snapper with
   Mayonnaise Sauce) 61
 Psari Mayoneza II (Red Snapper with
   Mayonnaise Sauce) 62
 Psari Plaki I (Baked Red Snapper with Vegetables). . 62
 Psari Plaki II (Baked Fish with Vegetables) 63
 Psari Plaki III (Fish with Vegetables) 63
 Psarosoupa (Fish Soup) 43
 Salmon Quiche. 185
Fraoles Glyko (Strawberry Preserves) 163
Frapa Glyko (Grapefruit Preserves) 164
Fried Kibbie 79
Fried Peppers and Onions 109

G

Galatoboureko (Custard Pastry) 170
Galatoboureko (Custard Pastry) 191
Galatoboureko (Margaret's Custard Dessert) . . . 155
Garides Pilaf (Shrimp with Rice Pilaf) 59
Garides Souvlakia (Skewered Shrimp) 58
Garides Tourkolimano (Shrimp Tourkolimano) 58
GARLIC SAUCE
 Skorthalia I (Garlic Sauce). 103
 Skorthalia II (Garlic Sauce) 104
 Skorthalia III (Garlic Sauce, Blender Method) . . . 104
Gibanica I (Strudel and Cheese Cake Combination) . . 50
Gibanica II (Cheese Peta). 52
Glyko Psomi (Holiday Sweet Bread). 114
Gomen Segá (Beef and Collard Greens) 186
GRAPEVINE LEAVES
 Dolmathakia (Stuffed Grapevine Leaves). 34
 Dolmathakia Me Avgholemono (Stuffed
   Grapevine Leaves with Egg-Lemon Sauce). . . . 87
 Dolmathes Yialandji (Stuffed Grapevine
   Leaves, Lenten). 107
GREEK RECIPES
 Ahladakia (Cookie Pears) 145
 Amigthalota Flogeres (Almond Flutes) 153
 Amygthalota (Ergolavi) (Almond Cookies). 190
 Angie's Easter Eggs 32
 Anginares Avgholemono (Artichokes with
   Egg-Lemon Sauce) 106
 Arni Fricassee (Lamb in Egg-Lemon Sauce) 74
 Arni Me Spanaki (Lamb with Spinach) 74
 Arni Psito (Roast Lamb) 75
 Arni Tis Souflas
   (Whole Lamb Barbecued on a Spit). 76
 Artos I (For Artoklasia). 12
 Artos II (For Artoklasia) 13
 Aspri Saltsa (Bechamel Sauce) 100
 Avgholemono Soupa (Egg-Lemon Soup) 40
 Baked Orzo 88
 Baklava I (Honey Nut Pastry) 154
 Baklava II (Honey Nut Pastry). 156
 Bamyes Me Domates (Okra and Tomatoes) . . . 106
 Basic Avgholemono Sauce (Egg and
   Lemon Sauce). 100

Breezoles Tis Skaras (Charcoal Broiled
   Lamb Chops) 77
Cabbage Slaw 176
Cephalonian Meat Pie (Kreatopeta). 179
Cheeses, Commentary 168
Christina's Delight (Nut Cake). 124
Copenhi (Custard Pastry with Crust and Filo) . . . 192
Crema (Cream Sauce). 100
Crema Gleeki (Sweet Custard). 147
Crema Karamela I (Caramel Custard). 147
Crema Karamela II (Caramel Custard) 148
Crema Karamela III (Caramel Custard). 148
Cypriot Cheese Bread. 117
Diana's Galatobouriko (Custard Pastry) 157
Diples (Rolled Honey Pastries) 162
Dolmathakia (Stuffed Grapevine Leaves). 34
Dolmathakia Me Avgholemono (Stuffed
   Grapevine Leaves with Egg-Lemon Sauce). . . . 87
Dolmathes (Stuffed Cabbage Leaves) 86
Dolmathes Yialandji (Stuffed Grapevine
   Leaves, Lenten). 107
Domates Yemistes (Stuffed Tomatoes) 93
Domatosalata (Tomato Salad) 46
Easy Tiropeta 54
Faki (Lentil Soup). 42
Fasoulakia Yiahni (Greek Style Green Beans). . . 107
Fasoulatha (Bean Soup) 40
Finikia (Honey Dipped Cookies). 133
Fraoles Glyko (Strawberry Preserves). 163
Frapa Glyko (Grapefruit Preserves). 164
Fried Peppers and Onions. 109
Galatoboureko (Custard Pastry). 170
Galatoboureko (Custard Pastry). 191
Galatoboureko (Margaret's Custard Dessert) . . . 155
Garides Pilaf (Shrimp with Rice Pilaf) 59
Garides Souvlakia (Skewered Shrimp). 58
Garides Tourkolimano (Shrimp Tourkolimano). . . 58
Glyko Psomi (Holiday Sweet Bread) 114
Halva I (Spiced Wheat Pudding). 150
Halva II (Halva Provincial) 150
Hamalia (Almond Cookies). 134
Horiatiki Salata (Provincial Salad) 46
Hortosoupa (Vegetable Soup) 43
Jimmy's Arni Psito (Roast Lamb). 194
Kadaife (Shredded Pastry with Nuts) 158
Kalamarakia (Sautéed Squid) 59
Kalamarakia Yemista (Stuffed Squid). 60
Karithopeta I (Almond Cake) 125
Karithopeta II (Walnut Cake) 127
Keftethakia (Cocktail Meatballs). 35
Keftethes (Meatballs) 75
Kema I (Meat Sauce) 101
Kema II (Meat Sauce) 102
Kema III (Meat Sauce). 102
Koliva (Memorial Wheat Offering) 10, 13, 14
Kolokithakia (Squash Casserole) 180
Kolokithakia (Squash in Tomatoes) 108
Kolokithopeta Gliki (Sweet Pumpkin Peta) 160
Kota Anginares Ke Manitaria (Chicken with
   Artichokes and Mushrooms) 69
Kota Kapama I (Chicken in Tomato Sauce
   with Spaghetti) 68
Kota Kapama II (Chicken in Tomato Sauce) 69
Kota Me Bamyes (Chicken with Okra) 67
Kota Melanaise (Chicken with Melanaise Sauce). . 70
Kota Pilaf (Chicken Pilaf). 71
Kota Riganato (Chicken with Oregano) 71
Kotopetakia Avgholemono (Chicken Rolls with
   Egg-Lemon Sauce) 66

Koulourakia I *(Easter Cookies)* 136
Koulourakia II *(Traditional Easter Cookies)* 137
Kourabiedes I *(Sugar Coated Butter Cookies)* . . . 138
Kourabiedes II *(Sugar Coated Butter Cookies)* . . 139
Kreatopetakia *(Meat Triangles)* 35
Lagana *(Feta Cheese Bread Roll)* 51
Litsa's Halva *(Spiced Wheat-Almond Pudding)* . . 151
Loukoumathes *(Sweet Fritters)* 161
Makaronopeta I *(Macaroni and Cheese Peta)* 52
Makaronopeta II *(Macaroni and Cheese Peta)* . . . 53
Marithes *(Fried Smelts)* 60
Mavromatika Fasolia Salata *(Blackeyed Pea
    Salad)* 46
Mayeritsa I *(Traditional Easter Soup)* 41
Mayeritsa II *(Easter Soup)* 42
Mayeritsa III *(Easter Soup)* 190
Meat Dressing 88
Melidzana Caviar *(Eggplant Canape)* 36
Melomakarona I *(Honey Dipped Cookies)* 140
Melomakarona II *(Honey Cookies)* 141
Menus 22-24
Mousaka I *(Eggplant Casserole)* 89
Mousaka II *(Eggplant-Meat Casserole)* 90
Mousaka Patata 180
Moustalevria *(Grape Pudding)* 149
Nefra Krasata *(Bill's Lamb Kidneys)* 81
Olive Bread 183
Olympian Cake 174
Pan Broiled Chicken 72
Pantespani Portokali *(Orange Sponge Cake)* . . . 127
Panzaria Salata *(Beet Salad)* 47
Papoutsakia Zucchini *(Stuffed Zucchini)* 91
Pasta Flora *(Fruit Squares)* 142
Pastitso 176
Pastitso I *(Macaroni and Meat Sauce Casserole)* . . 92
Pastitso II *(Macaroni and Meat Sauce Casserole)* . . 94
Pastitso III *(Macaroni and Meat Casserole)* 95
Patates Briani *(Greek-Style Potatoes)* 108
Patatosalata *(Greek Potato Salad)* 181
Paximathia I *(Tea Cookies)* 144
Paximathia II *(Greek Tea Cookies)* 146
Phanouropita *(Saint Phanourios Cake)* 19, 195
Plaki IV *(Baked Fish)* 64
Portokali Glyko *(Orange Preserves)* 163
Poutinga *(Cake with Pudding Topping)* 126
Prosphora *(Antidoron)* 10
Psari Marinato *(Marinated Fish)* 61
Psari Mayoneza I *(Chilled Snapper with
    Mayonnaise Sauce)* 61
Psari Mayoneza II *(Red Snapper with
    Mayonnaise Sauce)* 62
Psari Plaki I *(Baked Red Snapper with Vegetables)* . . 62
Psari Plaki II *(Baked Fish with Vegetables)* 63
Psari Plaki III *(Fish with Vegetables)* 63
Psarosoupa *(Fish Soup)* 43
Psito Kreas *(Roasted Meat)* 84
Psomi I *(Greek Bread)* 115
Psomi II *(Greek Bread)* 116
Psomi Sta Tessara *(Nick's #4 Bread)* 120
Psomi Tou Spitiou *(Bread for the Home)* 177
Ravani *(Almond Cake)* 128
Rizi Me Manitaria *(Rice with Mushrooms)* 110
Rizogalo I *(Rice Pudding)* 149
Rizogalo II *(Rice Pudding)* 152
Roast Lemon Lamb 175
Saganaki *(Fried Cheese)* 36
Salata *(Green Salad)* 47
Satziki *(Cucumber Dip)* 189
Savayiar *(Mocha Torte)* 173

Shrimp and Feta Cheese à la Grecque 175
Shrimp with Spinach 181
Sikotaki *(Grecian Style Calf's Liver)* 82
Sikotakia *(Fried Chicken Livers)* 72
Skaltsounakia *(Nut Filled Cookies)* 143
Skorthalia I *(Garlic Sauce)* 103
Skorthalia II *(Garlic Sauce)* 104
Skorthalia III *(Garlic Sauce, Blender Method)* . . 104
Soutsoukakia *(Meatballs in Tomato Sauce)* 82
Souvlakia I *(Shish-Ka-Bob)* 83
Souvlakia II *(Shish-Ka-Bob)* 83
Spanakopeta I *(Spinach Peta)* 110
Spanakopeta II *(Spinach Peta – A Third
    Generation Way)* 111
Spanakopetakia *(Spinach Puffs)* 37
Spanakorizo *(Spinach with Rice)* 112
Spice Paximathia 172
Spinach Cheese Casserole *(Lazy Day
    Version of Spanakopeta)* 178
Spinach Peta with Cornmeal Crust 196
Squash Soup 44
Stafili Glyko *(Grape Preserves)* 163
Steak Greek Style 95
Stefatho *(Stew)* 85
Tarama Keftethes *(Caviar Cakes)* 64
Taramosalata *(Caviar Dip)* 37
Tiropeta *(Cheese Peta)* 53
Tiropitakia *(Cheese Triangles)* 38
Tiropsomo *(Cheese Bread)* 54
Toursi *(Pickled Vegetables)* 38
Tourta Chocolata *(Chocolate Torte)* 171
Traditional Nog 168
Tradition of the Vasilopeta 24
Trigona *(Nut Filled Triangles)* 159
Tsoureki *(Sweet Bread)* 116
Tzatziki *(Yogurt and Cucumber Appetizer)* 183
Vasilopita *(Matula's New Year's Cake)* 121
Vasilopita *(New Year's Sweet Bread)* 122
Vegetable Casserole 112
Xantho Melachrino *(Yellow Cake with
    Spiced Meringue)* 132
Yaourti *(Yogurt)* 103
Yaourtopeta I *(Yogurt Nut Cake with
    Lemon-Honey Syrup)* 130
Yaourtopita II *(Yogurt Nut Cake)* 131
Yemistes Melidzanes I *(Stuffed Eggplant)* 97
Yemistes Melidzanes II *(Stuffed Eggplant Deluxe)* . 98
Yianniotiki Patsiariá 182
Yiaourtopeta *(Yogurt Cake)* 173
Youvarelakia *(Meatballs in Egg-Lemon Sauce)* . . . 85
Youvetsi *(Oven Stew)* 84
Zvinges *(Sweet Fritters)* 161

GREEK-AMERICAN RECIPES
Easy Avgholemono *(Easy Egg-Lemon Sauce)* . . 101
Hortosoupa *(Vegetable Soup)* 43
GREEN BEANS
Fasoulakia Yiahni *(Greek Style Green Beans)* . . 107
Loob–Yee Ib Lahm *(Lamb and String Bean Stew)* . .81
Vegetable Casserole 112

H

Halva I *(Spiced Wheat Pudding)* 150
Halva II *(Halva Provincial)* 150
Hamalia *(Almond Cookies)* 134
Hashwa *(Kibbie Stuffing)* 80
Horiatiki Salata *(Provincial Salad)* 46
Hortosoupa *(Vegetable Soup)* 43

I

Ionian Dinner 23

J

Jimmy's Arni Psito *(Roast Lamb)* 194

K

Kadaife *(Shredded Pastry with Nuts)* 158
Kalamarakia *(Sautéed Squid)* 59
Kalamarakia Yemista *(Stuffed Squid)* 60
Karithopeta I *(Almond Cake)* 125
Karithopeta II *(Walnut Cake)* 127
Keftethakia *(Cocktail Meatballs)* 35
Keftethes *(Meatballs)* 75
Kema I *(Meat Sauce)* 101
Kema II *(Meat Sauce)* 102
Kema III *(Meat Sauce)* 102
Kibbie. 78
Kibbie, Baked 78
Kibbie, Fried 79
Kifle *(Crescent Cookies)* 134
Kolachky *(Frozen Dough Cookies)* 135
Kolachky *(Nut Roll Bread)* 119
Kolbasa *(Sausage)* 80
Koliva *(Memorial Wheat Offering)* 10, 13, 14
Kolokithakia *(Squash Casserole)* 180
Kolokithakia *(Squash in Tomatoes)* 108
Kolokithópeta *(Squash and Feta Casserole)* 109
Kolokithopeta Gliki *(Sweet Pumpkin Peta)* 160
Kota Anginares Ke Manitaria *(Chicken with
    Artichokes and Mushrooms)* 69
Kota Kapama I *(Chicken in Tomato Sauce with
    Spaghetti)* 68
Kota Kapama II *(Chicken in Tomato Sauce)* 69
Kota Me Bamyes *(Chicken with Okra)* 67
Kota Melanaise *(Chicken with Melanaise Sauce)* . . . 70
Kota Pilaf *(Chicken Pilaf)* 71
Kota Riganato *(Chicken with Oregano)* 71
Kotlety *(Baked Meat Cutlets)* 79
Kotopetakia Avgholemono *(Chicken Rolls
    with Egg-Lemon Sauce)* 66
Kouloura *(Basic Techniques)* 30
Kouloura with Eggs *(Basic Techniques)* 30
Koulourakia I *(Easter Cookies)* 136
Koulourakia II *(Traditional Easter Cookies)* 137
Kourabiedes I *(Sugar-Coated Butter Cookies)* 138
Kourabiedes II *(Sugar-Coated Butter Cookies)* 139
Kousharie *(Lentils with Rice)* 189
Kreatopetakia *(Meat Triangles)* 35

L

Lagana *(Feta Cheese Bread Roll)* 51
LAMB
Arni Fricassee *(Lamb in Egg-Lemon Sauce)* 74
Arni Me Spanaki *(Lamb with Spinach)* 74
Arni Psito *(Roast Lamb)* 75
Arni Tis Souflas *(Whole Lamb Barbecued
    on a Spit)* 76
Baked Orzo 88
Breezoles Tis Skaras *(Charcoal Broiled
    Lamb Chops)* 77
Cephalonian Meat Pie *(Kreatopeta)* 179
Cevapcici *(Serbian Sausage)* 77
Hashwa *(Kibbie Stuffing)* 80
Jimmy's Arni Psito *(Roast Lamb)* 194
Kema I *(Meat Sauce)* 101
Kibbie 78

Kibbie, Baked 78
Kibbie, Fried 79
Loob–Yee Ib Lahm *(Lamb and String Bean Stew)* . . 81
Mayeritsa I *(Traditional Easter Soup)* 41
Mayeritsa II *(Easter Soup)* 42
Mayeritsa III *(Easter Soup)* 190
Mousaka II *(Eggplant-Meat Casserole)* 90
Nefra Krasata *(Bill's Lamb Kidneys)* 81
Psito Kreas *(Roasted Meat)* 84
Roast Lemon Lamb 175
Souvlakia II *(Shish-Ka-Bob)* 83
Youvarelakia *(Meatballs in Egg-Lemon Sauce)* . . . 85
Youvetsi *(Oven Stew)* 84
LEBANESE RECIPES
Baba Ga-Nooj *(Eggplant Appetizer)* 34
Baked Kibbie 78
Fried Kibbie 79
Hashwa *(Kibbie Stuffing)* 80
Kibbie 78
Loob–Yee Ib Lahm *(Lamb and String
    Bean Stew)* 81
Saf-Soof *(Cracked Wheat Salad)* 48
Tabouleh *(Cracked Wheat Salad)* 48
Litsa's Halva *(Spiced Wheat-Almond Pudding)* 151
Liturgical and Traditional Offerings 10
Loob–Yee Ib Lahm *(Lamb and String Bean Stew)* . . . 81
Loukoumathes *(Sweet Fritters)* 161
Luncheon with Friends 23

M

Makaronopeta I *(Macaroni and Cheese Peta)* 52
Makaronopeta II *(Macaroni and Cheese Peta)* 53
Marithes *(Fried Smelts)* 60
Mavromatika Fasolia Salata *(Blackeyed Pea Salad)* . 46
Mayeritsa I *(Traditional Easter Soup)* 41
Mayeritsa II *(Easter Soup)* 42
Mayeritsa III *(Easter Soup)* 190
Mazurki *(Fruit Cookies)* 144
Meat Dressing 88
MEATS/MEAT COMBINATIONS
Arni Fricassee *(Lamb in Egg-Lemon Sauce)* 74
Arni Me Spanaki *(Lamb with Spinach)* 74
Arni Psito *(Roast Lamb)* 75
Arni Tis Souflas *(Whole Lamb Barbecued
    on a Spit)* 76
Baked Orzo 88
Beef Stroganoff 77
Breezoles Tis Skaras *(Charcoal Broiled
    Lamb Chops)* 77
Cephalonian Meat Pie *(Kreatopeta)* 179
Cevapcici *(Serbian Sausage)* 77
Dolmathakia Me Avgholemono *(Stuffed
    Grapevine Leaves with Egg-Lemon Sauce)* 87
Dolmathes *(Stuffed Cabbage Leaves)* 86
Domates Yemistes *(Stuffed Tomatoes)* 93
Gomen Segá *(Beef and Collard Greens)* 186
Hashwa *(Kibbie Stuffing)* 80
Jimmy's Arni Psito *(Roast Lamb)* 194
Keftethakia *(Cocktail Meatballs)* 35
Keftethes *(Meatballs)* 75
Kibbie 78
Kibbie, Baked 78
Kibbie, Fried 79
Kolbasa *(Sausage)* 80
Kotlety *(Baked Meat Cutlets)* 79
Kreatopetakia *(Meat Triangles)* 35
Loob–Yee Ib Lahm *(Lamb and String Bean Stew)* . . 81
Meat Dressing 88

Mousaka I *(Eggplant Casserole)*. 89
Mousaka II *(Eggplant-Meat Casserole)* 90
Mousaka Patata 180
Nefra Krasata *(Bill's Lamb Kidneys)* 81
Papoutsakia Zucchini *(Stuffed Zucchini)* 91
Pastitso 176
Pastitso I *(Macaroni and Meat Sauce Casserole)*. . 92
Pastitso II *(Macaroni and Meat Sauce Casserole)*. . 94
Pastitso III *(Macaroni and Meat Casserole)*. 95
Psito Kreas *(Roasted Meat)*. 84
Roast Lemon Lamb 175
Sarma *(Cabbage Rolls)* 96
Sikotaki *(Grecian Style Calf's Liver)*. 82
Sikotakia *(Fried Chicken Livers)* 72
Soutsoukakia *(Meatballs in Tomato Sauce)* 82
Souvlakia I *(Shish-Ka-Bob)* 83
Souvlakia II *(Shish-Ka-Bob)*. 83
Steak Greek Style. 95
Stefatho *(Stew)*. 85
Yemistes Melidzanes I *(Stuffed Eggplant)* 97
Yemistes Melidzanes II *(Stuffed Eggplant Deluxe)*. 98
Youvarelakia *(Meatballs in Egg-Lemon Sauce)*. . . 85
Youvetsi *(Oven Stew)*. 84
Melidzana Caviar *(Eggplant Canape)* 36
Melomakarona I *(Honey Dipped Cookies)* 140
Melomakarona II *(Honey Cookies)* 141

MENUS
A Carpatho-Russian Christmas Eve 18
Aegean Cocktail Buffet *(Greek)* 22
Easter Sunay Feast *(Greek)* 20
Ionian Dinner *(Greek)*. 23
Lenten Meal *(Greek)* 21
Luncheon with Friends *(Greek)* 23
St. Basil's Feast Day Dinner *(Greek)*. 24
Sunday Lunch at Home *(Greek)* 22
Mousaka I *(Eggplant Casserole)*. 89
Mousaka II *(Eggplant-Meat Casserole)*. 90
Mousaka Patata 180
Moustalevria *(Grape Pudding)* 149
Muhallebi *(Armenian Custard)* 185

MUSHROOMS
Kota Anginares Ke Manitaria *(Chicken with*
Artichokes and Mushrooms) 69
Rizi Me Manitaria *(Rice with Mushrooms)*. 110

N
Nefra Krasata *(Bill's Lamb Kidneys)* 81
Niter Kebbeh *(Spiced Butter)* 186

O
OKRA
Bamyes Me Domates *(Okra and Tomatoes)* . . . 106
Kota Me Bamyes *(Chicken with Okra)* 67
Olive Bread. 183
Olympian Cake 174
Orechnik *(Nut Cake)* 126
Orzo, Baked 88

P
Pan Broiled Chicken 72
Pantespani Portokali *(Orange Sponge Cake)* 127
Panzaria Salata *(Beet Salad)*. 47
Papoutsakia Zucchini *(Stuffed Zucchini)*. 91
Pascha *(Traditional Easter Dessert)* 55
PASTA
Baked Orzo 88
Kota Kapama I *(Chicken in Tomato Sauce*
with Spaghetti) 68

Makaronopeta I *(Macaroni and Cheese Peta)*. . . . 52
Makaronopeta II *(Macaroni and Cheese Peta)* 53
Pastitso 176
Pastitso I *(Macaroni and Meat Sauce Casserole)*. . 92
Pastitso II *(Macaroni and Meat Sauce Casserole)*. .94
Pastitso III *(Macaroni and Meat Casserole)*. 95
Pasta Flora *(Fruit Squares)*. 142
Pastitso 176
Pastitso I *(Macaroni and Meat Sauce Casserole)*. 92
Pastitso II *(Macaroni and Meat Sauce Casserole)*. . . . 94
Pastitso III *(Macaroni and Meat Casserole)* 95
PASTRIES
Amigthalota Flogeres *(Almond Flutes)*. 153
Baklava I *(Honey Nut Pastry)* 154
Baklava II *(Honey Nut Pastry)*. 156
Copenhi *(Custard Pastry with Crust and Filo)* . . . 192
Diana's Galatobouriko *(Custard Pastry)* 157
Diples *(Rolled Honey Pastries)* 162
Galatoboureko *(Custard Pastry)*. 170
Galatoboureko *(Custard Pastry)*. 191
Galatoboureko *(Margaret's Custard Dessert)* . . . 155
Kadaife *(Shredded Pastry with Nuts)* 158
Kolokithopeta Gliki *(Sweet Pumpkin Peta)* 160
Loukoumathes *(Sweet Fritters)* 161
Trigona *(Nut Filled Triangles)* 159
Zvinges *(Sweet Fritters)* 161
Patates Briani *(Greek-Style Potatoes)* 108
Patatosalata *(Greek Potato Salad)* 181
Paximathia I *(Tea Cookies)*. 144
Paximathia II *(Greek Tea Cookies)*. 146
PEPPERS
Fried Peppers and Onions. 109
Toursi *(Pickled Vegetables)* 38
Phanouropita *(Saint Phanourios Cake)*. 19, 195
Piroshki *(Stuffed Dumplings)* 56
Plaki IV *(Baked Fish)* 64
PORK
Cevapcici *(Serbian Sausage)* 77
Kolbasa *(Sausage)* 80
Psito Kreas *(Roasted Meat)* 84
Sarma *(Cabbage Rolls)* 96
Portokali Glyko *(Orange Preserves)*. 163
POTATOES
Mousaka Patata. 180
Patates Briani *(Greek-Style Potatoes)*. 108
Patatosalata *(Greek Potato Salad)* 181
POULTRY
Doro Wot *(Chicken Sauce)*. 188
Kota Anginares Ke Manitaria *(Chicken with*
Artichokes and Mushrooms) 69
Kota Kapama I *(Chicken in Tomato Sauce with*
Spaghetti) 68
Kota Kapama II *(Chicken in Tomato Sauce)* 69
Kota Me Bamyes *(Chicken with Okra)* 67
Kota Melanaise *(Chicken with Melanaise Sauce)*. 70
Kota Pilaf *(Chicken Pilaf)*. 71
Kota Riganato *(Chicken with Oregano)* 71
Kotopetakia Avgholemono *(Chicken Rolls*
with Egg-Lemon Sauce) 66
Pan Broiled Chicken. 72
Sikotakia *(Fried Chicken Livers)* 72
Poutinga *(Cake with Pudding Topping)* 126
Povitica *(Walnut and Date Sweet Bread)*. 118
PRESERVES
Fraoles Glyko *(Strawberry Preserves)* 163
Frapa Glyko *(Grapefruit Preserves)* 164
Portokali Glyko *(Orange Preserves)* 163
Stafili Glyko *(Grape Preserves)*. 163

Proscuri *(Individual Church Altar Breads)* 11
Prosphora *(Antidoron)* 10
Psari Marinato *(Marinated Fish)* 61
Psari Mayoneza I *(Chilled Snapper with
   Mayonnaise Sauce)* 61
Psari Mayoneza II *(Red Snapper with
   Mayonnaise Sauce)* 62
Psari Plaki I *(Baked Red Snapper with Vegetables)* . . 62
Psari Plaki II *(Baked Fish with Vegetables)* 63
Psari Plaki III *(Fish with Vegetables)* 63
Psarosoupa *(Fish Soup)* 43
Psito Kreas *(Roasted Meat)* 84
Psomi I *(Greek Bread)* 115
Psomi II *(Greek Bread)* 116
Psomi Sta Tessara *(Nick's #4 Bread)* 120
Psomi Tou Spitiou *(Bread for the Home)* 177
PUDDING
   Halva I *(Spiced Wheat Pudding)* 150
   Halva II *(Halva Provincial)* 150
   Litsa's Halva *(Spiced Wheat-Almond Pudding)* . . 151
   Moustalevria *(Grape Pudding)* 149
   Rizogalo I *(Rice Pudding)* 149
   Rizogalo II *(Rice Pudding)* 152
Pysanky *(Ukrainian Easter Eggs)* 32

Q

QUICHES
   Artichoke Quiche 182
   Salmon Quiche 185

R

RABBIT
   Stefatho *(Stew)* 85
Ravani *(Almond Cake)* 128
RED EASTER EGGS
   Angie's Easter Eggs 32
   Easter Eggs 32
RED SNAPPER
   Psari Marinato *(Marinated Fish)* 61
   Psari Mayoneza I *(Chilled Snapper with
      Mayonnaise Sauce)* 61
   Psari Mayoneza II *(Red Snapper with
      Mayonnaise Sauce)* 62
   Psari Plaki I *(Baked Red Snapper with
      Vegetables)* 62
   Psari Plaki III *(Fish with Vegetables)* 63
RICE
   Dolmathes Yialandji *(Stuffed Grapevine
      Leaves, Lenten)* 107
   Garides Pilaf *(Shrimp with Rice Pilaf)* 59
   Kota Pilaf *(Chicken Pilaf)* 71
   Kousharie *(Lentils with Rice)* 189
   Rizi Me Manitaria *(Rice with Mushrooms)* 110
   Rizogalo I *(Rice Pudding)* 149
   Rizogalo II *(Rice Pudding)* 152
   Spanakorizo *(Spinach with Rice)* 112
Rizi Me Manitaria *(Rice with Mushrooms)* 110
Rizogalo I *(Rice Pudding)* 149
Rizogalo II *(Rice Pudding)* 152
Roast Lemon Lamb 175
RUSSIAN RECIPES
   Beef Stroganoff 77
   Kolachky *(Frozen Dough Cookies)* 135
   Kolachky *(Nut Roll Bread)* 119
   Kolbasa *(Sausage)* 80
   Kotlety *(Baked Meat Cutlets)* 79
   Mazurki *(Fruit Cookies)* 144
   Orechnik *(Nut Cake)* 126

Pascha *(Traditional Easter Dessert)* 55
Piroshki *(Stuffed Dumplings)* 56
Proscuri *(Individual Church Altar Breads)* 11
Pysanky *(Ukrainian Easter Eggs)* 32
Russian Tea 174
Russian Tea 174

S

Saf-Soof *(Cracked Wheat Salad)* 48
Saganaki *(Fried Cheese)* 36
SALADS
   Cabbage Slaw 176
   Domatosalata *(Tomato Salad)* 46
   Horiatiki Salata *(Provincial Salad)* 46
   Mavromatika Fasolia Salata *(Blackeyed Pea
      Salad)* 46
   Panzaria Salata *(Beet Salad)* 47
   Patatosalata *(Greek Potato Salad)* 181
   Saf-Soof *(Cracked Wheat Salad)* 48
   Salata *(Green Salad)* 47
   Tabouleh *(Cracked Wheat Salad)* 48
   Yemiser Selatta *(Lentil Salad)* 184
Salata *(Green Salad)* 47
Salmon Quiche 185
Sarma *(Cabbage Rolls)* 96
Satziki *(Cucumber Dip)* 189
SAUCES
   Aspri Saltsa *(Bechamel Sauce)* 100
   Basic Avgholemono Sauce
      (Egg and Lemon Sauce) 100
   Crema *(Cream Sauce)* 100
   Easy Avgholemono *(Easy Egg-Lemon Sauce)* . . 101
   Kema I *(Meat Sauce)* 101
   Kema II *(Meat Sauce)* 102
   Kema III *(Meat Sauce)* 102
   Skorthalia I *(Garlic Sauce)* 103
   Skorthalia II *(Garlic Sauce)* 104
   Skorthalia III *(Garlic Sauce, Blender Method)* . . 104
   Yaourti *(Yogurt)* 103
SAUSAGE
   Cevapcici *(Serbian Sausage)* 77
   Kema III *(Meat Sauce)* 102
   Kolbasa *(Sausage)* 80
   Savayiar *(Mocha Torte)* 173
SEAFOOD
   Garides Pilaf *(Shrimp with Rice Pilaf)* 59
   Garides Souvlakia *(Skewered Shrimp)* 58
   Garides Tourkolimano *(Shrimp Tourkolimano)* . . 58
   Kalamarakia *(Sautéed Squid)* 59
   Kalamarakia Yemista *(Stuffed Squid)* 60
   Marithes *(Fried Smelts)* 60
   Plaki IV *(Baked Fish)* 64
   Psari Marinato *(Marinated Fish)* 61
   Psari Mayoneza I *(Chilled Snapper with
      Mayonnaise Sauce)* 61
   Psari Mayoneza II *(Red Snapper with
      Mayonnaise Sauce)* 62
   Psari Plaki I *(Baked Red Snapper with
      Vegetables)* 62
   Psari Plaki II *(Baked Fish with Vegetables)* 63
   Psari Plaki III *(Fish with Vegetables)* 63
   Salmon Quiche 185
   Shrimp and Feta Cheese à la Grecque 175
   Shrimp with Spinach 181
   Tarama Keftethes *(Caviar Cakes)* 64
Serbian Christmas Customs 16
SERBIAN RECIPES
   Cevapcici *(Serbian Sausage)* 77

Cicvara *(Cornmeal Dish)* 178
Gibanica I *(Strudel and Cheese Cake
    Combination)* 50
Gibanica II *(Cheese Peta)* 52
Kifle *(Crescent Cookies)*. 134
Povitica *(Walnut and Date Sweet Bread)* 118
Sarma *(Cabbage Rolls)* 96
SHRIMP
Garides Pilaf *(Shrimp with Rice Pilaf)* 59
Garides Souvlakia *(Skewered Shrimp)* 58
Garides Tourkolimano *(Shrimp Tourkolimano)*. . . 58
Shrimp and Feta Cheese à la Grecque 175
Shrimp with Spinach 181
Shrimp and Feta Cheese à la Grecque. 175
Shrimp with Spinach. 181
Sikotaki *(Grecian Style Calf's Liver)* 82
Sikotakia *(Fried Chicken Livers)* 72
Skaltsounakia *(Nut Filled Cookies)* 143
Skorthalia I *(Garlic Sauce)* 103
Skorthalia II *(Garlic Sauce)* 104
Skorthalia III *(Garlic Sauce, Blender Method)* 104
SMELTS
Marithes *(Fried Smelts)*. 60
SOUPS
Avgholemono Soupa *(Egg-Lemon Soup)* 40
Faki *(Lentil Soup)* 42
Fasoulatha *(Bean Soup)* 40
Hortosoupa *(Vegetable Soup)* 43
Mayeritsa I *(Traditional Easter Soup)*. 41
Mayeritsa II *(Easter Soup)* 42
Mayeritsa III *(Easter Soup)* 190
Psarosoupa *(Fish Soup)* 43
Squash Soup 44
Soutsoukakia *(Meatballs in Tomato Sauce)* 82
Souvlakia I *(Shish-Ka-Bob)* 83
Souvlakia II *(Shish-Ka-Bob)* 83
Spanakopeta I *(Spinach Peta)* 110
Spanakopeta II *(Spinach Peta – A Third
    Generation Way)* 111
Spanakopetakia *(Spinach Puffs)* 37
Spanakorizo *(Spinach with Rice)* 112
SPECIAL OCCASIONS
Angie's Easter Eggs 32
Artos I *(For Artoklasia)*. 12
Artos II *(For Artoklasia)* 13
Easter Bread 117
Koliva *(Memorial Wheat Offering)* 10, 13, 14
Koulourakia I *(Easter Cookies)* 136
Koulourakia II *(Traditional Easter Cookies)* 137
Liturgical and Traditional Offerings 10
Mayeritsa I *(Traditional Easter Soup)*. 41
Mayeritsa II *(Easter Soup)*. 42
Mayeritsa III *(Easter Soup)* 190
New Year's 24
Pascha *(Traditional Easter Dessert)* 55
Phanouropita *(Saint Phanourios Cake)* 19, 195
Proscuri *(Individual Church Altar Breads)* 11
Prosphora *(Antidoron)* 10
Pysanky *(Carpatho-Russian/Ukrainian)* 32
Red Easter Egg *(Greek)* 32
St. Basil's Feast Day Dinner 24
Tradition of the Vasilopeta *(Greek)* 24
Vasilopita *(Matula's New Year's Cake)* 121
Vasilopita *(New Year's Sweet Bread)* 122
Spice Paximathia 172
SPINACH
Arni Me Spanaki *(Lamb with Spinach)* 74
Shrimp with Spinach 181

Spanakopeta I *(Spinach Peta)* 110
Spanakopeta II *(Spinach Peta – A Third
    Generation Way)* 111
Spanakopetakia *(Spinach Puffs)* 37
Spanakorizo *(Spinach with Rice)* 112
Spinach Cheese Casserole *(Lazy Day
    Version of Spanakopeta)* 178
Spinach Peta with Cornmeal Crust 196
Yianniotiki Patsiariá 182
Spinach Cheese Casserole *(Lazy Day Version
    of Spanakopeta)* 178
Spinach Peta with Cornmeal Crust 196
SQUASH
Kolokithakia *(Squash Casserole)* 180
Kolokithakia *(Squash in Tomatoes)*. 108
Kolokithópeta *(Squash and Feta Casserole)*. . . . 109
Squash Soup 44
Yianniotiki Patsiariá 182
SQUID
Kalamarakia *(Sautéed Squid)* 59
Kalamarakia Yemista *(Stuffed Squid)*. 60
Stafili Glyko *(Grape Preserves)*. 163
St. Basil's Feast Day Dinner 24
Steak Greek Style 95
Stefatho *(Stew)* 85
STEW
Loob–Yee Ib Lahm *(Lamb and String Bean Stew)*. 81
Stefatho *(Stew)* 85
Youvetsi *(Oven Stew)* 84
Stroganoff, Beef 77

T

Tabouleh *(Cracked Wheat Salad)*. 48
Tarama Keftethes *(Caviar Cakes)*. 64
Taramosalata *(Caviar Dip)* 37
Tiropeta *(Cheese Peta)* 53
Tiropitakia *(Cheese Triangles)*. 38
Tiropsomo *(Cheese Bread)*. 54
TOMATOES
Bamyes Me Domates *(Okra and Tomatoes)* . . . 106
Domates Yemistes *(Stuffed Tomatoes)* 93
Domatosalata *(Tomato Salad)* 46
Horiatiki Salata *(Provincial Salad)* 46
Kolokithakia *(Squash in Tomatoes)*. 108
Toursi *(Pickled Vegetables)* 38
TORTES
Savayiar *(Mocha Torte)*. 173
Tourta Chocolata *(Chocolate Torte)* 171
Walnut Torte. 129
Toursi *(Pickled Vegetables)*. 38
Tourta Chocolata *(Chocolate Torte)*. 171
Traditional Nog 168
Trigona *(Nut Filled Triangles)*. 159
Tsoureki *(Sweet Bread)*. 116
Tzatziki *(Yogurt and Cucumber Appetizer)*. 183

U

UKRAINIAN RECIPES
Easter Bread 117
Pysanky Legend. 32
Walnut Torte. 129

V

VARIETY MEATS
Mayeritsa I *(Traditional Easter Soup)*. 41
Mayeritsa II *(Easter Soup)*. 42
Mayeritsa III *(Easter Soup)* 190
Nefra Krasata *(Bill's Lamb Kidneys)* 81

Sikotaki *(Grecian Style Calf's Liver)*..........82
Sikotakia *(Fried Chicken Livers)*............72
Vasilopita *(Matula's New Year's Cake)*..........121
Vasilopita *(New Year's Sweet Bread)*...........122
Vasilopita *(Tradition)*.......................24
VEAL
Stefatho *(Stew)*.......................85
Vegetable Casserole.....................112
VEGETABLES
Anginares Avgholemono *(Artichokes with
    Egg-Lemon Sauce)*..................106
Bamyes Me Domates *(Okra and Tomatoes)*...106
Dolmathakia *(Stuffed Grapevine Leaves)*.......34
Dolmathes Yialandji *(Stuffed Grapevine
    Leaves, Lenten)*....................107
Domates Yemistes *(Stuffed Tomatoes)*........93
Eggplant Parmesan.....................184
Fasoulakia Yiahni *(Greek Style Green Beans)*...107
Fried Peppers and Onions................109
Gomen Segá *(Beef and Collard Greens)*.......186
Hortosoupa *(Vegetable Soup)*..............43
Kolokithakia *(Squash Casserole)*..........180
Kolokithakia *(Squash in Tomatoes)*..........108
Kolokithópeta *(Squash and Feta Casserole)*...109
Kousharie *(Lentils with Rice)*..............189
Panzaria Salata *(Beet Salad)*...............47
Papoutsakia Zucchini *(Stuffed Zucchini)*......91
Patates Briani *(Greek-Style Potatoes)*........108
Rizi Me Manitaria *(Rice with Mushrooms)*.....110
Sarma *(Cabbage Rolls)*..................96
Satziki *(Cucumber Dip)*.................189
Spanakopeta I *(Spinach Peta)*.............110
Spanakopeta II *(Spinach Peta – A Third
    Generation Way)*....................111
Spanakorizo *(Spinach with Rice)*..........112
Spinach Cheese Casserole *(Lazy Day
    Version of Spanakopeta)*..............178
Squash Soup.........................44
Toursi *(Pickled Vegetables)*................38
Vegetable Casserole....................112

W

Walnut Torte..........................129
WHEAT
Halva I *(Spiced Wheat Pudding)*............150
Kibbie..............................78
Koliva *(Memorial Wheat Offering)*......10, 13, 14
Litsa's Halva *(Spiced Wheat-Almond Pudding)*..151
Saf-Soof *(Cracked Wheat Salad)*............48
Tabouleh *(Cracked Wheat Salad)*...........48
Wines and Cheeses....................166
WINES & CHEESES/BEVERAGES
Beverages
Russian Tea.......................174
Traditional Nog.....................168
Cheeses
Feta............................168
Kasseri.........................168
Kefalotiri.......................168
Mizithra........................168
Notable Libations
Kokkinelli *(Dark Rosé Wine)*.............167
Metaxa *(Greek Distilled Spirit)*..........167
Ouzo *(Greek Liqueur)*................167
Roditis *(Rosé Wine)*.................167
Red Wines
Castel Danielis.....................167
Chateau Claus....................167

Demestica.........................167
Hymettus.........................167
Mavrodaphne......................167
Mont Ambelos.....................167
Pendeli..........................167
White Wines
Demestica.........................166
Hymettus.........................166
Mantinia..........................166
Mont Ambelos.....................166
Retsina...........................166
Saint Helena.......................166
Saint Laoura.......................166

X

Xantho Melachrino *(Yellow Cake with
    Spiced Meringue)*...................132

Y

Yabesh Dabo *(Ethiopian Bread)*..............187
Yaourti *(Yogurt)*.......................103
Yaourtopeta I *(Yogurt Nut Cake with
    Lemon-Honey Syrup)*..................130
Yaourtopita II *(Yogurt Nut Cake)*............131
Yemiser Selatta *(Lentil Salad)*..............184
Yemistes Melidzanes I *(Stuffed Eggplant)*........97
Yemistes Melidzanes II *(Stuffed Eggplant Deluxe)*..98
Yianniotiki Patsiariá.....................182
Yiaourtopeta *(Yogurt Cake)*................173
YOGURT
Tzatziki *(Yogurt and Cucumber Appetizer)*.....183
Yaourti *(Yogurt)*......................103
Yaourtopeta I *(Yogurt Nut Cake with
    Lemon-Honey Syrup)*................130
Yaourtopita II *(Yogurt Nut Cake)*............131
Yiaourtopeta *(Yogurt Cake)*.............173
Youvarelakia *(Meatballs in Egg-Lemon Sauce)*.....85
Youvetsi *(Oven Stew)*.....................84

Z

ZUCCHINI
Kolokithakia *(Squash in Tomatoes)*..........108
Papoutsakia Zucchini *(Stuffed Zucchini)*......91
Squash Soup.........................44
Zvinges *(Sweet Fritters)*..................161

it's GREEK to me!

To order copies of this book, please write to:

It's Greek To Me!
573 North Highland
Memphis, TN 38122

Phone: (901) 327-8177
Fax: (901) 327-4440

Or visit our website:
www.itsgreektomecookbook.com